DIE RICH

ALSO BY STEPHAN R. LEIMBERG

A Comparison: Life Insurance Inside or Outside
    A Qualified Insurance Plan
Money and Retirement
The New Tax Law
Administration of Estates
An Introduction to the Tools and Techniques of Estate
    Planning
Federal Income Taxation
Funding Corporate Buy-Sell Agreements
The Public Life of a Private Annuity
The Tools and Techniques of Estate Planning
Presenting IRA
Computing the Federal Estate Tax

DIE RICH

Making It, Keeping It, and Passing It Along Under the New Tax Laws

CHARLES PLOTNICK AND
STEPHAN LEIMBERG

COWARD-McCANN, INC.
NEW YORK

Copyright © 1983 by Charles K. Plotnick and Stephan R. Leimberg
All rights reserved.
This book, or parts thereof, may not be reproduced
in any form without permission in writing from the publisher.
Published on the same day in Canada
by General Publishing Co. Limited, Toronto.

The "Checklist of Executor's Primary Duties," page 60, is reprinted with permission from Stephan R. Leimberg et al., *The Tools and Techniques of Estate Planning,* 4th edition, copyright © 1982, The National Underwriter Company, Cincinnati, Ohio.
Appendix A is adapted with permission from the American College's Advanced Estate Planning Course.

LIBRARY OF CONGRESS CATALOGING IN PUBLICATION DATA
Plotnick, Charles K.
  Die rich.
  1. Estate planning—United States. 2. Inheritance and transfer tax—Law and legislation—United States.
I. Leimberg, Stephan R. II. Title.
KF750.P57 1983   343.7305'32   82-18185
ISBN 0-698-11223-7   347.303532

Designed by Helen Barrow
Printed in the United States of America

ACKNOWLEDGMENTS

I would like to acknowledge Neil Hurowitz, my law partner, whose books on support and divorce inspired me to write this book. To Helen Ware and Karen Darin for their invaluable help in preparing this manuscript. And my children, Steve and Amy, for their constant support and encouragement. And to our super-agent Rick Balkin, without whose guidance and assistance this book would not have been possible.

CHARLES K. PLOTNICK

To my wonderful friends and secretaries, Jessie Torrelli and Pat Cresse, not only for having written and rewritten many chapters but also for being the thoughtful, vibrant and wonderful people that they are.

STEPHAN R. LEIMBERG

To my wife, Diane, for making my life so rich.
CHARLES K. PLOTNICK

To my parents, Edward and Sylvia Leimberg:
I love you both more than I've ever told you.
STEPHAN R. LEIMBERG

Contents

Preface 15

Introduction 17

1. Do You Really Need a Plan? 19
>   Who cares? . . . People planning . . . Asset planning

2. What Is Going to Stop You? 23
>   Don't know where to start . . . Fear and distaste . . . Too busy . . . General dislike of attorneys, banks and insurance men . . . Failure to realize magnitude of problem and tax consequences . . . Unwillingness to address family situations . . . Belief in lasting health and immortality

3. Identify the Enemy 29
>   Inflation—the odds against being adequately prepared . . . Lack of security for you and your family . . . An adequate income if disabled . . . Excessive transfer costs . . . Lack of liquidity . . . Your own special problem

4. The One and Only You 35
>   Why you are unique . . . Different strokes for different folks . . . What are you really worth?

5. A Blueprint for Your Future 41
>   Gathering the information . . . Analyzing the needs . . . Formulating a plan . . . Testing and implementing plan . . . Reviewing the plan . . . Put yourself on your own payroll

6. **What's in a Name?** 46

　　Like and dislike . . . So what's good about joint tenancies? . . . So what's not to like?

7. **Is a Will a Must?** 52

　　Without a will, what? . . . What does a will will? . . . I'd rather do it myself . . . Turn arounds . . . Do's and don'ts . . . Probate—what to avoid

8. **Trust Me** 63

　　How far does trust go? . . . Who should watch the store? . . . What's in it for me? . . . Arms in the arsenal . . . Revocable living trust . . . The irrevocable living trust . . . Testamentary trusts . . . A compromise—life insurance trust with a pour-over will . . . Other types of trusts

9. **Is It Better to Give?** 74

　　Why give when you've got? . . . What's it cost to give? . . . The little giant . . . Divide and conquer . . . The mighty marital . . . E pluribus unum . . . Putting it all together . . . A special bonus . . . Give what? . . . About time . . . How now? . . . A few final words

10. **Will You Die for All Your Worth?** 82

　　PART 1—WHAT THE FEDS GET (THE FEDERAL ESTATE TAX)
　　Computing the tax . . . What's in and how to get it out . . . *Category 1*—Property you own in your own name . . . *Category 2*—Gifts in which you retain the income or control over the property or income . . . *Category 3*—Gifts made conditional on surviving you . . . *Category 4*—Gifts you made but retained the right to alter, amend, revoke or terminate . . . *Category 5*—Annuities or similar arrangements you purchase (or that are purchased on your behalf) that are payable to you while living, and then to your designated survivor . . . *Category 6*—Jointly held property where someone else automatically receives your interest by surviving you . . . *Category 7*—General powers of appointment—an unlimited right to specify who receives someone else's property . . . *Category 8*—Life insurance that you own or have important rights over or that is payable to or for the benefit of your estate . . . What comes next? . . . About attorney's fees

　　PART 2—THE STATE OF STATE DEATH TAXATION—WORSE THAN YOU WOULD THINK . . . What to expect—not 57 varieties . . . The "inheritance" tax . . . The "estate" tax . . . The "credit" estate tax

Contents   **11**

. . . How to beat the system—or win by playing their game your way . . . Double trouble . . . Rates rate . . . Not all exemptions or deductions are created equal

11. *That's Life (Insurance)*   104

What's it all about? . . . Who needs it? . . . Chocolate, vanilla or strawberry? . . . Settling up . . . Very interesting (loans) . . . Say grace . . . Universal life—something new under the sun? . . . How high is up (how much insurance)? . . . Left or right (your rights in your policy)? . . . Horseless riders . . . Here's an upper G.I. (guaranteed insurability) . . . Getting it out and keeping it out (of your estate) . . . Is "out" in? . . . This transfer is a one-way wrong-way ticket . . . A.P.L.—apples, potatoes and lettuce? . . . Come again (reinstatement)? . . . Can't argue with this one (incontestable clause) . . . Life (insurance) is full of dividends . . . It's not what you've got but what you do with what you've got that counts (dividend options) . . . Easy rider . . . Some taxing questions . . . Which way to pay? . . . Combatting the ultimate certainty—change . . . How does adjustable life work? . . . How to fight the unfightable (inflation)

12. *More Taxpayers Mean Less Taxes*   133

Cheaper by the dozen . . . The long and the short of it (Short-term trusts) . . . Who cares? . . . Here's how . . . Tax-I? . . . Put or call? . . . Sidestepping a tax trap . . . Sales in your sunset (sale—or gift—leaseback) . . . Why, oh why? . . . What's it take? . . . Tie tax . . . Divide and conquer (incorporation) . . . Now you see it—now you don't . . . Sophisticated shuffles . . . Getting high on a sub (subchapter S corporations) . . . Putting the S on solid ground . . . Personal holding company . . . Hold on . . . What more could you ask? . . . To have fish for dinner, there must be a catch

13. *A Tax Shelter for Everyone*   152

Those ever-loving deductions . . . Pension and profit-sharing plans—the ultimate tax shelter . . . Not for everyone . . . What's available . . . How (income) taxing is it? . . . Death and taxes . . . The right way to borrow . . . Where there's life (insurance) . . . Buy the numbers (HR-10 plans) . . . Paying the price . . . Putting it in and taking it out . . . A not so tender trap . . . The people's pension (individual retirement account—IRA) . . . What's up? . . . It ain't necessarily so . . . Where does it all go? . . . Rolling over into clover . . . It's all in the timing . . . A super IRA (simplified employee pension plan—S.E.P.P.) . . . How high is up? . . . No free lunch . . . It all comes back to me now

14. Pay Later and Save Money 166

When a payout pays . . . A public idea? (the private annuity) . . . What will it take? . . . Down on the farm . . . What's in and what's out . . . I never promised you a rose garden . . . Why take your lumps? (installment sale) . . . Divide and conquer . . . Who a payout pays . . . Just how good is it? . . . Try the numbers . . . A word of warning . . . Good as gold—or better? (installment payments of estate tax—Section 6166) . . . 6166 by the numbers . . . Fool's gold . . . Paradise lost?

15. Everybody Likes a Bargain 179

Why all the interest in interest free (and low interest) loans? . . . Is it good for you? . . . How do you do? . . . Interesting yes—but taxing? . . . College bound through the reserve loan . . . A word of caution . . . Demand a sample . . . A rose by any other name (Flower Bonds) . . . Soft-peddling . . . There are thorns . . . Stem too stern?

16. Specific Techniques for Eliminating or Reducing Taxes 185

Last of the red-hot bargains (the marital deduction trust) . . . Why trust a trust? . . . P.O.A. versus Q.T.I.P.—what's it mean? . . . Options—old and new . . . The inter vivos (living) trust . . . Life or death? . . . String along . . . It's super . . . No free lunch . . . What happens next? . . . Learning to say no (disclaimers) . . . What you have to do to disclaim . . . Tax-imp-lications

17. If You Work for a Living 198

Keep up with the fringes . . . Would you like it with, or without? . . . Dollar for dollar . . . All of us together . . . An option worth thinking about . . . Social security . . . A good life policy . . . How secure is it? . . . Veterans' benefits . . . Civil service . . . Disability—the living death . . . Protecting your income . . . The choice is up to you . . . Fill in the gaps

18. Minding Your Own Business 212

A man alone (buy-sell agreements) . . . Your brother's keeper . . . Who needs it? . . . A few pennies' worth of planning makes a lot of sense . . . Just what is it we're trying to do here? . . . Finding funding . . . How much is enough? . . . What do we do next? . . . How taxing is it? . . . What about the estate taxation of proceeds? . . . How taxed is the seller? . . . Is part better than whole? (Section 303 stock redemptions) . . . The magic number . . . One more time with no hocus-pocus . . . How to make sure the trick works . . . Name of the

Contents 13

game—survivor's income benefit plan . . . Who would play this game? . . . Kicking off . . . What does it cost the firm? . . . Are you in or out? . . . Feelin' good (medical expense reimbursement plan) . . . A must for your MERP . . . Gotcha covered

19. *Youth, Old Age and Mental Illness* 232

What do you like? (Uniform Gifts to Minors Act) . . . What do you give and what does it take? . . . Tic tax . . . Who can play? . . . In tax savings we trust—the 2503(c) trust . . . Why trust 2503(c)? . . . How's that? . . . Rule-of-thumb tax . . . Consider the alternatives . . . Protecting you against old age . . . Nothing lasts forever—the power of attorney . . . Sensible shifts . . . On and on and on . . . When does it all end? . . . Is it taxing? . . . Don't count on it

20. *Charitable Gifts* 246

Keeping your eye on the ball . . . Giving it now . . . What a charitable contribution really costs . . . How high is up? . . . What's in the future? . . . You're probably wondering . . . Take stock in this gift . . . Where there's life there's hope—and charity . . . Records, records, records . . . Giving it later

21. *Dying and Death: What Can Be Done—Before and After* 259

Death is inevitable—taxes are not . . . What to do when your time is limited . . . Easing administration . . . A "living will" . . . How to increase the overall size of your estate . . . How to reduce transfer taxes . . . How to decrease income taxes . . . Personal touches . . . After death

22. *Wrapping It Up* 265

Taking stock of yourself . . . Getting it together and going for help . . . Get a lawyer you like . . . The addition of an accountant . . . The agent who works for you . . . Bank on the right man—or woman . . . Your executor—an appointment to be carefully considered . . . What does the executor do? . . . Trustees . . . Guardians . . . Educate your survivors—before they are . . . Die rich

Appendixes 275

    A. Your personal fact finder   276
    B. Income tax tables: rates for tax years beginning in 1982, 1983, and thereafter   306
    C. Unified rate schedule for estate and gift taxes: gifts made in 1982, 1983, 1984, and 1985   312

D. Determination of whether estate qualifies for Section 303 stock redemption   313
E. Inventory of important information needed by executors or administrators   315
F. Forms commonly involved in settlement of death   332

Glossary 341

Preface

If you are sincere about planning for your future and being able to "die rich":
1. Read this book thoroughly.
2. Complete "Your Personal Fact-Finder" that you will find in the Appendix.
3. Go back and reread those portions of the book that deal specifically with your situation.
4. Take the necessary action to implement your Plan.

Many get-rich-quick books have been written with abstract schemes that people in normal walks of life would never seriously think of following up. You will find this book completely different. All of the ideas and information contained here are practical and can be followed and adhered to by anyone serious about improving their own situation and safeguarding their family's future.

There is no magic in this book, but there are ideas and information that can save you and your family thousands and thousands of dollars and, at the same time, provide you with peace of mind and a definite plan for your future. This information is usually available only to top corporate executives and professional people, who pay considerable amounts of money for it. Now you have the opportunity to have the same information for the price you paid for this book.

The authors have a combined total of over forty years' experience dealing with all phases of estate planning. Their backgrounds include lecturing to qualified experts, teaching graduate college courses, lecturing to civic and social organizations, and guiding and advising legal clients. Because of the diversity of their contacts with the public, they have gained an understanding of the very wide gap that continues to exist between what can be accomplished to best plan for the future and what is in fact actually being done.

The purpose of this book is not to fill you with abstract concepts that very few people will understand, much less attempt to pursue. Rather, it is to advise you of the many ways in which careful estate planning can make the future much more enjoyable—for you, for the members of your family who will share the future with you, and for your heirs.

A reading of this book should give you an understanding of the countless ways in which you can improve your position today, and in the future, if you will systematically and seriously attempt to do so. When you are aware of the many different approaches that can be of significant value to you and the people who are important to you, then you will be motivated to follow through first on your own, and then with those other advisors whom we shall discuss with you in detail in the book.

In today's complex society, there are innumerable rules, regulations and taxes that affect everyone in America who has managed to accumulate property, regardless of its value. Won't you accept our invitation to attempt to increase the value of your property for your future, and then make certain that your family receives as much of this property as they can possibly get, without its being unnecessarily diluted, or even lost completely, because of lack of planning?

C.K.P.
and
S.R.L.

Introduction

We are writing this book because we firmly believe that anyone who has worked hard all of his/her life deserves to have something to show for it in the end. It is as simple as that. However, we will not attempt to tell you how to beat the system, how to cheat banks, or how to illegally avoid paying taxes. We feel that any individual who has the brains to accumulate property can work within the system to maximize his/her highest potential. The only problem is that very few people understand what the system is all about.

Therefore, our purpose in writing this book is to explain the system to you, tell you what you must know, and where you should go to get advice, so that in the end you can thoroughly reap the benefits that make the American capitalistic system a golden opportunity for those willing to attempt to understand it and to work within its framework.

Technically, we are talking about estate planning. Practically, we are talking about everyday planning that should be understandable to most people and takes into account the accumulation of property and the ability to give that property to whom you wish, in the way that you want to give it, without having it taken away, dissipated, or lost because you did not set things up properly.

There are tax laws with which everyone should be familiar so that he can take advantage of them. There are simple planning devices, like the way we set up our bank accounts, for example, that can save average people thousands of dollars, if only they spend a few minutes to learn what those devices are.

One more caution: while we sincerely believe that no one can read this book without gaining information that can possibly be worth hundreds if not thousands of dollars to them and to their families, we cannot truthfully state that merely by reading this book your personal situation will be greatly improved.

The many ideas in this book must be implemented as they apply to the reader, the reader's family, and his/her family's personal situation. To implement these ideas requires, in many cases, the services of a professional. However, we promise we will not stimulate you to action and then abandon you without giving you guidelines to help implement the ideas. We have therefore devoted part of this book to specific recommendations on how to choose the professionals: insurance men, accountants, lawyers and bankers, if any or all are indicated, to help you complete your plans.

We have also tried to be as nontechnical as possible. Lawyers and accountants get reams of information daily on new tax laws and new cases that seem to show one how to get around each new law as it is passed. It is absolutely impossible in one short, easily readable book to tell you everything there is to know about tax planning and tax laws. However, we have tried to combine essential information about estate planning that everyone should be aware of, with some technical information and down-to-earth practical advice that should be of considerable benefit to almost anyone who has anything of value.

Armed with these ideas, you will be in a much better position to realize the type of professional assistance and advice you need, and this fact alone should repay you many times over for the time you will spend reading the following pages.

Time is a very precious commodity. No matter how wealthy any of us are or how important we think we are in the scheme of life, we can never again recapture a lost minute. Life is the most important thing that we will ever have or could hope to possess. All of us owe it to ourselves and to our loved ones to take a little time to put our lives in order, so that when we come to the end of our lives, we will be able to feel in our hearts that we have done the very best that we could. If we have accomplished this much, then as the title indicates, we will be able to "die rich."

1.
Do You Really Need a Plan?

Do you really need a plan? The answer to that question is an unequivocal yes—as long as there is any person, including yourself, in whom you have the slightest interest. Life is a continuing process, and whether one likes to think about it or not, death is the inevitable conclusion to life. All of us are now in the process of making our way through our own lives, and at some point in time, our lives will come to an end regardless of whether or not we have made plans for ourselves and our families.

While death is inevitable, taxes are not. Almost everyone can reduce his tax burden. Many of us can legitimately avoid taxes altogether. And even worse, a large part of your estate won't go to your family or other beneficiaries, if you don't have a plan. What plans you make now to accumulate, preserve and distribute your estate will strongly influence whether or not your lifetime personal financial goals for yourself and your family will be achieved.

Planning, especially estate planning, is a continuous process of accumulating, conserving and distributing assets in the manner that most effectively accomplishes your objectives. Estate planning is a way to meet personal needs, desires and objectives including the use of tax minimization tools and techniques.

One of the most common fallacies today is the belief that estate planning is only for the wealthy. On the contrary, although vitally important for those persons who have accumulated substantial property, estate planning is just as important, if not more so, for individuals of modest to moderate means. A needless loss of assets to pay taxes or estate settlement costs hurts the survivors even more when the estate is smaller. A few dollars saved by the use of a well-thought-out tax shelter, even if it is only putting the proper title on a bank account, will have the greatest significance in those cases where the bank account in question represents a proportionately larger part of the person's property.

At this point you may be thinking, "What goals do I have that would fall into the category of estate planning?" Typically, most people are interested in estate planning in order to accumulate sufficient assets to provide for a comfortable retirement, take care of themselves and their families in the event of a long-term disability, assure financial security for family members in the event the head of the household should die, secure enough capital to meet college education costs or other special needs and to provide for favorite schools and charitable organizations.

Who cares?

Who really cares about whether or not you have an estate plan? Certainly not the IRS. In fact, if you don't care, nobody will. But you should be aware that somewhere, someone has a plan for you, and that this other plan will go into effect if you don't care enough to formulate one of your own.

In fact, if you do nothing about planning, the federal government and the government of the state in which you reside will plan your estate for you. This is often called "uncontrolled" planning. The cost can be quite high. If you do nothing, you forfeit the right to give your property to the individuals you select in the manner that you choose, to arrange your assets in a manner that would minimize taxes, and, in general, the right to arrange for the disposition of assets and a reduction of taxes and other settlement costs.

One of the most significant attributes of a free society is the fact that you can control the planning of your own estate. You, together with your professional advisors, can measure your needs, establish your own priorities and select your own goals. You can give first preference to accomplishing the needs, goals or objectives that you, and not the federal or state governments, feel are most important.

People planning

There are really two distinct reasons for making an estate plan. The first involves people. Begin with yourself. Look at your situation as it exists today and how it will progress through the years. Are you happy with it? Would you like to take some positive action to change its direction? Do you have a goal or goals you want to achieve?

Then look around you. Estate planning is extremely important for anyone who has minor children; who has an exceptionally artistic or intellectually gifted family member; who has a retarded, emotionally disturbed or physically handicapped child or other dependent. Estate planning is important for anyone who has a house and cannot or does not want to handle money or securities. How about the people who will handle your business or manage your property?

Clearly, everyone's situation is different, because no two people are really alike. Take the case of Ezra and Phyllis, who were both in their late sixties. They had worked hard all of their lives, had accumulated a great deal of property, but they had a very serious problem. The one person about whom they both cared most was their thirty-year-old son, who unfortunately had serious mental and psychological problems. All of the wonderful tax shelters they had been shown, and the many ways in which their estate could be set up to reduce taxes, really held no meaning for them unless their plan would be beneficial for their son.

While other people in their circumstances might have stayed home and felt sorry for themselves, Ezra and Phyllis took action. They contacted a lawyer who specialized in estate planning, and they established a trust with their bank to care for themselves in their old age, in the event they were not competent to care for themselves, and for their son at their deaths. When Ezra died and Phyllis later suffered a stroke, the bank, through the trust they had set up many years before, was able to invest their money and provide the necessary care and attention for both Phyllis and her son, for the rest of their lives. People planning must therefore be an essential element of your plan.

Asset planning

While most people think of asset planning in terms of large amounts of money, asset planning can be important in many situations. For example, in some states there is no state inheritance tax on property owned jointly by husband and wife. Therefore, if the only asset a family has is a $10,000 bank account, there would be no inheritance tax on this property if it were in the joint names of husband and wife. However, if the husband were to die and the property was solely in his name, then a tax would be imposed. Who owns property is therefore an essential element of planning, and here taxes can play a very important part. While taxes and the titling of property will be discussed at length in later chapters, it is important to realize that your plan must deal with the specific assets that comprise your estate. Not only must you be particularly aware of how your assets are titled and their value to you and to the government for tax purposes, but you must be concerned as to what happens to the assets at a later point. Will they stay in their present condition, or will they deteriorate? Will the value fall as the property ages, or will it appreciate because of its inherent value or because of inflation? You must also decide what will happen to the assets at your death and at the death of your spouse.

For federal death tax purposes, from an asset planning point of view, The Economic Recovery Tax Act of 1981 has made tax planning a whole new ball game. Where previously estate planning was indicated if you were single, widowed or divorced, and had assets of over $175,000, there is now a sliding scale increasing annually to 1987, at which time the tax exemption will equal $600,000. If you are married, it is now possible to give an unlimited amount of property to your spouse, estate-tax free.

You will learn why these particular amounts were chosen in the chapters dealing with the federal and state taxes, but at this point it is important to appreciate the necessity of asset planning in any over-all estate plan. You will see that while the above figures are quite large, there are many cases in which taxes can be saved for children, so as to increase the amount of the property they will ultimately receive. You will also see that the value of your property for estate tax purposes can include all or part of your home, the proceeds of life insurance, and just about everything you have. There are also various forms of tax and administrative costs that can be minimized if you own a business or property in more than one state. Certainly, if you own your own business, you have an asset that needs individualized attention. Again, we have specifically considered the effects of planning for your business in a later chapter, but you should realize at this point, that if you do own a business, or are a partner or a shareholder in a business, that the business itself is an asset that requires careful attention and proper planning.

Do you need a plan? The answer is yes, and the implication is that if you are not concerned enough to formulate a plan, then you will unfortunately be subject to a plan that others have made for you, and will impose on you and your family. It is essential to consider those people, including yourself, whose future can be positively affected by proper planning, as well as to consider your assets, and the tax implications of estate planning in regard to what will eventually happen to your property.

2.
What Is Going to Stop You?

You have now accepted the concept of the importance of a plan for you and your family. What now stands between you and the security you would like to provide for your family, or for yourself, or perhaps a friend or favored charity? There is a saying that an estate breaks up not because the estate owner has done anything wrong—but because he or she hasn't done anything—and that's wrong!

There are many reasons why people fail to take any action and formulate a plan, causing a breakup in their estate and a complete loss of security for the future of themselves and their families. If you can recognize these obstacles, you should be able to easily overcome them and get your plan underway.

Don't know where to start

It is certainly difficult to accomplish a given task if you don't know where to start. Estate planning for yourself and for your family is really an all-encompassing objective and an easy task to set aside because of its complexities and your inability to know how to attack the problem. One of the prime considerations in this book is therefore to illustrate precisely where to start, and the information contained in the next three chapters will provide you with this precise information, and you can then be well on your way to a more secure future.

Fear and distaste

One of the real tests of a successful person is the ability to perform distasteful tasks. Successful executives frequently start their day by first taking care of, and thereby eliminating from the workload, the most difficult or unpleasant item on their agenda. They realize that once this problem has been disposed of, they will have clear sailing to tackle those matters with which they feel more comfortable. This is in stark contrast to the individual who keeps putting off distasteful, though important, obligations, and in the end never does get to them. The same is true when it comes to planning your estate.

The prospect of dying is certainly not a pleasant subject. But the mere fact that death might be a rather unpleasant matter to think about will in no way lessen its impact upon the survivors who were dependent upon the deceased. For those who find planning for death a fearful and distasteful matter, it might be helpful to balance these feelings with the knowledge of what their thoughts would be in the future if they knew they were about to die and knew that they had made no plans at all in regard to the effect of their death on their families and other survivors.

Too busy

There is a constant demand on your time in today's society. Life appears to be much more complex than it was fifty years ago. Not only are there more specific jobs and tasks to be performed, but the accounting procedures for them, coupled with taxes, budgeting and other problems, can fill your day from morning to night. There is but one way to overcome the problem of this limitation on your available time and that is by instituting a system of priorities. If something is really important to you, it must be placed ahead of other tasks, even though they seem to be all-encompassing at the time. In this manner, the truly important items on your list will be accomplished, and you will find you still have time to take care of other more routine matters.

Have you ever noticed, when you read the newspaper, that those people with the most important and time-consuming positions are the ones that constantly take on new projects? Charitable and civic leaders are rarely retired, unemployed persons. They are mostly active leaders in business and the professions, whose backgrounds would seem to imply that they have absolutely no time available to take on any new projects. But they do, and they do it successfully. There is then, no excuse for being too busy to plan for your future and your family's future. If you are worried about what might happen to you if you don't put money away for yourself for retirement, and if you think the possibility of your becoming ill and dying is a matter of so little consequence that it is near the bottom of your priority list, then you probably would not have had the interest to buy this book. However, if you are genuinely concerned about the family's future, as well as your own, planning your estate will become your number one priority.

General dislike of attorneys, banks and insurance men

You are all psyched up to formulate an excellent plan, but you are hesitant about contacting a lawyer, an insurance man or someone from the bank. Perhaps this hesitancy is based on a prior unfortunate experience, but, in general, it is based on preconceived ideas without factual basis.

Later in this book, you will find specific advice on the selection of personal advisors. However, if your hesitancy about making plans for your future is caused by an unwillingness to deal with specific advisors, then you must first overcome this reluctance in order to take the steps necessary to protect your family. You are not only an important individual in your own right, but you are a potential client or customer. As such, you have the absolute right to select those individuals with whom you feel most comfortable and whose background, education and experience indicate that they can be most helpful to you. You are not obligated to do business with the first individual with whom you come in contact, regardless of the importance of his/her position or background. There are numerous experienced attorneys who deal with estate matters, and they will be most anxious to work with you in planning your future. If for any reason, after an initial conference it is your impression that the attorney whom you have consulted does not have either the background or experience, the fee schedule that meets with your approval, or the necessary concern about your situation, then you should not hesitate to pay that individual for his time for the initial conference, and seek counsel elsewhere.

In regard to insurance advisors, you have the choice of many professionals who will be more than pleased to assist you in formulating a plan. Insurance companies have long realized the necessity of formalized training for their agents, and experienced agents, especially those with the degree of Chartered Life Underwriter (CLU), have a history of offering quality services to prospective clients. Again, if after your initial contact you do not feel comfortable with the individual, you should have no problem in obtaining qualified help elsewhere.

The estate planning and trust departments of commercial banks offer services to their general banking clients in the field of estate planning that deserves your considered attention. Banks and bankers, like other successful businessmen, are usually quite anxious to make their commercial banking customers—those with checking accounts, savings accounts, loans, and so forth, familiar with the estate planning services that are available to their customers. It is therefore in the bank's interest, as well as your own, to discuss your plans with a representative of your bank's estate planning department. Again, be acutely aware of the fact that you are the individual whose "business" is being solicited and whose sense of approval is desired by the professional. Since you are, in fact, in the driver's seat, there should be no hesitancy on your part to associate yourself with a good professional advisor.

Failure to realize magnitude of problem and tax consequences

One reason that people often give for failure to plan for their future is that there really is no need for a plan. Stuart and Elaine were two young people who thought that no planning was necessary in their situation. They each worked for a large corporation, had excellent insurance and other fringe benefits, and had enough additional income to buy three pieces of real estate in addition to their home. Since they only had one son, who was already fifteen years old, and held all of their property in joint names, they were sure their company's insurance benefits and their own real estate would provide the funds to take care of any future problems.

Unfortunately, Stuart and Elaine were involved in an automobile accident in which Stuart was killed instantly. Elaine survived for twenty days and then died. The adverse tax consequences, as well as the emotional impact on their son, were of a magnitude that neither could have foreseen. In reconstructing their estate, it was discovered that by proper planning their son would have received $120,000 more than he eventually did. This very large amount was paid in taxes that could have been easily and legally avoided, if Stuart and Elaine had formulated a basically simple and quite inexpensive estate plan.

At the very least, you should have your situation professionally evaluated, if after reading this book, you have even the slightest indication of a potential problem area.

Unwillingness to address family situations

It is easy to plan when you have a husband, wife and child all living together in a happy, healthy and loving environment. The situation lends itself to a logical plan providing for the future of the husband and wife together, provisions for the surviving spouse in the event of the death of the other, and provisions for the future education, support and maintenance of the child in the event of the death of one or both of the parents. All families, however, are not created equal, and in some there are particular problems that need tough decisions. What do you do about providing for your spouse if you are separated but your spouse is caring for your minor child? What estate plans should you make where you have three children, all of whom you love, but one of whom has a disability that will handicap him/her for the rest of his/her life? How do you make provisions in your will for your dependent mother when you know that your wife and mother have never gotten along well together? These are serious decisions requiring delicate but responsible solutions. They are the types of problems that so many people continually set aside for some future date, at which time (they hope) the problem will have disappeared. In fact, should *you* disappear before the problem does, then you will have made a very difficult problem completely unmanageable. If the answers to these questions were hard for you to answer during your lifetime, how can you expect them to be logically and neatly solved if you are no longer here?

Why leave your family with the problem, when you could have solved it with some technical planning, some good advice, and by making some down-to-earth, tough decisions? If you had lived, wouldn't you have given more to the disabled child throughout the course of his/her life than to your other children, if they were self-sufficient? Wouldn't you have continued to give your mother some money, despite any differences between your wife and mother? In short, the very reason you might hesitate to take any action at this time is in fact the very reason that you must take action now. Otherwise, the difficult decisions that you have avoided making can result in a lifetime of difficulty for your surviving family members.

Belief in lasting health and immortality

Although no one has done it yet, some of us still think we will live forever, and when you are young and healthy, there really is no point in making plans for your old age or death. Unfortunately, when you are old it is usually too late to accomplish what otherwise could have been done. The time to save for your old age is when you are young. The time to buy life insurance is when it is cheap and you are insurable. The time to worry about disability is when you are well enough to buy disability insurance. And, of course, the time to make your will is *now!* One of the truly fine features of any estate plan is its flexibility. In other words, plans can be changed as situations change. But just because things will be different later does not mean that you should wait until later to make your plans.

You didn't have to buy this book to find out that death is inevitable, but even so, taxes are not inevitable. There is a very important distinction between death and taxes—death doesn't get worse every time Congress meets.

3.
Identify the Enemy

With the obstacles of ignorance, fear, work, indecision, hesitancy and indifference now behind you, you are ready to do battle with the enemy. But you must know exactly who the enemy is. Let's explore its many faces.

Inflation—the odds against being adequately prepared

Almost everyone can remember when, with a few dollars in our pocket, we set out to buy something for someone we cared about. After carefully choosing and selecting just that certain something we knew would be appropriate for the occasion, we found our balloon of happiness deflated when we learned that the money we had was not enough to purchase the particular object we had selected. We had everything we could possibly need to accomplish our goal, except that we just weren't quite prepared to pay for what we wanted.

Isn't this illustrative of what is happening to all of us today? We make plans to do certain things and buy certain things, and the price is always increasing, sometimes beyond our reach. Isn't it true that whether the economists tell us we are in good times or bad times, the price of everything keeps increasing?

The dictionary defines inflation as an increase of the amount of currency in circulation, resulting in a relatively sharp and sudden fall in value and rise in prices; it may be caused by an increase in the volume of paper money issued or of gold mined, or a relative increase in expenditures, as when the supply of goods fails to meet the demand.

If you find the above statement complicated and hard to understand, you are in good company. The leading economists of our day have obviously been unable to control inflation by their attempts to vary some of the components that they claim cause inflation, and about the only certain statement that can be made is that you should seriously consider the detrimental effects inflation can have on your future planning.

The cost of your basic family needs—food, clothing and housing—have been continually increasing. Therefore, any funds designed to cover these needs for yourself and your family at a later date must take into consideration that the amount of money needed to provide these basic necessities can be far greater than it is today. Therefore, it first makes good sense when providing for future expenditures to build in an increasing percentage factor, so that your future projection will be realistic.

Lack of security for you and your family

What a great feeling it would be to eliminate the fear of financial insecurity in the future. Unless you have already amassed sufficient funds to take care of yourself, and your family after you, this should be quite high on your priority list. Future financial insecurity is one of the overriding negative factors that you should pinpoint, and then attempt to eliminate or reduce to the greatest extent possible. But if life is so complex and changing in today's highly technological world, is there really anything that you as an individual can do to reduce, or attempt to eliminate, potential future insecurity? The answer is that there is a great deal you can do, and in fact certain things that you must do now.

First of all, while you don't have to be a clairvoyant who knows what will happen to you and your family during the coming years, who else is in a better position to project where you and your family will be five, ten or twenty years from now? If you have young children, there is a good chance that college educations will still be needed, the mortgage payments will still have to be paid, and, even if you can't be certain what costs will be for food, transportation, clothing, and so forth, you can be pretty certain that they will be at least the same as they are now if not more. Your plan must therefore be started now, utilizing the information and past history that you have amassed, with a projection of what you think will happen as of the time the plan is put into effect. Even if your assumptions aren't 100 percent accurate, 80 percent secure is certainly better than complete insecurity.

How much is security? That will, of course, vary with the goals and needs of the people involved. A $100,000-a-year executive who spends $125,000 a year can be much more insecure than an individual who makes $20,000 a year and still manages to put aside $1,500 a year for his future security. Fortunately there are many avenues open by which you may provide this future security, and after you have completed this book, you should be in a position to attempt to alleviate most of your serious concerns about the future.

An adequate income if disabled

Unless you personally know someone who has been seriously or permanently disabled, you can't appreciate the enormity of the problems that can arise. Disability has been called, and rightly so, a living death. It is an enemy to be greatly feared and one that requires careful planning to protect against.

Susan and David Hyatt are in their mid thirties. They have two children in their middle school years, live in a nice home, have good friends and consider themselves to be quite secure in regard to the future. David has been employed by a small company for the past ten years, where he has worked himself up to a managerial position, and Susan plans to resume teaching within the next few years. It is hard for them to save money, but David's income does cover their needs with some savings for college and vacations. David has purchased life insurance, and his employer provides hospitalization coverage and group life insurance. No one could have foreseen that David would become the victim of a tragically crippling disease that would force him to be removed completely from the work force and eliminate his earned income. Unfortunately, disability was the one contingency for which Susan and David were not prepared, and the mental effect upon David of staying home and watching his once fortunate family eke out a meager existence was just as hard on him as the effects of his physical illness.

Fortunately there are ways to plan for such contingencies, as indicated in Chapter 19, and these ideas should be incorporated in your future planning.

Excessive transfer costs

One of the areas in which you can greatly reduce future costs for your family is in the area of probate costs, inheritance and state taxes. In Chapter 10 you will find tax saving ideas that can help to reduce or eliminate most if not all taxes in modest estates and also ideas that can save many thousands of dollars, if the amount of your property at the time of your death would be such as to warrant implementation of these important tax saving ideas.

Unfortunately, for those persons who have not explored the financial consequences associated with death and the transfer of property, these taxes remain an unknown enemy, and therefore one against which they fail to prepare.

For example, there is different tax treatment of property held jointly between husband and wife, as indicated in Chapter 6, compelling reasons for a will, as indicated in Chapter 7, excellent ways to reduce transfer costs by gifts, as indicated in Chapter 9, and ways that you can reduce transfer costs by creating tax-exempt wealth, as indicated in Chapter 12. In addition to the above suggestions, the latter Chapters contain other specific recommendations that can save you money and save transfer costs to your family, regardless of whether you are worth a few dollars or a few million dollars. In fact, the less you have, the greater the percentage of your property it is possible to save by utilizing this information.

It is therefore incumbent upon you to know exactly what taxes will be imposed upon your estate at your death and what costs your family or heirs will be called upon to pay for the privilege of having your property transferred to them. As you will see in this book, once you know what is involved, you can implement the cost saving and tax ideas so that you can give to your family that amount you wanted them to receive, instead of having your assets severely depleted by excessive transfer costs.

Lack of liquidity

One enemy that manages to shoot down so very many well-thought-out plans is that "money-squeeze-crunch" known as "lack of liquidity." One of the most common known applications of lack of liquidity is the situation we find ourselves in when the bills keep coming in and we don't have the liquidity to take care of these obligations. (By liquid assets we mean cash or other property such as certificates of deposit or "E" bonds that can be readily converted to cash.) However, in most cases we are all too well aware of the fact that the obligations exist and that funds have to be made available to take care of our obligations.

There are, however, situations that arise where money is required to meet certain obligations and in which the need for the funds was not anticipated and so not planned for. This failure to anticipate the need for liquidity can have unfortunate consequences, even over and above the need for the specific amount involved. Consider the following—

Joe and Elaine were what their neighbors considered to be "well off." They had raised their children and were now enjoying the benefits of a comfortable business that they ran together in a small town. They had saved enough money to buy the building in which the business was located, and, now that the children were away from home, Elaine was also working in the business. They had cancelled their life insurance because the children were on their own and because Elaine could really take care of most of the business herself and felt she didn't need the insurance money. They both believed that their store was their future and that no other planning was necessary.

Even after Joe's untimely death, Elaine felt that the business was her security. In fact, Elaine didn't realize that she would have any financial problems until she discovered the amount of death taxes that were due and the fact that there was no money available to pay them, since everything was tied up in the store and the business. Although Elaine's assets had considerable value, Joe's estate did not provide the amount of liquidity that would have enabled Elaine to satisfy the costs and expenses arising from Joe's death, and then pay all of the taxes that were due. Elaine therefore had to look to the business and real estate in order to obtain the necessary funds to satisfy the obligations arising from Joe's death, including the possibility of a forced sale of the store or building. Lack of liquidity was an enemy Joe and Elaine had failed to consider.

"How liquid should you be?" The answer depends on your knowledge of approximately what the costs, expenses and taxes will be in your estate. You will be in a much better position to know what your liquidity problems will be after reading this book, and particularly Chapter 10 on what the Feds get and the state of state death taxation.

Your own special problem

Up to this point, this chapter has presented some of the most serious problems against which your plan should consider protecting you and your family. However, your own situation might call for protection from an "enemy" against which you will have to formulate your own specific plan.

For example, you might have a parent or in-law residing with you and dependent on your income. What happens to that dependent parent when you die? Does he/she become your wife's or children's obligation? Isn't there a better way to plan ahead to provide the necessary money and care for your loved one, while at the same time not imposing a burden or economic hardship on your spouse and children? You might need your plan to include a lifetime arrangement for this situation, and your utilization of one of the ideas set forth in Chapter 19 on Youth, Old Age, and Mental Illness. At the very least, the problem calls for you to make plans to solve it now, as opposed to leaving the problem for your heirs to solve, with the resulting emotional and financial difficulties that a later decision would impose on all of the participants.

Your special problem might instead be a child whose funds will require long-term supervision, or perhaps your domestic situation is such that an individualized approach is necessitated. If you are divorced and have children, then your plans and your children's needs will certainly differ from the plans that might otherwise be made had you been married at the time of your death. Regardless of your situation, you can't put these potential problems on the back burner and hope they disappear. Identify them as problems, and recognize that your plans must provide a solution for them. Only in this manner will your plan be one that truly will satisfy your needs and those of your family and those other individuals for whom you wish to adequately provide.

4.
The One and Only You

Why you are unique

You are a very unusual person. You have many characteristics similar to your neighbors', but you are still separate and distinct from everyone else. That is not to say that you don't have things in common with other people. You may live next door to someone who works in the same place of employment, and you may live in the same type of home. Your spouse and children may be the same ages as your neighbors', but even with all that in common, you know that you are different from your neighbor. Your likes and dislikes, your savings habits, your health, your outlook on life, your background, your ambition, and your goals for yourself and your family all may be different. In short, you are you, and you are unique.

If this is in fact the case, then why are you often treated as if you were the same as everyone else, or at least everyone else in your economic circumstances, religious group, geographical area, or place of employment? The answer is that it is easier to categorize people and to generalize about peculiar attributes that certain groups in society share. These generalizations are often built on myth, can be created as an advertising promotion, or can be arrived at after some type of research has been performed but with a sampling that doesn't really consider all of the many possible variables involved.

Not only are you unique, but you are a very important person. You have your own thoughts, your own ideas, and your own plans and goals for your future and for your family. If this is so, then why do people constantly try to place you into a group without considering your personal wishes and desires?

The telephone rings. The insurance representative introduces himself politely and tells you that his company has just designed a new plan that he thinks would be an excellent one for you. In fact, it's such a good plan that your business associate, Ed Robinson, had suggested that the agent review the plan with you.

What in fact has really taken place? You have been relegated to a group comprising thousands of persons. The group can be as large as all males between ages twenty-one and sixty-five, or as small as the employees of Johnson's Vacuum Cleaner Repair Company. The fact of the matter is that what you are buying, if you subscribe to the plan, is a packaged product. Now there are many products not built specifically to your individual requirements that are desirable. We buy automobiles, television sets, even dinner at a restaurant. But when it comes to designing and implementing a plan for yourself and your family, you really can't afford to go into the clothing store and take a suit off the rack. You should have a made-to-measure plan, tailored specifically to your needs and those of your family. If a tailor-made suit could sell for the same price as a ready-made one, chances are you might think long and hard before buying the same thing everyone else is wearing. There is no requirement that a plan tailor-made to your specifications need cost more than the package plan that anyone can buy.

The lawyer who prepares your will can also be as guilty as the insurance man with a prepared package. If, for example, you are merely asked to furnish the names of your beneficiaries, how much they are to receive, and who will supervise the distribution of the assets, then in effect, you are getting a packaged will. Before preparing your will, and any trust instruments or other documents that will be an integral part of any plan you might make, whoever has the responsibility for preparing all or part of your plan must know two specific things. First, he/she must know all of the facts concerning the people involved and the assets to be distributed and second, must know your specific goals, ideas and plans for your family and yourself.

There is a story about a very successful insurance agent who insisted on prying beneath the surface to obtain all of the information possible concerning his prospective client before making a recommendation that would be geared to the client's specific needs. He had been talking to a successful businessman who had gone on at great length to describe his business, his other assets, the names of his family members, his wife, his children, how much money he was making now, how much he would need in the future, and how much money he had available to spend for insurance. Finally, after coming to the end of inventorying his family and business, he turned to the insurance representative and said to him, "Well, now that you have absolutely all of the information I could possibly give you about my situation, how much insurance would you recommend I buy?" To which the agent replied in a courteous and deliberate fashion, "But there is one thing you haven't told me, Mr. Jones— you haven't told me how much you love your wife." Make sure that your plans truly represent the real you.

Different strokes for different folks

If everyone is different, then it follows that everyone deserves to be treated as an individual, or even as a family unit with its own distinct property, goals and objectives. You should keep a big distance between yourself and the "estate planner" who has the solution to your problem before he really knows the problem. In fact, you should also be wary of someone who is ready to jump in with a solution before you have completely finished advising that person of all the facts, or, if you are aware that some key elements are not known to your purported advisor at the time that he makes suggestions concerning your estate plan.

In the next chapter we will deal specifically with what information must be assembled and analyzed before any solutions can be recommended. Once all of the available information is known, you can be in a position to decide the best arrangements for you and your family, and then, and only then, can anyone else be in a position to offer you guidance to help you formulate a plan based on your goals and needs.

Before the Tax Act of 1981 was passed, a simple but effective way of removing property from an estate was by transferring ownership of a life insurance policy as discussed later in this book. It was a tax-saving device often recommended by insurance men and other estate planners to reduce estate taxes in the husband's estate. However, general recommendations of this type of "plan" made without inquiring into the many variables involved often resulted in unfortunate and unexpected results.

In those situations where the parties later divorced and the ex-wife became the owner of the policy on the life of her former husband, serious problems arose. If the husband became uninsurable and remarried and had children who needed protection from a policy he no longer owned, a simple estate planning device could become a domestic relations nightmare. The new tax law has changed the necessity for this type of transfer, as will be discussed, but where the damage has been done, it may be too late to change it.

Don't rush to get involved in new tax-savings plans unless you are certain that you personally will in fact benefit from them. Savings plans, real estate and stock plans that often promise higher returns "after taxes" may in fact deliver these "higher returns" only to those persons in a higher income tax bracket than you. And of course, a major consideration must be, does the plan in question help you achieve your goal—which may or may not be entirely financial. Do you want safety as opposed to the opportunity for the highest possible return?

Should the emphasis be on retirement, death benefits, or what you'll need next year to get by on? Different goals, different people, different situations—and therefore no one else should substitute their goals and aspirations for yours.

What are you really worth?

Now that you have clearly established that you are a unique individual, that your needs are different from those of everyone else, take a good look at yourself and make a determination as to what you are really worth. It is not an easy question to answer, so perhaps it would be best to break it down into several different categories. For example: (1) what are you really worth today, assuming that you keep working at what you are now doing and your assets remain fairly constant? (2) what are you really worth if you were not to consider your earned income but had to rely solely on the return from your investments and capital? (3) what are you really worth to your family if something were to happen to you today?

As a working individual, you receive a return for your work that is called earned income. Some people have compared the working individual to a machine, which is a capital investment that throws off a certain return (earnings) as a result of the work performed. The answer you already know. It gets paid to you in the form of your salary or in the form of the money that you take from a business that you own yourself. In most cases this is by far the

The One and Only You

largest source of income presently available to you and your family.

The next category is the return on your capital or investments. To obtain this answer requires some work. There are forms at the end of this book, which you can use to make an inventory of all your assets. In Chapter 5, A Blueprint for Your Future, the forms will be discussed in greater detail. In order for you to make a determination as to what you are really worth, you will have to gather all the information relating to your property. Use these forms to simplify assembling the data, and you can arrive at an amount that will represent the current market value of the assets that comprise your present estate. What is the real worth of these assets? The only way to make a determination as to the real value to you and your family of your "capital assets" is to review them so that you can arrive at a figure that would represent the amount of income that this property could throw off to you and your family. In these days of rapidly changing interest rates, it is difficult if not impossible to select an exact figure that would represent the amount of return you could expect to receive on your capital investments. For example, say you were to add up a list of all your assets and the resulting figure was $40,000; if this $40,000 could be converted to cash and invested, what return could you reasonably expect? Formerly, most planners would use a conservative 5 percent or closely related figure. Today, it might be permissible to go as high as 8 percent, keeping in mind that if security is your goal, you should take a conservative approach to the amount of expected return without the risk of overestimating the potential income that could be realized from your assets.

Therefore, if you hope to retire in twenty years, your plan must take into account the fact that at that point your earned income will stop, and the return on your investments, plus whatever other retirement plan will be in effect at that time, must equal the amount of income you hope to receive at that time. Other retirement income would come from whatever company or individual retirement plan you might have (discussed in detail in Chapters 12, 14, 15, 19, and 20) as well as any help you might receive from your government plan (covered in Chapter 19). If it looks as though you might fall short, then you will have to take steps to increase your income, utilizing the many saving techniques in this book, so that you can achieve your goal.

Lastly, if you were to die tomorrow, what would you really be worth to your family? Since the income derived as the result of your working would stop, while the value of your other assets would remain relatively constant, it is obviously necessary for you to arrange to offset this lack of income. Life insurance, social security, if applicable and available, can go a long way toward filling this gap. But today, right now, what are you worth to your family in the event of your death? Take your assets, the amount of your insurance or other death benefits, use 8 percent or whatever conservative figure you select, and you will have the answer. If you have $50,000 in insurance, at 8 percent your family will receive $4,000 a year; $100,000 in insurance and other benefits would produce an income of $8,000 per year or $667 a month. $250,000 invested at 8 percent would provide a weekly income of $385. Of course, higher rates of return would necessitate accumulating a smaller amount of principal, but you are dealing with your future and your family's, so keep abreast of the current rates of return by all means, but act conservatively. Certainly, if you consider the potential decrease in purchasing power that inflation can bring, a conservative estimate would be closer to reality. In any event, it is always better to have a little too much than not quite enough.

5.
A Blueprint for Your Future

Gathering the information

Now that you are aware of the necessity for planning, the obstacles that stand in your path, and the need for individualizing your plan, you are ready to begin. Like the architect whose soaring skyscraper must first be planned and sketched out in detail, you too must have a blueprint for your future. Nothing of lasting consequence can be accomplished on a trial and error, hit or miss basis, and therefore your plan for the future of your family and yourself must also be built on a firm foundation.

In order to chart a course, it is important to know where you stand at the present time. Chances are you have already accomplished quite a bit to date, and whatever property you do have will serve as a base for future acquisitions.

What information do you need? How do you go about gathering it? Appendix A to this book is called Your Personal Fact-finder. The information requested in the fact-finder should encompass most if not all of what will be necessary to give you a complete picture of your present situation. The fact-finder asks you to complete information about yourself, your family, the names of your personal advisors, updated information as to any present estate planning documents such as wills, marital agreements, trusts, custodianships, social security information and the like. It requires you to list specific information concerning your real estate, securities and mortgages, and personal property such as household furnishings, automobiles, and jewelry. Information is requested about bank accounts, savings, checking, cash, and miscellaneous property. Space is provided for specific information about all of the life insurance policies owned by you, policies insuring your life and the lives of the members of your family.

Information is requested about hospitalization insurance and disability coverage. In the event that you are self-employed or have an interest in a closely held business, there are forms provided to complete this information.

If you work for a salary, specific information is requested concerning employee group insurance, qualified and nonqualified pension benefits, as well as other specific employee–employer type arrangements.

Lastly, you are asked to list the various sources of your family income. While the forms might take some time to prepare, you should find that completing them, instead of being a routine task, can be quite an enlightening experience. For example, by reviewing your insurance and company benefits thoroughly in order to furnish the required information, you might find that they are not set up precisely as you thought they were and, in fact, might actually be set up improperly. Stock certificates that you thought were in joint names might be in your name or your wife's name alone. Deeds to property can sometimes be typed incorrectly, and beneficiary provisions of company-sponsored plans may be outdated. Quite often, business agreements may become outmoded, mostly from sheer neglect rather than from any intentional desire to deprive a business associate, or yourself, of what either might otherwise be entitled to. Again, it is much better to discover any inaccuracies that may exist at this time rather than at some point in the future when it might be too late to change them to accomplish the purposes for which they were originally made.

Analyzing the needs

You now have a clear picture of what you have and how it is set up. You've more or less frozen a period in time and, for that given moment, constructed a balance sheet of your family's current assets. Now let's look at your financial picture, not in terms of what you now have or don't have, but in terms of your continuing family finances. Do you live on a monthly budget? How much do you save annually? What methods of savings or investing do you prefer? The next section in your family fact-finder will enable you to detail how your present family finances are conducted and will also give you the opportunity to analyze for yourself those forms of savings or investments that you now prefer.

Next, you are asked to state, in terms of your own priorities, the importance of adequate funds for disability, retirement, college

A Blueprint for Your Future

education, or your own specific needs. Space is provided to detail any educational needs that your family might have.

Formulating a plan

Now for the all-important task of formulating a preliminary plan.

First, let's look at what your income and capital needs will be so that you can have financial independence without working. At what age would you like to retire and what do you estimate at the present time your required monthly retirement income should be? What sources of funds do you at present expect to fulfill the above requirements? And how do you propose to fill in any difference between what you hope to have and what your present plans will provide?

A thorough plan must cover all contingencies, and therefore you should include provision for income and capital needs during any possible future disability. In such a case, what would you estimate your required monthly income to be at retirement age and what sources of funds at present are expected to fulfill these needs and requirements? Again, your confidential fact-finder will help you make these determinations.

Lastly, what income and capital needs do you foresee following your death? What will your surviving spouse and dependent children require for their income during any adjustment period, until your youngest child is self-supporting, and what will it take to provide a life income for your surviving spouse after your youngest child is self-supporting? How about capital or lump-sum needs? Should there be money set aside for emergencies, to cancel an outstanding mortgage, to clear up any outstanding notes and taxes, or for education? What sources of income will help satisfy these needs? What government benefits or company pension plans can you count on? What other sources of capital do you have? Can you expect them from insurance, or the proceeds of business agreements? Again, the fact-finder will assist you in eliciting the above information and in making any determination.

The last page in your plan calls for you to list your present liabilities and any additional factors affecting your plan other than those already considered.

Testing and implementing plan

You have now prepared what should be considered a first

draft of what your plan will eventually be. However, your plan must be tested against the many factors beyond your control that can affect your future, your family's future, and the financial position of everyone involved. In order for your blueprint to be properly useful, it must be able to withstand unexpected problems, expenses and taxes. Therefore, before you can begin to implement the plan, you have to be aware of the legal and tax implications of what can happen in the future to your property in the course of transferring it to your family in the event of your death. The taxes and cost consequences can, in effect, prevent your property from going to your family in the way you want it to and a large percentage may go either to the government by way of taxes or for unnecessary probate costs and other expenses that should have been avoided by planning. Therefore, you have to test your plan to see if it maximizes your tax advantages and reduces, to the greatest extent possible, any costs or expenses that will have to be paid. In order to do this you have to know what the federal estate tax will be and what the state death taxes are, as set forth in detail in Chapter 10. You have to know how to keep up with your fringe benefits and get the most from your government sponsored plan, as indicated in Chapter 19. If you are in business for yourself, you must take the proper precautions to maximize and stabilize the value of your business and to eliminate death and disability problems.

There are specific ways that money can be set up for your children—and for your parents if they are dependent on you for their income.

What's really the best way to utilize life insurance to maximize its benefits for your family? How can one create tax-exempt wealth? And what are some of the specific tax saving techniques that you personally can use to reduce your taxes?

Lastly, to whom do you turn for the proper advice and guidance to help you finalize and implement your plan? The answers to all these questions are contained in the following chapters. Armed with the information they contain, and counseled by the types of advisors recommended in this book, you will have taken a giant step toward future financial independence for your family and yourself.

Reviewing the plan

When a new building is finished, the architect's blueprint hasn't served its entire purpose; it may be needed as a starting point for remodeling the building later to serve a new purpose. The subject matter of your blueprint does not stay fixed, either, but is constantly changing. Your life, and the lives of your family, friends, and potential heirs and beneficiaries, are always evolving. Because of this, your plan must not remain static. It should be reviewed and evaluated whenever there is a change in the personal situation of any of the people whose lives the plan touches. Certainly, it should be reviewed and revised if necessary when there is a change in the property or tax laws that will affect the plan. At the very least, a periodic review should be made every three years to be certain that your plan will accomplish its intended purpose.

Put yourself on your own payroll

You've heard it many, many times: It's just impossible to keep up with present expenses without going further into a hole. How can I possibly take any steps, or set aside even a minimum amount of money, to accomplish any of these future goals?

There are two ways you can accomplish your ambitions for the future. First, by utilizing some of the ideas contained in this book, you may find that you have more money available to you to accomplish the goals that you have set for yourself. Better planning can mean less taxes. It can mean more after-tax dollars to you. However created, these additional funds can help provide a meaningful part of your future financial security.

There is also a second way. If you feel that all of your money is going out and none of it manages to stick to your fingers, then you apparently have everyone on your payroll. The mortgage company or your landlord is on your payroll. The supermarket is on your payroll. The department store or clothing store is on your payroll. The government that collects your taxes is on your payroll. The utility company is on your payroll. In fact, just about everyone is on your own personal payroll with the exception of one very important person—yourself. Therefore, why not put yourself on your own payroll. If your plan calls for you to put an extra $25 a week into securities, insurance, or in the bank for a future home or real estate investment, then make certain that you do it. In fact, put yourself high up on the payroll, so that you don't overlook yourself when it comes time to pay your obligations. If you do, you'll find that there still might not be anything left at the end, but at least you will have provided the funds necessary to protect one of your most valuable assets—your interest in the future of your family and yourself.

6.
What's in a Name?

How you take title to property is extremely important. Should your car be in your name alone? Why does almost every married couple who owns a home have title in both names? When should property be in one name alone and what's the difference anyway? Most important, what's the best way for you to take title to your assets?

Jack and Donna Pursel recently purchased a new home. The title to their home reads, "Jack and Donna Pursel, tenants by the entireties." What does a "tenancy by the entirety" mean and what are the tax implications? How does a tenancy by the entirety differ from a "joint tenancy with right of survivorship"? And what's the difference how their property is titled?

Like and dislike

Let's start by examining the similarities and distinctions between a tenancy by the entirety and a joint tenancy with the right of survivorship.

First, in both cases, if either Jack or Donna (the joint tenants) should die, the interest of the decedent passes by law directly to the survivor. So if Jack dies first, Donna automatically owns both her interest and the interest Jack had owned. In either case the property she'll own will be free from the claims of Jack's personal creditors.

Since both forms of property ownership either implicitly or directly give the co-owners "rights of survivorship," the survivor doesn't have to worry about what the decedent's will says—or does not say. Because Jack's interest passes by law and not under his will, Donna will not have to worry that Jack's other heirs may attack his will. She takes her interest in these two forms of jointly held property automatically at his death.

Another similarity between the two forms of joint tenancy is that in both cases the property passes outside of probate, the legal process under which a will is proved to be the decedent's last will and under which the estate is administered (discussed in detail in Chapter 7). Avoiding probate may save costs in some cases and avoid delays.

A distinction between a tenancy by the entirety and a joint tenancy with a right of survivorship is that the latter may consist of any number of persons and can exist whether or not those persons are related by marriage. Jack's two brothers and three cousins could join Jack and purchase property jointly and each co-tenant could have rights of survivorship. But a tenancy by the entirety can exist only between a husband and wife.

Most important, each joint tenant of a "rights of survivorship" tenancy can, without anyone else's approval or signature, sever ("partition") the tenancy. In the example above, one of Jack's cousins could unilaterally decide to sell her interest—or give it away—say to her friend Sadie. Sadie, the purchaser, would then be a "tenant-in-common" with all the other co-tenants. The contractual relationship of Jack and his cousins toward each other would not change. They are *still* joint tenants with rights of survivorship. But as to Sadie, the new tenant, they would be tenants-in-common. That means, if Sadie dies, her interest does not go automatically to the survivors. Instead, it would go to her beneficiaries under her will or, if she didn't have a valid will, to her heirs under her state's intestacy laws. If Jack (or any of the other tenants with rights of survivorship) died, his property interest would be redistributed among the survivors—except for Sadie who didn't have survivorship rights.

Another way for several people to hold property is therefore "in-common" as opposed to "with right of survivorship." In those situations in which title is held as "tenants-in-common," even if originally set up this way, upon the death of one co-tenant, his/her estate (and eventually the beneficiaries of that estate) will own the share that had belonged to the deceased co-owner.

A spouse who owns a property interest as tenant by the entirety cannot unilaterally sever (sell or give away) his/her interest. Severance can only occur by mutual agreement, termination by divorce, or conveyance by both spouses to a third party. For example,

Donna could not sell or give away her share of the house unless Jack agreed to the sale in writing.

So what's good about joint tenancies?

What's good about tenancies by the entirety or joint tenancies with rights of survivorship? Why do so many people own property in one of these ways? The answer is, lots of reasons.

First, you can be sure if your co-tenant dies that the property will be quickly, easily, and (in most states) automatically transferred to you. So you have the psychological sense of family unity and security. That's why most financial advisors recommend that the family home and small checking and savings accounts be held in this manner.

Second, as was mentioned above, in many states the personal creditors of a co-owner cannot make claims against jointly owned property. Donna can be sure that her home and other jointly held property is safe from Jack's business and personal creditors.

A third advantage of jointly owned property pertains to state death-tax savings: Some states exempt jointly owned property from state death taxes. This can be significant and become particularly important if there is no state limit to the amount of jointly held property that is exempt. For instance, Jack and Donna live in Lancaster, Pennsylvania. Pennsylvania's inheritance tax for property owned by one spouse and left to the other spouse is 6 percent. But if the same property is jointly held, when one spouse dies there is no inheritance tax. So if their home, purchased solely with Donna's earnings, is worth $200,000, the state inheritance tax savings is $12,000. In other words, had Donna owned the same house solely in her name, at her death Jack could have been subjected to a $12,000 state death tax. But because it is jointly held between spouses, it is totally exempt (as is all the other property Jack and Donna own jointly with each other) from Pennsylvania inheritance taxes.

Freedom from probate is a fourth advantage. Since jointly owned property with right of survivorship does not pass through probate, there is no possibility that the change of ownership will be delayed in estate administration.

A fifth advantage is a by-product of the fourth—property that passes by survivorship is not subject to the same public scrutiny or publicity that accompanies the probate of a will, which then becomes a public document. This aspect is particularly important if you don't want well meaning (and sometimes not so well meaning) and often misguided friends, relatives, and other "advisors" telling your survivor how to handle his or her assets.

So what's not to like?

One big disadvantage is that property held in joint ownership can't be disposed of in your will. So regardless of what Jack says—or does not say—in his will, if he was a joint tenant with right of survivorship in land in Wildwood with his brothers and cousins, at his death the property would pass to them—and not to Jack's wife, Donna. (Many people have elaborate wills and trusts that will be totally useless at the death of the first of two co-tenants to die, since the decedent's will does not operate on joint tenancy property.) The bitter irony is, even though the property will go to Jack's cousins rather than his wife, Jack's estate will have to pay estate taxes on the property.

Second, neither Donna nor Jack could unilaterally rent their home, sell it, or give it away (this "disadvantage," of course, serves to protect the other joint owner, and from that viewpoint is advantageous).

Title to jointly held property passes immediately and automatically to the surviving co-tenant. Although this sounds good, Jack can't provide for any management of the property (in other words, he can't have it go to a trust to assure that it will be handled wisely). This may force Donna to make investment and management decisions she may not want to make (or be capable of making).

Hidden state gift tax costs (not all states have gift taxes) can be an unpleasant surprise at both the creation and the severance of a joint tenancy or tenancy by the entirety. (Federal law provides for an unlimited "marital deduction" for gifts one spouse makes to another—you can literally give your entire estate to your spouse and pay no gift tax.) Say Donna calls her stockbroker and has him purchase one hundred shares of Zee Rocks stock "in my name and my husband Jack's name as joint tenants with the right of survivorship." Jack is being given an interest he did not have before. Donna is making a gift of about half the value of the property. If it is large enough, this gift may generate state gift taxes in many states.

Now assume the stock appreciates substantially and Jack and Donna decide to sell it. Jack tells Donna to put the proceeds in her bank account. He may be making her a gift of his interest. So it is possible that your state's tax authority will claim that two taxable gifts have been made: one when the property was titled jointly and Donna gave Jack his interest, and another when Jack gave his interest back to Donna.

Still another problem inherent in too much jointly held property is what estate planners call "overqualification" of the marital deduction. It means you have needlessly subjected too much property to taxation at your surviving spouse's death. How? By passing more property than is necessary to maximize the use of the "marital deduction."

For example, assume Jack's estate at the time of his death in 1987 was worth $900,000. Deductible debts and expenses total $100,000. What would happen if Jack's entire $800,000 net estate were held jointly with Donna? Everything would pass to Donna at his death. The federal estate tax law allows Jack to leave Donna (through will or otherwise) an unlimited amount of property. The catch is, when Donna dies, the property she's received from Jack (assuming she hasn't given it away or used it up) is added to her own assets and taxed. Worse yet, Jack's estate was allowed—and could have taken—a "unified credit" that would shelter up to $600,000 from tax; Jack could have passed $600,000 to his children that wouldn't have later been taxed when Donna died. But he didn't. By "overqualifying the marital," that is, by passing too much to Donna, he "underutilized the unified credit." That's all legal jargon for saying that $600,000 that didn't have to be subject to tax when Donna dies will be subjected to tax.

How could this "overqualification" have been avoided? If the property was owned only in Jack's name, Jack could have given Donna an amount equal to his net estate ($800,000), less the amount he could pass tax free under the unified credit to anyone he wanted ($600,000). She could have received this $200,000 outright or in a so-called "marital" trust. This trust would have provided management protection and investment advice for the $200,000, but would have made the funds available to Donna at her request. Alternatively, Jack could have given the property to Donna outright. The other $600,000 could have been left by Jack to a "family" (estate planners call this a *"non*-marital") trust. That family trust would provide further security for Donna during her lifetime. She would receive all income from the trust as well as certain other rights and privileges. But at her death, property in that trust would go directly to their children and—because of the way the trust was arranged—it would not be taxed again in Donna's estate.

It is possible, therefore, through a so-called zero tax marital deduction "formula clause" in a will or trust, to pass just the right amount of property (no more and no less) to a surviving spouse so that the utility of both the estate owner's unified credit and the marital deduction is maximized, and so that the surviving spouse does not receive more than the amount of property that will maximize tax savings at the first spouse's death, while at the same time removing from the surviving spouse's estate property that can now pass tax free to the children or other heirs at the death of the surviving spouse. This technique can save—literally—tens of thousands of dollars from taxes.

7.
Is a Will a Must?

Without a will, what?

Do you really need a will? What can a will do for you in your particular circumstances?

Technically, a will is a legal expression of what you want to happen to your property when you die. With a will, you can accomplish three vitally important things:

First, you can decide who gets your property at your death;

Second, you can decide the manner in which the property shall be given; and

Third, you personally can select the people to help carry out your plans.

To truly understand the importance of a will, just see what can happen where there is none. Take the case of Joan and Alan. Joan and Alan were in their early thirties and had two healthy, normal children, Susan, nine, and Jeffrey, seven. Alan had a good job and Joan stayed in their attractive middle-income home and raised the children. Without any advance warning, Joan contracted a blood disease and died within six months. Four months later, Alan was killed in an automobile accident.

Immediately following Alan's death, Joan's sister took Jeffrey and Susan home to live with her. Three weeks later, when Alan's brother had the children visiting with him, he and his wife decided the children should remain with them. He therefore refused to return them to Joan's sister. A court fight then took place between Joan's sister and Alan's brother to decide with whom the children would live.

Meanwhile, since neither Joan nor Alan had a will, the court

Is a Will a Must?

appointed a friend of Alan's lawyer to serve as executor of Alan's estate. He had a difficult time locating Alan's property, since Alan had money scattered in different banks, and only he and Joan knew where everything was. After considerable time and expense, the court determined that the children should remain with Alan's brother, who was formally named their guardian. But it still was necessary for Alan's brother to appear in court whenever he needed money for the children.

As a result of the jockeying back and forth between the two families for the children's affections, not to mention the trauma of losing their parents, both children developed serious emotional problems that remained with them for many years. But the really sad part of the story is that if Alan and Joan each had made a will, had designated the person or persons whom they wished to act as guardian for their children, and then had informed the guardian(s) where their property was located, many of these unfortunate problems could have been eliminated.

Wills are also necessary where there are no children involved. In Edgar's case, his father had left the family business to him, and he was running it quite efficiently. There was more than enough money available to take very good care of Edgar and his only sister, Elizabeth. This was in keeping with his father's wishes, even though the father had left the business entirely to Edgar.

However, circumstances change, and even though he was in his late forties and had never married, Edgar did meet someone, married and had a child. When Edgar died shortly after the birth of his son, everyone was surprised to learn that a successful businessman like Edgar had never made a will. Unfortunately, the most surprised person was Edgar's sister, Elizabeth, because under the laws of Edgar's state, his wife and son shared equally in his estate, while his sister, Elizabeth, who was not on the friendliest terms with Edgar's wife, received nothing. She was now completely cut off from her sole source of income—the business that had been her father's. The business was now being run for the benefit of her brother's new wife and infant son. Certainly not the result desired or ever contemplated by Edgar or his father.

The above true stories indicate the absolute necessity of a will. Actually, everyone has a will; if you don't draw one, your *state*—through its intestacy laws—"will draw the will you failed to make." This absence of a valid will is called "intestacy." In other words, the laws of the state in which you live will determine automatically, and regardless of what you really wanted, the disposition of your property.

Typically, intestacy laws spell out certain preferred classes of survivors. Usually, if you die survived by a spouse, that person will receive the bulk of your estate. Any children and other descendants you have will share what is left. They will divide your estate in the proportions and manner specified by your state's intestacy laws. Other relatives or organizations you care about may receive nothing, as was the case of Elizabeth in the story above.

Generally, if no spouse, children or other descendants survive you, your parents, brothers and sisters will receive equal shares of your estate. (One quick and inexpensive way of finding out how your state's intestacy laws work is to visit your local bank's trust department. They generally have free brochures as well as a helpful staff that can explain, in general terms, the intestacy laws of your state.)

Without a will, you cannot direct that any of your property go to a nonrelated individual or a charity. You have lost control not only over who will receive your property at your death but also over how or when they will receive it. You have forfeited the privilege of naming a personal representative to guide the disposition of your estate and make sure things go as you want them to. The court-appointed administrator of your estate will have minimum flexibility in dealing with your assets or your loved ones.

Without a will you cannot name guardians for minor or disabled children, and your children will then be in the same position as Jeffrey and Susan were when the last of their parents died. If you let the state draw your will, you give up the right to minimize the administrative expenses, and federal, state and estate death-tax shrinkage through the use of certain deductions, exclusions and various planning techniques.

A valid will—regardless of how large or how small your estate—is a cornerstone of the estate planning process because it allows you, rather than the state, to control the disposition of your personal property.

What does a will will?

Your estate is your property. It is whatever you own. Your probate estate is the real and personal property you own in your own name that you personally have a right to transfer according to the terms of the will that you write and which takes effect at your death. Essentially, probate property consists of the assets you own solely in your own name.

There is some property that will not be affected by your will. For example, life insurance is not probate property because it passes by contract and not under your will. Regardless of what your will says, life insurance proceeds pass directly to the beneficiary you have named in your policy. (Unless you have named your estate as beneficiary, a designation that is rarely recommended.) Likewise, jointly held property with rights of survivorship and property passing under certain employee benefit plans are nonprobate assets. They will not be probate property because you cannot dispose of those assets by will.

I'd rather do it myself

Who needs an attorney? Why not draw my own will? There are many reasons why homemade wills are good examples of the old adage "He who has himself for an attorney has a fool for a client."

No matter how small your estate or how simple your desires, it's worth the expense to employ a qualified attorney. The complexity and interrelationships of tax, property, domestic relations and other laws make a homemade will a frivolous, dangerous and highly expensive way to cut corners. The ultimate cost of a homemade will can typically be much greater than one drawn by a qualified attorney, but it will be your heirs, and not you, who pay the price. Consider the case of Margaret Alice Johnson, who wanted to be certain that she treated her two daughters, Sylvia and Gladys, as fairly and equally as possible.

Margaret Alice's husband had died some years before, leaving her with some insurance proceeds, a home and a life insurance policy on her life on which she continued to pay the premiums. When daughter Gladys was married, Margaret Alice lent Gladys and her husband, Phil, $20,000 to help them buy their home and recorded a mortgage on their home in that amount. Her insurance policy was also in the amount of $20,000. Before the loan to Gladys, both Gladys and Sylvia were named as co-beneficiaries of the policy so that each would receive $10,000.

Wanting to be fair, Margaret Alice made her own will. She first made a provision in her will that Gladys and Phil did not have to pay back the $20,000 she loaned them for their home. She then provided in her will that since she had forgiven the $20,000 that Gladys owed on the house, to be fair, she was now going to leave Sylvia the full $20,000 from her life insurance, and not just the $10,000 that the policy presently provided. Margaret Alice, despite her good intentions, could not have made a worse mess of her affairs.

When Margaret Alice died, Gladys and Phil were separated and in the process of getting divorced. By forgiving the $20,000 owed on the house jointly by Gladys and Phil, Margaret Alice handed Phil an instant profit of $10,000, since the laws of their state held that the property being owned jointly by Gladys and Phil was half Phil's. Therefore, when the $20,000 mortgage was marked satisfied, Phil, the ne'er-do-well, soon to be ex-son-in-law, was $10,000 richer.

The life insurance policy, as indicated above, was a separate contract between Margaret Alice and the insurance company. The insurance company was bound by law to pay the $20,000 equally to Gladys and Sylvia, because this was what the policy said, and while Margaret Alice had made other provisions in her will, she had neglected to change the beneficiaries on her life insurance policy—the only change that would have had a legal effect on who would receive the proceeds.

In addition, the $20,000 owed on the home was still an asset of Margaret Alice's estate and was taxed by the state for inheritance tax purposes, when this might have been avoided had Margaret Alice consulted a qualified attorney.

What would it cost to have a will drawn by someone who knows how to do it? The answer is, that depends. The more assets, the more complex your dispositive desires, and the more facts that have to be considered, the more money you have to pay. Quite often, a two- or three-page will may be adequate and you should be billed approximately $150. In many other cases, the will may be much longer, and the bill higher, because of the time the attorney must spend in drafting it. Don't forget, your will must not only effectively accomplish the personal objectives you specified with respect to how your assets are to be distributed, but must also take into consideration the federal and state income, estate and gift tax laws.

No matter how few or how many pages, a properly prepared will must provide a plan for distributing your assets the way you want them distributed. But that will must also consider the needs of your beneficiaries as well as the federal and state laws which impact upon your dispositive plans. Obviously, your will must be unambiguous and completely describe what you want accomplished. Furthermore, the will must be flexible enough to take into consideration any of the many changes in family circumstances which might occur after you sign your will.

Don't forget to ask the attorney's hourly charge before he/she begins the work—or agree on a total fee in advance. Just like any other contract for services to be performed, have the attorney put the agreement in writing so there will be no misunderstanding.

Turn arounds

The one thing you can be sure of is change. Your feelings about your property and the people you want to receive your property will change—and so will they—and their needs. Fortunately, a will is inoperative until you die, and, therefore, you can change it any time until then.

There are many very good reasons why people change or revoke their wills. For example, modification should be considered if your health or your beneficiary's health or financial circumstances have changed. A birth, a death, a marriage or a divorce all change to some extent the circumstances that were operative at the time you signed your will. Furthermore, when the tax law changes in a significant manner, your will should, at the very least, be reexamined.

How can you change your will? Changing the will can be as simple as having the attorney draft a codicil. A codicil is a legal means of modifying an existing will without rewriting the entire document. It is typically used when the will needs only minor modifications. A codicil is often a single page document that reaffirms everything you have already stated in your will except the specific provisions that need to be changed. Just like your will, your codicil should be typed, signed and properly witnessed according to the requirements of your own state's laws.

If substantial changes are needed, you probably should have a new will. You may want to draw a new will in some cases even though you have not made substantial changes. For example, if you decide not to leave property to someone who is named in your original will, you may want to avoid offending the omitted beneficiary by destroying the old will after a new will is drawn and properly executed.

State law, in many cases, will *automatically* revoke or modify your will if certain events occur. The most common automatic will revoking triggers are: (1) marriage, (2) divorce, (3) birth or adoption of a child, and (4) slaying. For instance, if you legally divorce your spouse, in many states all provisions in your will relating to your spouse become inoperative. Or if you were single when you made your will and then marry, automatically, regardless of what you do or do not say, your spouse has a right to receive that portion of your estate that would have been received had you died without a valid will. Your spouse has a right to his/her intestate share—unless your will actually gives your spouse a larger share.

What if you did not provide for a child born or adopted after you wrote your will? In many states, the state "writes" that child into the will for you. Your state may provide that a child born or adopted after you wrote your will will receive that share of your estate not passing to your spouse that would have been given to the child if you did not have a will (unless it appears in the will by specific direction that you intended that child should not benefit under your will).

Almost all states have "slayers' statutes." These laws forbid anyone who participates in a willful and unlawful killing from acquiring property as a result.

There is one further way your will can be changed. You may not like it, but many states give a surviving spouse what is known as a "right of election." In other words, your surviving spouse might have a right to "take against your will"—to take a specified portion of your estate regardless of what you gave your spouse in your will. One state, for example, allows a surviving spouse to demand at least that share that would have been allowed had the decedent died without a valid will. For example, in one state, if an individual leaves his entire estate to his son, absent a pre- or postnuptial agreement to the contrary, his wife can take the same one-third share of his estate she would have received had her husband died intestate.

Some states even give these "rights of election" to children. There are ways to avoid these rights of election but they cannot be accomplished by your executor. You must do the planning.

Do's and don'ts

Do remember that both you and your spouse should have wills. Those wills should be coordinated. Insist that your attorney examine documents relating to all your assets including your life insurance policies, the deeds to jointly held property such as your home and bank accounts, and your certificates for company-sponsored pension and group insurance benefits, before your will is drafted. A will should not be drawn in a vacuum. It must consider and be tied to the values and ownership arrangement of your assets, your overall employee benefit program, and your personal financial plans.

Do keep your will where it can be found quickly. The person you have named as executor should know where it can be found. Make sure your attorney, or perhaps some other advisor, has a copy.

Don't name anyone as guardian or executor without conferring with them first. Both jobs involve awesome responsibilities, are highly time-consuming, can be extremely complicated and, if handled improperly, can be personally costly to your executor.

For these reasons, many people choose a bank or trust company to act as their executor so that their family will have the benefit of a professional and impartial personal representative to handle their affairs. In those cases where an individual is chosen, you should name a back-up executor, guardian and trustee, such as a bank or trust company, in case the person you have named for some reason will not or cannot serve or, having agreed to serve, is unable to continue to serve.

Most importantly, don't make changes in your will—even minor changes—without consulting your attorney.

Probate—what to avoid

When you die, you probably will own property and owe debts. You may have claims against other persons such as accounts receivable or lawsuits in progress. Your executor has the duty of collecting the money that is owed to you.

He/she then must satisfy any debts to your creditors (including the federal and state governments to whom you or your estate owe taxes).

The next major duty of an executor is to distribute what is left to the appropriate individuals or organizations. This process is called "probate" and is generally supervised by a local court known as the Probate Court, the Surrogate's Court or Orphan's Court.

You may have designated a person in your will to take charge of this process. That person is called an "executor." If you die intestate, that is, without a valid will, the Court will appoint someone to do the executor's job. That person will be called an "administrator" and has essentially the same duties and legal privileges as an executor.

Your executor or administrator (quite often also referred to as decedent's personal representative) must perform a number of extremely important and often highly complex tasks. For example, your executor may have to bring suit on your estate's behalf or release someone from liability. Without the probate process, there would be no one legally entitled to do these things. Titles to real estate could not be made marketable because no one would be legally empowered to act on behalf of your estate. Probate is therefore a very important process in which your executor carries out his/her tasks under court supervision and scrutiny. In fact, your personal representative will not be discharged from his or her duties by the court until an accounting of all assets, liabilities and dispositions has been made.

CHECKLIST OF EXECUTOR'S PRIMARY DUTIES
1. Probate of will.
2. Advertise Grant of Letters.
3. Inventory of safe deposit box.
4. Claim for life insurance benefits—obtain Form 712.
    a. Consider mode of payment.
5. Claim for pension and profit-sharing benefits.
    a. Consider mode of payment.
    b. Obtain copies of plan, IRS approval and beneficiary designation.
6. Apply for lump sum Social Security benefits and V.A. benefits.
7. File Form 56—Notice of Fiduciary Relationship.
8. Open estate checking and savings accounts.
9. Write to banks for date of death value.
10. Value securities.
11. Appraisal of real property and personal property.
12. Obtain 3 years of U.S. individual income tax returns and 3 years of cancelled checks.
13. Obtain 5 years financials on business interest plus all relevant agreements.
14. Obtain copies of all U.S. gift tax returns filed by decedent.

Is a Will a Must?

15. Obtain evidence of all debts of decedent and costs of administering estate.
16. Were any of decedent's medical expenses unpaid at death?
17. Has the estate received after death income taxable under Section 691 of the IRC?
18. Prepayment of inheritance tax—check local state law to determine if permissible and if so, the applicable deadlines.
19. Consider requesting prompt assessment of decedent's U.S. income taxes.
20. File personal property tax returns—due February 15 of each year estate in administration.
21. File final U.S. and state individual income tax return (IRS Form 1040)—due April 15 of the year after the year in which death occurs.
22. Is the estate subject to ancillary administration?
23. Are administration expenses and losses to be claimed as an income or estate tax deduction?
24. Obtain alternate valuation date values for U.S. estate tax.
25. Payment of U.S. estate tax with flower bonds—must be tendered to Federal Reserve with Form within 9 months of death.
26. Consider election of extension of time to pay U.S. estate tax—must be filed on or before due date of U.S. estate tax return.
27. Consider election to defer payment of inheritance tax on remainder interests—where permitted, determine deadline for election.
28. Consider election for special valuation of farm or business real estate under IRC Section 2032A—must be made with timely filed U.S. estate tax return.
29. File form notice to IRS required by Section 6039A of IRC—due with final U.S. individual income tax return or U.S. estate tax return.
30. File inheritance and federal estate tax return—federal due within nine months of death—extensions may be requested—check local state law for due date and possible extensions.
31. File inventory—check local state law for requirements and due date.
32. Consider requesting prompt assessment of U.S. estate tax return.
33. Apply for U.S. I.D. number if estate will file U.S. income tax return.
34. File U.S. Fiduciary Income Tax Return (Form 1041)—choice of fiscal year.
35. Consider redemption under IRC Section 303.
36. Apply for tax waivers.
37. File account or prepare informal family agreement.
38. Prepare audit notices and statement of proposed distribution.
39. File schedule of distribution if applicable.

Source: *The Tools and Techniques of Estate Planning,* 4th edition, The National Underwriter Co., Cincinnati, Ohio.

Why then do you hear so much talk about avoiding probate? Frankly, because at one time, courts charged high probate fees, and lawyers based their fee on the size of your probate estate. In most states, probate is now a relatively inexpensive process (call your local probate court for a list of the charges). Attorneys are more commonly billing clients by the hours they actually spend rather than a percentage of the probate estate.

There are still good reasons, however, for avoiding probate with respect to certain assets. For example, if you own property in more than one state, multiple probates (these are called "ancillary administrations") will be required. Property will have to be probated in each state where property is owned.

Another reason for avoiding probate with respect to assets such as the family home or checking accounts is that the probate procedure can be time consuming. Typically, the entire procedure takes from a minimum of nine months to as long as two or three years in some cases. Your attorney will point out those assets which should be held in a manner that will not pass through probate.

If privacy is important (once the will is probated, it becomes a public document), then avoiding probate is essential.

Two last comments about probate: First, the fees your estate will pay the estate's attorney can (and should) be negotiated by your executor *before* hiring the attorney. (This is one good reason that any attorney should seldom be named as executor. In most states, the executor you have nominated can use any attorney he/she would like to use and is not bound to use the attorney who drew your will—regardless of what the attorney wrote into the will.)

Second, although there are many advantages to passing property outside of probate (for example, property passing through a life insurance contract is less likely to become subject to contest than property passing under the provisions of a will), probate equates to court supervision. That means a disinterested party will be safeguarding the interests of your beneficiaries. This "watchful" control over the executor often outweighs the relatively minor costs involved in probate.

8.
Trust Me

How far does trust go?

"Trust"—could a word be more descriptive—and yet say less? Just what is a trust? How does it work? What are the advantages and disadvantages of a trust?

Let's start by defining the term. A trust is not really a "thing" as much as it is a "relationship." It's the relationship that exists when one party (a "grantor" or "settlor" or "trustee" or "donor") transfers money or other property (called the trust "corpus" or "principal") to a second party (a "trustee"), who must use that money or property solely for the benefit of a third party (the beneficiary). The essential concept is that the trustee (which can be one or more persons or a corporate financial institution) holds (for administration, management and investment purposes) the legal title to the property you place in the trust but may use the property and the income it produces only for the benefit of the beneficiaries you have selected.

How do you set up a trust? Let's take the case of Bob and Nancy as an example. Their attorney, Mark, prepared a written document called a "trust agreement." The attorney spelled out in the trust agreement Bob's and Nancy's wishes as to how the assets of the trust were to be managed and invested, who was to receive the assets and income, how that money or property was to be paid out, and at what ages (and upon what events) each of their beneficiaries was to receive his or her share. The trust also indicated the names of the trustees.

Who should watch the store?

Mark pointed out several important points to Bob and Nancy before he drafted their trust. First, he told them that they could have more than one trustee. If they selected several parties (such as more than one person or a person and a bank), each party would be a co-trustee and they would make decisions jointly.

Nancy wanted to know what characteristics a good trustee should have. Mark suggested that their trustee or trustees should have sound business and financial judgment, a knowledge of the principles of asset investment and management, and an intimate knowledge of the needs of each beneficiary. Another important aspect is that the trustee should be able to survive through the term of the trust, regardless of how long that might be (some trusts last for two or three generations).

Mark suggested that a trust company, or bank authorized to perform trust duties, is often the best choice to meet these requirements. When Bob asked why Mark felt a bank would make a good trustee, he replied that most trust companies and banks have investment experience and would not be incapacitated by death or disability, or become unavailable (banks take holidays but never vacations).

More important, Mark added, unlike a family member, a corporate trustee can carry out the directions of the trust instrument objectively and impartially. The value of this objectivity is particularly important in avoiding intrafamily conflicts of interest that often occur where the trustee and one or more beneficiaries are members of the same family. A corporate trustee can say "no," where appropriate, without starting a family feud.

Bob asked if a corporate trustee, acting alone, might be impersonal and lack a familiarity and understanding of family needs. The attorney's reply was that if Bob and Nancy felt that was a problem, the solution was to name both a corporate and one or more individuals as trustees. He also suggested that they or their beneficiaries could reserve or be given the power to change to another corporate trustee.

What's in it for me?

At this point you may be wondering why Bob and Nancy set up their trust. What are the advantages of a trust, and how could you benefit from one? Bob and Nancy, like most people who set up a trust, wanted to accomplish a number of objectives.

There are many reasons other than tax savings for making gifts in trust, rather than giving property outright to your beneficiaries. These "people oriented" objectives can be divided into three categories—management of assets, conservation of assets and disposition of assets.

Quite often, a property owner will feel that the beneficiary is unwilling or unable to invest, manage or handle the responsibility of an outright gift. For example, Bob and Nancy don't want to give outright gifts to their minor children, but they do want to provide for their financial security. Another good example where trusts should be considered is in the case of recipients who are legally adults but who lack the emotional or intellectual maturity, physical capacity, or technical training to handle large sums of money. Many individuals can't or don't want to handle assets (such as a business) that require constant and high-level decision-making capacity. A trust is often used to postpone full ownership until the donees are in a position to handle the property properly.

Many donors want to achieve the income and estate tax advantages of gifts but are reluctant to place all the ownership rights in the hands of the donee. They utilize trusts as the solution to the ambivalent position of wanting to institute a program of gifting but fearing the possible results of an outright "no strings attached" transfer, which lessens the donees' dependence on them.

The use of a trust is also indicated where the proposed gift property does not lend itself to fragmentation, but the donor desires to spread beneficial ownership among a number of people. For example, a large life insurance policy (and the ultimate proceeds it generates when the donor dies) is better held by a single trustee than jointly by several individuals. Another example of such property is real estate. Typically, land will be more valuable if it is not divided. A ten-acre tract of land may be worth substantially more than ten one-acre tracts. If a trust is used as a receptacle for the gift, ten beneficiaries could share in the growth and income from the land without necessitating an actual division of the property itself. An apartment house is still another example of an asset that is much more efficiently and profitably handled through a single unified management. Of course, at whatever specified given event, the trustee could sell the property and divide the proceeds or split up the property itself.

Trusts will often be used in lieu of outright gifts where conservation of assets and particular dispositive plans are important. For instance, where control is essential, a donor will often want to limit the class of beneficiaries and prevent the donee from disposing of property to persons outside the family. In fact, one of the reasons Bob and Nancy are setting up their trust is to prevent their daughter's spouse from acquiring rights to Bob and Nancy's chain of flower shops. A gift in trust for their daughter Barbara, or for the benefit of "Barbara and her children" (or even for "Barbara and her husband as long as they are married") provides protection against an unsuccessful marriage.

A closely held business is often the major (or only practical) asset an individual can use to make meaningful and significant gifts. If the business is a corporation, a trust provides a vehicle for such a person to make gifts of the corporation's stock with minimal loss of control.

A trust is often used instead of an outright gift, because a gift in trust can provide protection against creditors of both the donor and donee. Trusts are often used to familiarize a trustee (who eventually will be managing assets "poured-over" from the donor's will or paid by contract to the trust from life insurance and pension proceeds) with the donor's assets, his family, his plans and his relationship of each to the other. Smaller gifts in trust can be made immediately. If the trustee invests and manages the property wisely, more property can be placed into the trust at later times or at the estate owner's death. In other words, lifetime gifts to the trust give the donor an opportunity to watch the trustee in action and make suggestions as to property investment, management, and income and capital payments.

Parents will often use a trust as a means of providing income for a child (and principal at the trustee's discretion for emergencies) without making that child a fortune hunter's target.

Where an individual owns several pieces of property of equal value, he could make outright gifts of parcel "A" to his son and parcel "B" to his daughter. However, he may be treating the children unequally since one property could increase in value while the value of the other could fall, or the properties could increase (or decrease) at different rates. But by placing both properties in trust and giving both children equal shares in trust property, he could equalize benefits between the children.

Property that requires management or "watching" should not be placed directly into a minor's hands. Why? Because major decisions cannot be made and the property cannot be sold, exchanged or mortgaged without the appointment of a guardian. This is often an expensive, inflexible and troublesome procedure. Once an outright distribution is made, a child is free to spend or use it upon reaching majority but often doesn't have the financial maturity to invest, manage or spend it wisely.

Still a further reason for a trust is that an outright gift will often return to the child's parents (or to the child's spouse) should the minor child predecease the parents. This would defeat many of the donor-parent's tax and personal objectives.

Finally, when compared with an outright gift, which is subject to the "probate" process (explained in Chapter 7), a trust can provide privacy and relative security from a will contest.

In summary, a trust is one of the best ways the donor can give a gift and at the same time achieve flexibility to meet future contingencies and attain his or her personal objectives with respect to the beneficiaries.

What are the tax reasons for setting up a trust? The answer is that significant income and tax savings can be realized through trusts. In an "irrevocable trust" (you can't change the terms or get the property back once it is set up), you can actually shift the burden of income taxes from you—at your income tax rates—to the trust itself and/or its beneficiary, both of whom typically are in lower income tax brackets than you are. The difference in income tax rates could amount to substantial annual savings. Coupled with the personal income tax exemption allowed to each beneficiary, these savings can be significant. For example, in 1984 Bob and Nancy file jointly; they are in a 42 percent income tax bracket. That means on taxable income of $60,000 they pay $15,168 in tax. But every additional dollar over $60,000 that the couple receives, such as income from interest, rent or dividends, will be taxed at a 42 percent rate, or higher. That means that 42 cents of every additional dollar of taxable income from such sources as dividends, or interest, or rental income, will be lost in federal income taxes (and state income tax). But if unearned taxable income could be shifted to a trust, it would be taxed at much lower rates. For example, if Bob and Nancy received an additional $5,000 in interest and dividends, approximately $2,100 would be lost in taxes. But if they gave the property producing the income to a trust for their children and the trust paid taxes on that $5,000 of income, the tax would be $662, a saving of about $1,438 a year. That income tax savings alone over a period of years could fund a year or two of a child's college education, if the trust was established soon enough.

You can often save federal estate taxes and state death taxes when you place property into a trust. That's because, if you arrange the trust properly and the trust is irrevocable, the property (and the income it produced) is no longer in your estate. (There may, however, be gift tax implications when you put the property into the trust. That's because the transfer of property to the trust is really an absolute gift to the beneficiaries of the trust. If the gift is large enough, you'll have to pay gift taxes.)

Trusts are often set up by people perfectly capable of handling assets but who can't—or don't want to—take the time to do so. These people want to relieve themselves of property management and do so by using trusts. Your trustee will assume the responsibility of investing, managing and conserving the property on behalf of the beneficiaries (including you, if that's what you want). Furthermore, a trust may be a great way for you to protect yourself in the event you are unexpectedly disabled due to a sickness or injury and become unable to manage your assets.

Arms in the arsenal

What are the various types of trusts that you can use to meet your objectives?

There are a number of types of trusts. The terms of those trusts can be as wide and varied as the imagination of your tax counsel and the needs and desires of the parties you want to benefit.

The two most common types of trusts are the "living" (often called inter vivos) trust and the "testamentary" (created under your will and taking effect at your death) trust. A third type is a combination of the two. It's called a life insurance trust/pour-over will combination.

Let's look at each of these types of trust and see how they work.

Revocable living trust

A "revocable" trust is one that allows you to change your mind and regain property you have put into the trust at any time or change the terms of the trust. If you have made a trust "revocable," you can also specify who is to receive income or principal at any time. Because you have complete control of the property and the income it produces, for federal income and estate tax purposes, when you establish a revocable trust you are treated just as if you never gave up the property you've placed in the trust. Therefore, if Bob establishes a revocable trust, and Bob puts property in the trust, and that property earns income, Bob will be taxed on it. Even if their children actually receive the income, Bob would still be subject to income tax since he is treated as if he never gave the property away. This same result would apply for federal estate tax purposes. The property would be taxed in Bob's estate.

But note the effect of what is happening in this example. Bob and Nancy's children are receiving the income. The IRS would treat Bob as if he had received the income and then gave it away to his children. So they not only may be taxed on the income produced by the assets in the trust but also may be liable for gift taxes on the income they "received" and "gave away."

Why then would Bob and Nancy set up a revocable "living" (set up during lifetime) trust? One reason is that a living trust makes it possible to provide management continuity and income flow even after Bob and Nancy die. No probate of the assets in the trust would be necessary since the trust would continue to operate after they die in the same way it did while they were alive.

Bob and Nancy will obtain a second advantage from a living revocable trust. The burdens of investment decisions and management responsibility can—when they want them to—be shifted from their shoulders and assumed by their trustees. Bob and Nancy could still control investment decisions and management policy as long as they were alive and healthy, but they could use the trust as a "backup" in case they become unwilling or unable to manage their own assets. Often, this type of revocable living trust is called a "step-up" trust. That's because the trustee would step-up to take Bob and Nancy's place in decision-making and in day-to-day management if they want to be relieved of the burden of managing trust property. A step-up trust would also be of considerable help if Bob and Nancy became incapable of acting on their own behalf in later years, because of a sickness or accident, and could not manage or invest their property.

Another advantage of a revocable living trust is that, unlike the terms of the wills they signed, the terms of the trust and the amount of assets that Bob and Nancy place into it will never become public knowledge at their death. The public will never have a right to know the terms and conditions of a revocable living trust. Only their trustees and beneficiaries will have access to the trust instrument.

There are, of course, disadvantages to a revocable living trust. Typically the trustee will charge fees to manage and invest property placed into the trust. Since such a trust should be drawn by a competent tax attorney, legal fees are involved in drafting a revocable living trust. "The person who acts as his or her own attorney has a fool for a client." Nowhere is this axiom more applicable than in the drafting of wills and trusts. Homemade wills, and trusts torn out of form books, have caused incredible amounts of litigation and court costs. It's almost impossible for a lay person to understand all the intricacies of both federal and state tax law, and the other procedural state law requirements for drafting and executing wills and trusts. More often than not, the legal fees involved in straightening out homemade wills and trusts will greatly exceed the small fee an attorney would have charged to prepare the proper documents.

The irrevocable living trust

Many individuals have established "irrevocable" living trusts. Why would anyone ever establish a trust if you couldn't recover the property you have placed into it, and you are not permitted to make changes in the terms of the trust? Once you put property into an irrevocable trust, you relinquish the right to receive the property back, terminate the trust or change its terms. Another drawback is that you may be making taxable gifts. For example, if Bob and Nancy had set up such a trust, each time they put property into the trust, they would really be making a gift to each of the trust beneficiaries. If the gifts were large enough, they could even be liable for gift taxes. Furthermore, a trustee would charge fees for asset management. Worse yet, Bob and Nancy would lose the use of trust property and any income that property may produce. Why then would anyone ever establish an irrevocable living trust?

The answer is that such a trust can substantially reduce (or even eliminate) income taxes and possibly save massive amounts of federal estate tax. That's because when property is placed into such trust, the property and income it produces no longer belong to the grantor. After the transfer of the property to such a trust, if the trust is properly arranged, the assets in it and the income produced by it will no longer be in the grantor's estate for federal (and often state) death tax purposes.

Testamentary trusts

Both the revocable and irrevocable living trusts, as their names imply, are trusts established when you are living. Another type of trust, the "testamentary" trust, is established at death through the terms of your will. The major advantage of a testamentary trust is that fewer documents are needed to put this type of trust into effect. For example, if Bob and Nancy had their attorney draw an irrevocable living trust or a revocable living trust, a trustee would have to draw two sets of documents, the trust and their wills. With a testamentary trust the will and the trust are all one document. So there may be a slight savings in legal fees. (Although, in this case, the savings will be minimal, with the risk that is taken that the testamentary will might never come into existence if the will is not probated or if it is attacked.)

A compromise—life insurance trust with a pour-over will

One of the most popular types of trust is the type which is coupled with the provisions of your will. This is called a life insurance trust and pour-over will combination. A living trust is established immediately. It can be either revocable or irrevocable. You can "fund" it by putting cash or other income-producing property into it immediately, or choose to leave it "unfunded," that is, not put any significant amount of cash or other property into the trust. Many states allow a trust to come into existence even though no property is put into it when it is set up, except the right of the trust to receive life insurance proceeds. In other words, you name the trust as beneficiary of life insurance policies on your life.

When you die, your will provides that probate assets—after payment of debts, expenses, taxes and specific bequests—are to go ("pour-over") into the life insurance trust, together with the proceeds (death benefits from the policies) of the insurance that has the trustee named as the beneficiary (the person to whom the insurance money is to be paid).

Why a life insurance trust? The trust contains provisions as to how your life insurance and all your other assets will be administered and distributed. The big advantage of the life insurance trust/pour-over will combination is that all your assets are easily coordinated and administered in a unified manner according to your wishes. Although the trust is termed a "life insurance" trust, other assets, such as employee benefits and assets you leave in your will, can easily be paid to the trust. The trust will be effective after your death even if your will is held to be invalid.

Other types of trusts

There are other types of trusts. In fact the number of trusts that can be designed is limited only by the creativity and imagination of the attorney. Some of the more popular types of trusts are the "marital" and "family" trusts, commonly referred to as the "A"–"B" trusts; a "C" trust, which can qualify for the estate tax marital deduction but assures you that your property will eventually go to the party of your choice; a 2503(c) trust; and a short-term (Clifford) trust.

The marital/family trust is an arrangement to give your surviving spouse full use of the family's economic wealth, while at the same time minimizing, to the greatest extent possible, the federal estate tax payable at the death of both spouses. It's actually two separate trusts. The first trust, or the marital trust, is designed to qualify for the estate tax marital deduction. This is the deduction allowed for the net value of gifts passing at death from one spouse to a surviving spouse in a qualifying manner. Property in the marital trust, to the extent it is still owned by the surviving spouse or forms part of the principal of the marital trust when the surviving spouse dies, will generally be taxable at the surviving spouse's death for federal estate tax purposes.

The second trust is called the "family" or "nonmarital" trust. This trust "bypasses" the surviving spouse and for that reason is sometimes referred to as a bypass trust. It is designed to hold assets for the economic well-being of both the surviving spouse and other family members. The property in the family trust will pass free of federal estate taxes at the death of the surviving spouse. In fact, it is this family or the bypass trust that is primarily responsible for minimizing the overall impact of death taxes, upon the death of both spouses, and therefore maximizing the amount passing to surviving children.

It's important that even though assets in the family trust will not be taxed when the surviving spouse dies, creative drafting on the part of your attorney can provide a substantial amount of economic security (without estate taxation) for your surviving spouse. For example, the surviving spouse can be given the right to receive all the income annually or more frequently from this family trust without causing its assets to be includable in his or her estate. Likewise, the trustee can be given discretion to give additional amounts of capital to your surviving spouse. The surviving spouse can even be given certain discretion as to the amount and form of payment to the next trust beneficiaries (the children). So this trust can be made quite flexible and is one that should be given careful consideration if the size of the estate warrants its use.

A "short-term" trust (often called a Clifford trust) is an inter vivos irrevocable (lifetime, nonchangeable) trust, that is established by an individual for a limited duration. Usually, a short-term trust will last either for the lifetime of the beneficiary or for at least ten years and one day or more. But when the terms you have specified expires, property in the trust automatically returns to you.

The advantage of a short-term trust is that it permits a high-income tax bracket taxpayer to shift income to a relatively lower bracket individual. For example, if you have the financial responsibility for supporting another person such as a widowed aunt, a child or other relative, and you would like to provide financial security and income for that individual, you may want to shift income from your bracket to the beneficiary's tax bracket through the trust. Yet, when the trust term is over, you receive back the property you placed into the trust. For example, if Bob and Nancy placed property that produced an annual income of $5,000 (as previously discussed in this chapter) in a short-term trust, they could shift the income tax with similar tax savings for the length of the trust.

The third type of commonly used trust is known as the "Section 2503(c)" trust. This is a gift tax tool that enables an individual to make a gift to a minor in trust and still obtain the $10,000 annual gift tax exclusion. The use of this irrevocable funded trust for gifts to minors eliminates many of the practical objections to outright gifts and at the same time makes it possible to obtain gift tax savings.

Each of these trusts is covered more extensively in other chapters.

9.
Is It Better to Give?

Why give when you've got?

When you've got all you need to provide you with adequate income and financial security, it may be the time to think about "intentional defunding" of your estate. Intentional defunding is another way of saving; it is better to give assets—and income—to keep them from being taxed (and probated) in your estate. So giving (we'll call it "gifting") is a way to reduce your estate taxes and probate costs. Giving away assets to save estate taxes is especially useful where you have an asset that is likely to appreciate substantially, and you'd like to have the growth occur in someone else's hands. For instance, Sam Corey recently formed an insurance agency. He might want to give stock in the business to his children, Sam, Jr., and Lee, before the business becomes successful.

Another advantage of lifetime giving is that you know the person—or charity—that you want to get your gift will receive it. Wills can be broken, and in most states a surviving spouse or child is entitled to a portion of your estate regardless of what your will says (this is called the right to "elect against" your will). A lifetime gift is a sure thing.

Your lifetime gift is private. No one but the "donee," the recipient of your gift, has to know any of the details. On the other hand, property that passes under your will must be inventoried, and that list is filed with the county "Register of Wills." It therefore becomes public information. This makes your beneficiaries prey to the well (and sometimes not so well) intended but often harmful advice of those people who always know how to invest someone else's money. This is not a problem with a lifetime gift.

Making a gift while you are alive gives you the pleasure of seeing the recipient(s) enjoy it. It also makes it possible to see what

Is It Better to Give?

your donee does with the gift. For example, you can watch how your son handles and invests cash. That can help you make decisions about whether, when, and how to make larger additional gifts, either during your lifetime or at your death.

A gift provides financial security for loved ones and at the same time insulates that property from the claims of your creditors.

Estate taxes are not the only taxes you can save by lifetime gifts. In fact, more gifts are motivated by potential income tax savings than estate tax savings. Sheryl Madelman's salary puts her in the 50 percent income tax bracket. That means that 50 cents of every additional dollar of salary she earns will be lost in taxes. Worse yet, if she has dividends from stocks or receives rental income or even earns interest from a bank account, at least 50 cents, and maybe more, of every dollar wouldn't go to her but go to the federal (and probably more to the state) government. But if she gives the stock to her daughter, Lynn, the income from the stock is no longer taxed to Sheryl. Instead, it's taxed to Lynn at Lynn's much lower bracket. If Lynn was in a 20 percent bracket, the 30 percent difference is the tax savings the family unit realizes.

To summarize, giving is an important estate planning technique because it can save estate taxes and probate costs, guarantee that the party you want to receive your gift will do so, and assure everyone that the details of the gift will be completely private. Making a lifetime gift gives you an opportunity to enjoy the pleasure of your recipients and to see how well they handle and manage the gift. Finally, gifts of income-producing property shift the tax on the income and are easy ways to save income taxes.

What's it cost to give?

It may not cost a cent in taxes—even to make substantial gifts. The reason? Before one cent in tax is due, you may qualify for one or more of these:
1. An annual $10,000 per donee gift tax exclusion;
2. The right to "split" gifts;
3. A "marital deduction"; or
4. A "unified credit."

Let's see how these four gift tax reducers work.

The little giant

Anyone, married or single, can give up to $10,000 in cash or other property each year to any number of parties with no gift tax liability whatsoever. This is called the annual gift tax exclusion. These gifts can be made to individuals (whether or not they are related to you) or to other parties (such as a charity or club). Here's an example:

John Talone, a wealthy twenty-eight-year-old bachelor, has three nephews, Jim, Andy and Nick. John can give each of his nephews $10,000 in cash or other property each year. That means he can remove $30,000 a year ($10,000 × 3) from his estate at no federal tax cost to himself or to them. If John marries his girlfriend, Westie, and as his wife, she agrees to "split" the gift (split gifts are discussed in more detail later in this chapter), the amount the couple can give—per donee, per year—doubles. So John and Westie together can give up to $60,000 a year, $20,000 to each of John's three nephews.

The annual exclusion is called the "Little Giant" because—over time—it can remove massive amounts of property from your estate. Since John's life expectancy is about forty-five years, he could avoid estate taxes on $2,700,000 ($60,000 × 45). In fact, if his nephews invest the money each year and only earn 10 percent, the $60,000 a year gifts will increase dramatically. If John's top federal estate tax bracket is 50 percent, the federal estate tax savings from these "no cost" gifts will be substantial.

Divide and conquer

"Split gifts" are just one more of the many pleasures of married life. When a husband or wife makes a gift to a third person (that person does not have to be a relative), the IRS treats the gift as if each spouse made half the gift—even if they didn't. In the example above, even if all the money that John and Westie give John's nephews comes from John's personal assets, the couple can split the gifts. It's as if John and Westie each gave $30,000 a year, $10,000 to each nephew, even though all the money came from John's personal bank account.

There's more than one reason to split gifts. Obviously, doubling the amount you can give away each year is advantageous. But what makes gift "splitting" even more important is that it causes the gift tax—if there will be one—to be lower. The reason is that the rates are "progressive." (That doesn't mean better—it means disproportionately higher.) For example, as you can see in the Table, page 77, if John made a taxable gift of $100,000 while he was single, it would result in a $23,800 gift tax. But the same taxable $100,000

Unified Rate Schedule for Estate and Gift Taxes

If the amount with which the tentative tax to be computed is:	The tentative tax is:
Not over $10,000	18% of such amount
Over $10,000 but not over $20,000	$1,800 plus 20% of the excess over $10,000
Over $20,000 but not over $40,000	$3,800 plus 22% of the excess over $20,000
Over $40,000 but not over $60,000	$8,200 plus 24% of the excess over $40,000
Over $60,000 but not over $80,000	$13,000 plus 26% of the excess over $60,000
Over $80,000 but not over $100,000	$18,200 plus 28% of the excess over $80,000
Over $100,000 but not over $150,000	$23,800 plus 30% of the excess over $100,000
Over $150,000 but not over $250,000	$38,800 plus 32% of the excess over $150,000
Over $250,000 but not over $500,000	$70,800 plus 34% of the excess over $250,000
Over $500,000 but not over $750,000	$155,800 plus 37% of the excess over $500,000
Over $750,000 but not over $1,000,000	$248,300 plus 39% of the excess over $750,000
Over $1,000,000 but not over $1,250,000	$345,800 plus 41% of the excess over $1,000,000
Over $1,250,000 but not over $1,500,000	$448,300 plus 43% of the excess over $1,250,000
Over $1,500,000 but not over $2,000,000	$555,800 plus 45% of the excess over $1,500,000
Over $2,000,000 but not over $2,500,000	$780,800 plus 49% of the excess over $2,000,000

For 1982 – *In the case of decedents dying and gifts made in 1982:*

Over $2,500,000 but not over $3,000,000	$1,025,800 plus 53% of the excess over $2,500,000
Over $3,000,000 but not over $3,500,000	$1,290,800 plus 57% of the excess over $3,000,000
Over $3,500,000 but not over $4,000,000	$1,575,800 plus 61% of the excess over $3,500,000
Over $4,000,000	$1,880,800 plus 65% of the excess over $4,000,000

For 1983 – *In the case of decedents dying and gifts made in 1983:*

Over $2,500,000 but not over $3,000,000	$1,025,800 plus 53% of the excess over $2,500,000
Over $3,000,000 but not over $3,500,000	$1,290,800 plus 57% of the excess over $3,000,000
Over $3,500,000	$1,575,800 plus 60% of the excess over $3,500,000

For 1984 – *In the case of decedents dying and gifts made in 1984:*

Over $2,500,000 but not over $3,000,000	$1,025,800 plus 53% of the excess over $2,500,000
Over $3,000,000	$1,290,800 plus 55% of the excess over $3,000,000

For 1985

Over $2,500,000	50%

gift made from John's money after John and Westie were married would be treated as if they each made a $50,000 taxable gift. That drops the gift tax to a total of $21,200 ($10,600 for each). Splitting saves $2,600. If you live in a community property state, such as Texas, Louisiana, California, Idaho, Arizona, New Mexico and Washington, gifts of community property by a husband and wife to a third party are not eligible for gift splitting, since such property has already—in essence—been "split."

The mighty marital

Another advantage of marriage—at least from the recipient spouse's viewpoint—is that before a gift from one spouse to another becomes taxable, a marital deduction is allowed (over and above any annual exclusion).

Gift-tax laws allow one spouse to give another an unlimited amount gift-tax free because of this mighty marital deduction. So if John gives Westie $120,000 (in addition to his $10,000 gift tax annual exclusion, not one dime will be subject to gift tax. If he gives her $1,200,000, it's still 100 percent gift-tax free. There's no upper limit on how much you can give—or leave—your spouse.

E pluribus unum

Even that part of a gift which is taxable may not generate an actual tax liability. A dollar for dollar reduction in the gift tax payable is allowed to every taxpayer. This is called the "unified credit" because it is allowed against gift taxes, or estate taxes, or both. But unlike the $10,000 per donee annual exclusion, which regenerates each year, the unified credit ($47,000 in 1981, $62,800 in 1982, $79,300 in 1983, $96,300 in 1984, $121,800 in 1985, $155,800 in 1986, and $192,800 in 1987 and later years)—once used, is gone. So you can use it now to eliminate the tax on lifetime gifts—or later to wipe out the estate tax. Let's put that another way: The $79,300 credit is roughly equivalent to an exemption of $275,000 in 1983 and will be equivalent to a $600,000 exemption by 1987.

Putting it all together

If John and Westie make a $600,000 gift in 1983 to their son, Russell, each spouse would compute gift tax liability as follows:

Gift (split)	$300,000
Less: Annual exclusion	10,000
Net gift	$290,000
Tax on net gift	$ 84,400
Less: Unified credit in 1983	79,300
Net tax due	$ 5,100

Since the credit used during lifetime reduces the credit available against the estate tax by 1987, John and Westie each will have $113,500 ($192,800 − $79,300) of credit left. They can use that credit at any time and against any taxable lifetime gift—or it can be used by each spouse's executor to offset any estate tax liability.

A special bonus

Under prior law, any gift you made within three years of your death was brought back into your estate regardless of your motive for making the gift. But this harsh treatment no longer applies. For example, if John should die within three years of a cash gift of $10,000 to a cousin, the gift would not be brought back into his gross estate. It would escape estate tax entirely even though he made it deliberately to avoid the tax.

Because gifts that qualify for the annual exclusion are gift tax free and are not brought back into the gross estate, the trick is to give such outright unrestricted gifts to as many donees as possible each year. You can use this special bonus to avoid estate taxes even if you are on your death bed while you are making the gifts.

Give what?

You're probably wondering at this point what's the best property to give away. The answer is, that depends on your circumstances and objectives.

Typically, if you are in a high income tax bracket and your donee is in a relatively lower bracket, the best type of property for you to give is high-income producing property.

Another prime property for gifting is an asset that is likely to grow substantially in value. The gift should be made when the gift tax values—and therefore the gift tax transfer costs—are lowest. So if John was incorporated and thought his business was about to acquire a substantial customer, a gift of the stock before profits rose, (and, with it the value of the business) would be an inexpensive way to shift assets to his son, Russell.

You should give property away even if it's already appreciated if you are thinking about selling the property and your donee is in a lower income tax bracket than you are. For example, John bought stock ten years ago at $20 a share. Now it's worth $100. John is going to sell it to finance his son's private school tuition. He'd be better off giving it to a custodian for his son (gifts to minors are discussed in Chapter 19) and having the custodian sell it. The $80 of growth would be taxed to his son, Russell, at his low tax bracket rather than to John at his high rates. (This same technique can be used even if your children are not minors.)

Another type of property that makes an excellent gift is life insurance. That's because it has a relatively low gift tax value but a high estate tax value. For instance, if you own a $100,000 term policy on your life, you could remove $100,000 from your estate at practically no gift tax cost (but don't forget you are giving up control) by transferring ownership to your spouse or child or to a trust for them.

Don't give away "loss" property, property which would result in a loss if you sold it. That's because your donee can't use your loss to offset his/her income. You should sell the property, deduct your loss against other income, and give away the proceeds of the sale.

If you can't decide what type of property to give away and you own assets in more than one state, give away property in a state other than the one in which you live. That prevents what's known as "ancillary administration," a costly and duplicative process involving probate not only in the state of your domicile but also in the state where the property is. If John and Westie owned a sailboat in Maryland and they lived in Pennsylvania, the sailboat would be a better gift to their son (other things being equal of course) than cash of identical value.

About time

When is the best time to make a gift? One answer is, "Never," if you can't afford to part with the property for psychological or financial security reasons. If you are depending on that property or the income it produces, or think you might need it at some time in the future, don't give it away no matter how much savings you may realize.

Another answer is, if you feel you can afford to make a gift, then the time to make the gift was yesterday but the next best time is right now. Get it out of your estate as quickly as possible. The reason is to shift the tax on the income to your donee as quickly as you can. That way, income tax savings compound the advantages of making the gift.

Generally, if the assets you own fluctuate widely in value, you should give them away when the market is low.

How now?

There are many ways of making gifts. One way is outright. John might give Westie $10,000 in cash. If John wanted to give her stocks, he might tell his broker to put the title in her name. Quite often gifts are made by putting real estate or other property in joint names with a "right of survivorship." (If John buys land in

Wildwood, for instance, and titles it jointly with Westie with rights of survivorship, should one spouse die the other automatically becomes the sole owner.)

Often, the problem with outright or joint gifts with rights of survivorship is that the recipient can't—or doesn't want to—handle or manage the asset. In a nutshell, the form of your gift should match your donee's financial abilities and desires. John may be thrusting an unwelcome burden on Westie that she is ill-equipped to handle if he gives her property outright or if he titles property jointly and then dies.

When the recipient of a proposed gift is a minor or mentally or emotionally disabled child (or adult), care must be taken to arrange for property management and investment advice. A temporary solution to this problem is the Uniform Gifts to Minors Account. A better long-term solution is a 2503(c) trust. (See Chapter 19.)

Another consideration is how soon you want your donee to have the property. Not everyone wants the recipients of their gifts to have absolute and immediate control. John, for example, may want his nephews to reach greater emotional maturity before they receive substantial gifts. Yet, he might want to remove those gifts from his estate and have the income taxed to them immediately. For this reason, many property owners set up trusts. You can set the terms of the trust. The law gives you wide discretion as to how and at what time (or times) trust property will be paid out to your beneficiaries and still allows substantial estate and income tax savings.

A few final words

It's important that gifts—like any other tool or technique you use in planning your family's financial future—be used wisely. Putting too much in the wrong hands at the wrong time may be more costly in the long run than not making gifts. On the other hand, many estate owners foolishly try to hold on to all their property "until the last minute." Often, the result is that thousands of dollars of income and estate taxes are needlessly paid (and therefore not available to your loved ones).

Both mistakes can be avoided by thinking out the consequences of even the smallest gifts—and talking it over with members of the estate planning "cooperative." Discuss the pros and cons of gifts with them and have them chart out a gift giving program that fits into your personal objectives for yourself and your family.

10.
Will You Die for All You're Worth?

PART 1: WHAT THE FEDS GET (THE FEDERAL ESTATE TAX)

Confiscatory! That's one word that has often been used to characterize the federal estate tax. It's not far from the truth in many cases. If you don't plan, the federal government—rather than your family—will be the "beneficiary" of a large part of your estate.

Knowing how the federal estate tax works is the key to beating the system. We'll examine what to do—and what not to do—as we look at the case of Jim Martin and his wife, Grace. Jim is forty-two. Grace is thirty-eight. Jim is a senior executive in the Providence Investors Corporation, a small but highly profitable investment company. The Martins have three children, Ted, Jeff and Jonathan. We'll do a quick overview of the computation process and then come back and look at how each tax provision works.

Computing the tax

Here in a nutshell is how the federal estate tax would be computed at Jim's death.

First, Jim's executors would have to compute his "gross estate." This is the total of all property Jim owned when he died. It also includes some property that Jim didn't own technically but which the tax law requires his executor to include in his estate.

After Jim's executor computes his gross estate, deductions can be taken for funeral and administrative expenses as well as for certain debts and taxes. The result is Jim's "adjusted gross estate."

Then, (one or more) deductions may be allowed for (1) property passing to a surviving spouse (this is called the "marital" deduction), and (2) property passing to a charity (the "charitable" deduction). The result, after taking these deductions, is the "taxable estate."

But the term "taxable" estate is slightly misleading because certain gifts Jim made during lifetime (so-called "adjusted taxable gifts") must be added back at this point. The federal estate tax rates are applied to the total.

Fortunately, even the result of this calculation is not the bottom line: Jim's executor may reduce the tax otherwise payable by one or more credits. The credits, which provide for a dollar for dollar reduction of the tax, are:

1. The "unified credit" (a credit in 1983 equivalent to the tax on roughly $275,000 worth of assets allowed to every taxpayer regardless of how that property is left or to whom. The unified credit may be used during lifetime to offset gift taxes for lifetime gifts or at death to offset estate taxes);

2. The "credit for state death taxes" (Jim's estate will be allowed a federal credit for the state death taxes his estate actually pays—up to specified limits);

3. The "credit for foreign death taxes" (if Jim owned property subject to tax in another country); and

4. A credit for estate taxes paid by the estates of other decedents for assets included in Jim's estate (this is called the "credit for tax on prior transfers" and is allowed only if the two deaths occur within a short time of each other).

What's in and how to get it out

Jim could save estate taxes if he knew what was includable in his estate and why. Then with the advice of his advisors, he could remove the appropriate assets. Let's go back to the beginning of the computation process and see what would be includable and how we could prevent or minimize estate tax inclusion. As we go along, make a list of the property you own that would be includable under each category and state the approximate value. We'll run what estate planners call a "hypothetical probate," a financial X ray of how much tax and other expense your estate would have to pay if you died today.

Category 1—Property you own in your own name

Jim's executor must include all the property he owned in his own name at the time of his death. Any cash, stocks, bonds, notes, real estate or mortgages payable to Jim, as well as any "tangible personal property" (essentially this is "touchable," "movable" property) Jim owns, such as watches, rings and other personal effects, must be included. Bank accounts Jim keeps in his own name (both checking and savings) are includable. Even the right to future income is includable (so if Jim had the right to partnership profits, dividends, interest payments or bonuses that he hadn't actually received when he died, the value of these amounts must be included in Jim's estate).

How could Jim avoid taxation on property he owns in his name? One way is to get it "out of his name" and have someone else own it. Jim could make small gifts each year to his wife, Grace, and to his three children. A better way is to purchase assets in their names right from the start. That way the appreciation grows in their hands. That's another way of saying that Jim wouldn't have to pay a gift tax on any future growth since he's given away cash and therefore removed the asset it's used to purchase at the lowest possible cost. For example, instead of buying stock at $10 a share and then giving it away when it's worth $100 (and paying gift tax based on the $100 date-of-gift value), Jim should give cash now to a custodian or trustee for his children. Then the stock could be bought in their names so that if it grows from $10 a share to $100 over the next five years, neither the initial value nor the growth would occur in Jim's estate.

Approximate value of assets I own in this category $_____

Category 2—Gifts in which you retain the income or control over the property or income

The best way to explain this category is to say, You can't give away your cake and expect to continue to eat it—and still avoid the estate tax. If Jim gives away property but keeps the right to the income it produces or the right to determine who will receive the income or the right to use or possess or enjoy the property itself, that retained right will cause the entire value of the property—measured on the date of Jim's death—to be includable in his estate.

The logic for this seemingly harsh rule is that the right to enjoy or control property or determine who will receive the property or its income is a key characteristic of property ownership. To an important degree, giving away property but keeping the income is an incomplete disposition; your donee's full and complete possession or enjoyment of the property doesn't start (and therefore your ownership does not end) until you die.

How can you avoid inclusion under this category? The answer is to make each gift absolute and with no strings attached. For example, according to a number of cases, you could give your home to your spouse and continue to live in it as long as you made her absolute owner of the property. You could give your home to your children, but it's very important that you either move out or pay them a reasonable rent and have all documents changed to indicate that they are—in fact—the new owners. (It also helps if they pay real estate taxes and the other expenses of running the home.)

Approximate value of assets that fit into this category $_____

Category 3—Gifts made conditional on surviving you

Say Jim ostensibly gives an asset to one of his sons in trust but conditions the son's right to it on surviving him. For instance, Jim might put real estate worth $100,000 in trust for his son, Jonathan. Assume the trust provides that "the property is to go to my son, Jonathan, if he survives me, otherwise to the person I name in my will." If there is a meaningful probability that the property will return to Jim (or a beneficiary of Jim's estate), the value of the property transferred will be includable in Jim's estate.

Jim's right to regain the property (or the right to say who will receive it) if his son does not survive him is called a "reversionary interest." This type of transfer is includable in Jim's estate because it is considered to be—in substance—a substitute for disposing of the property by will.

How do you defeat this section of the tax law? Very simple. Your attorney should specify that the property will go to some party other than you or your estate if the condition you've established isn't met. For instance, you might say, "If my daughter is not alive at the time of my death, my land in Wildwood is to go to my nephew, Farnsworth."

Approximate value of assets that fit into this category $_____

Category 4—Gifts you made but retained the right to alter, amend, revoke or terminate

Most of us make our gifts outright. We give our children or relatives presents on their birthdays or holidays. We give them stocks or bonds or set up bank accounts for them.

But sometimes, because of the size of the gift or the lack of maturity or the financial management or investment ability of our recipients, we want to tie up the gift or place certain limitations or restrictions on it. Usually such gifts are made through a custodial account (like the Uniform Gifts to Minors Account) or in trust.

Jim Martin, for example, might set up gifts in trust for his minor children. So far so good. He's been wise to provide management protection and investment advice for them. But if Jim retains a right to change the gift he's made, or to alter it, amend it, revoke or terminate it, the value of the property subject to that power will be in his estate. Worse yet, it will be in his estate at its value when he dies—not when he made the gift. For instance, if Jim put $10,000 into a trust for his children and it grew to $80,000 by the date of his death, the entire $80,000 would be in Jim's estate if he held one of the prohibited powers.

What are the forbidden rights that will cause estate tax inclusion?

The mere power to control the date a beneficiary will receive his interest will cause inclusion. So if Jim, in the trust instrument, retains the right to accelerate one son's interest so that he receives it sooner than another, the property will be in Jim's estate (even if Jim can't personally benefit in any way).

Worse yet, the IRS construes this rule broadly. That means that even if Jim held an "alter, amend, revoke or terminate" right as trustee or co-trustee, the property would still be in his estate.

How do we avoid inclusion under this law? Be sure you are not trustee or co-trustee or custodian for a gift you make or a trust you establish. Also, provide in the trust or custodial instrument a substitute (other than yourself) in case the "fiduciary" (the person with the responsibility of safeguarding your beneficiary's interests) you named, cannot or will not serve.

Approximate value of gifts that fall into this category $_____

Category 5—Annuities or similar arrangements you purchase (or that are purchased on your behalf) that are payable to you while living, and then to your designated survivor

If you are receiving an "annuity" (a systematic liquidation of principal and interest) that will last as long as you live and payments are to continue for the lifetime of a survivor you have selected, at your death the "present value" of your survivor's interest will be in your estate.

Say Jim purchased an annuity (or Jim's employer, Providence Investors Corporation, buys one or creates one for him as an employee benefit) that would pay him $600 a month for life and at his death continue to his wife, Grace, as long as she lives. The value of what Grace is expected to receive is discounted (there are IRS tables used to make this calculation) and included in Jim's estate.

Fortunately, there are three qualifications:

First, if you purchase an annuity (or your employer provides one for you as an employee benefit) and it ends at your death, nothing will be in your estate. This is because the federal estate tax is a levy on the privilege of transferring property. If there is no transfer or shifting of rights when you die, nothing is includable in your estate.

Second, to the extent that your survivor furnished part of the original cost of the annuity, that portion of the value of the survivor's annuity will not be in your estate. So if Grace paid for 25 percent of the annuity, only 75 percent of the present value payable to her at your death will be in your estate. (If your employer paid part of the price, that contribution is treated as if made by you.)

Third—and this is a "biggy" for most of us—it is possible to exclude up to $100,000 of the death benefit from a pension or profit sharing plan set up by our employer. In other words, if Jim was covered under the Providence Investors Pension Plan and the plan paid a $350,000 death benefit to his wife, Grace, $100,000 of the $350,000 can be federal estate (and in some states, state death) tax free. This federal estate tax exclusion rule applies to up to $100,000 of cash, insurance, or other property generated in the pension or profit-sharing plan by employer dollars.

But there's a catch! For death benefits under your employer's pension or profit sharing plan (death benefits under an "HR-10 Plan," a self-employed individual's retirement plan, also follow these rules) to be estate tax free:

1. *Don't* make your estate the beneficiary. Be sure you've named a person or trust you set up while you were living as beneficiary. Be sure to name a secondary beneficiary in case the one you've named dies before you do.

2. Be sure your beneficiary knows that he or she must receive payments spread over more than one tax year (two years is good enough). Otherwise, the benefit will be in your estate. If your beneficiary does choose to take the pension money in a lump sum, the estate tax exclusion can still be saved if he/she elects to forgo the right to "ten year income average" the death benefit. In other words, some or all of the money your beneficiary will receive under your pension or profit sharing plan will be subject to income tax when it is received. By electing to forgo special ten year income averaging (normal five-year income averaging may still be available), your beneficiary can receive the pension benefits in a lump sum without causing the death benefit to be in your estate.

If you are covered under an "IRA" (Individual Retirement Account) or a "SEPP" (Simplified Employee Pension Plan), up to $100,000 of the death benefit can still be excluded from your estate. But the exclusion is available only if your beneficiary takes the money in the form of an annuity, that is, spread out in substantially equal payments over at least 36 months.

Approximate value of benefits that fall into this category... $_____

Category 6—Jointly held property where someone else automatically receives your interest by surviving you

Many of us own property "jointly with the right of survivorship" or as "tenants by the entireties" (basically the same thing, only this form of ownership exists between husband and wife). Most of us own our houses this way. It means that upon the death of either joint owner, the survivor automatically (regardless of what our wills say) becomes owner.

There are two rules that affect this category of property. The first is the "50–50" rule. It provides that only half of jointly held property with right of survivorship will be in your estate—regardless of who contributed what to the purchase price. For instance, even if Jim and Grace had purchased their $130,000 home entirely from Jim's income, under the 50–50 rule, only $65,000 or 50 percent, will be includable in Jim's estate. (Of course, if Grace died first, 50 percent of the value of the home would be in her estate even though she made no contribution.)

This 50–50 rule can only be used if the property is owned by you and your spouse (and no one else). So it wouldn't work for property that is owned by you and your brother as joint tenants.

The 50–50 rule will work for personal as well as real property. For instance, if Jim calls his stock broker, Ed Sigmond, and purchases 100 shares of Xerox as joint tenants with the right of survivorship with Grace, the property qualifies under the 50–50 rule.

How then is property that isn't taxed under the 50–50 rule treated? The answer is, under the "percentage of contribution" (also called the "consideration furnished") rule. This rule is simple—but sometimes harsh. In a nutshell, it taxes jointly held property entirely in the estate of the first joint tenant to die—except to the extent the survivor can prove contribution (out of funds other than those acquired by gift from the decedent).

Say Jim and his brother, John, bought property worth $30,000. John used $10,000 he inherited as his share of the contribution to this property, which was titled jointly with Jim. Since John could prove contribution—from his own funds—of one-third of the purchase price of the property, then only two-thirds of the value would be in Jim's estate. If John died first and Jim could prove he paid for two-thirds of the purchase price for the original property, only one-third would be in John's estate under this rule.

The "percentage of contribution" rule is used in every case where the 50–50 rule does not apply. This makes it extremely important that joint tenants, other than spouses, keep meticulous records—and separate bank accounts—and a financial diary as to whose funds purchased what.

Picture a brother and sister working an entire lifetime, side by side. The brother dies and the government wants to tax all their jointly held property in his estate. Without records (we suggest a "partnership" or corporate agreement that "splits" profits and assets where the joint tenants are in business together or making investments jointly), the survivor may have little chance of success in proving contribution. Often a farm or small business is lost because the decedent's estate cannot afford the federal estate tax on the entire property.

Approximate value of assets that fall into the 50–50 category (put only 50%) .... $_____

Approximate value of assets that would be taxed under the percentage of contribution rule (multiply your original percentage contribution times today's fair market value) .... $_____

Category 7—General powers of appointment—an unlimited right to specify who receives someone else's property

When Jim's grandfather died, his will established a trust and placed $400,000 of stocks and other securities into it. Jim's father, Marty, was given a "general power of appointment" over the assets in the trust. That means that even though Marty didn't technically own the property, Marty could specify who was to receive it. This power to appoint (choose the recipient of someone else's property) was so broad that it was considered "general." Marty could have named anyone, even himself or his estate or his creditors, as the recipient(s) of his father's property.

If Marty's father had provided that Marty could only choose between his children (Jim and his sister, Martha) or some other preselected class of beneficiaries and could not appoint the property to himself or his estate, the power would be "limited" or "special."

The difference between a general and a limited power is important: If you have a "general" power over the assets in someone else's trust, the value of those assets are includable in your estate. But if your power is "limited," the assets will not be in your estate.

Jim plans to set up two trusts for Grace in his will. One trust will give her a general power of appointment over trust assets. So she can demand everything in the trust for herself or anyone else immediately and without limitation. This will be called the "marital" trust since it is designated to qualify for the "marital" deduction described below. Any assets remaining in this trust when Grace dies will be in her estate, since her rights to the property in it are tantamount to outright survivorship.

The second trust Jim will create is a "nonmarital" (often called a "family" trust). Although it provides additional income and security for Grace, its assets will *not* be includable in her estate. That's because she'll be given a limited power of appointment. She has the right to "appoint" trust income or principal to any one of their children; she can pick the child she thinks needs or deserves it most (or is in the lowest tax bracket). In this way, the limited power adds additional financial flexibility without causing these assets to be subject to a second estate tax when Grace dies (they will be taxed once when Jim dies).

Both general and special powers of appointment are important estate planning tools that your attorney can build into your estate plan with little trouble.

Approximate value of assets subject to a general power of appointment that I control .... $_____

Category 8—Life insurance that you own or have important rights over or that is payable to or for the benefit of your estate

If, at the time of your death, you own life insurance on your life (or you gave it away within three years of your death), it will be included in your estate regardless of whom you have named as beneficiary.

In fact, if you merely have the right to benefit in any meaningful way—or determine who will enjoy that benefit in an economic sense—the policy will be in your estate. For instance, even if Jim had given away a policy on his life but kept the right to name the policy beneficiary or surrender the policy or borrow its cash value or almost any other so-called "incident of ownership," the entire death proceeds (and not just the value of the right he retained) would be in his estate. Inclusion of the entire death benefit would be required even if Jim couldn't exercise the power for his own benefit.

The second rule that applies to life insurance is, no matter who owned the policy or held "incidents of ownership" in it, it will be includable in your estate if it is payable to your estate or benefits your estate. So if Grace purchased a policy on Jim's life but named Jim's estate as beneficiary, the entire proceeds would become subject to federal estate tax.

Inclusion of life insurance can be avoided by "assigning" it (transferring it irrevocably) by gift ("love and affection") or for "valuable consideration." But there is an insidious tax trap to be avoided in transfers where the new owner pays any amount of valuable consideration. The problem is, all or a substantial portion of the insurance, which is normally income tax free, becomes subject to ordinary income tax. For instance, if Jim or Jim's employer sold a $100,000 policy on his life to Jim's wife, Grace, or to a trust for her benefit, the proceeds would be subject to ordinary income tax when

Jim died (no matter how little was paid on the policy). If the trust purchased the policy, the tax on $100,000 could be as high as $55,000.

The point is, never make a transfer of life insurance for any consideration (other than "love and affection") without first consulting both your insurance agent and tax counsel.

Approximate value of life insurance I own or that is payable to my estate .... $_____

Now total up all the approximate values you have entered on the boldface lines above. The sum is roughly your "gross estate." (Don't worry that the figures are not exact or precise. We're just trying to "guesstimate" your estate's probable "liquidity" need—its need for cash.)

What comes next?

Fortunately, the federal government doesn't base the estate tax on your gross estate. That's only the starting point for computing the tax as you'll see by the tables, page 93 and 94.

Stage 2 is an artificial point called the "adjusted gross estate." In other words, your executor makes an adjustment to the gross estate.

Funeral expenses (subject to "reasonable limits") are deductible. These expenses include interment, burial lot or vault, grave marker and perpetual care costs.

Administrative costs are deductible. Administrative costs include expenses incurred in administering property in your estate. This means your executor can deduct expenses incurred in the collection and preservation of assets that will pass under your will, costs incurred in paying off your debts, and the expenses incurred in distributing what's left to your beneficiaries.

These administration expenses include court costs, accounting fees, appraiser's fees, brokerage costs, executor's commissions and attorney's fees. How much will they be? That depends.

Estate settlement costs will vary widely from location to location. They'll also be affected by both the size of your estate and the complexity of the administrative problems. For instance, if all your assets were "liquid," that is, if everything you owned was cash or could be converted into cash quickly and without cost or trouble, your attorney would have an easy job and the costs would be low.

Determination of Cash Requirements

	(1)	Gross Estate.....................	$ _____
Minus	(2)	Funeral and Administration Expenses (estimated as ____ % of ____).. ____ √	
	(3)	Debts and Taxes .... ____ √	
	(4)	Losses .... ____	
		Total Deductions..... ═══	____
Equals	(5)	Adjusted Gross Estate	____
Minus	(6)	Marital Deduction .... ____	
	(7)	Charitable Deduction .... ____	
		Total Deductions..... ═══	____
Equals	(8)	Taxable Estate	____
Plus	(9)	Adjusted Taxable Gifts (post-1976 lifetime taxable transfers not included in gross estate) .... ____	
Equals	(10)	Tentative Tax Base (total of taxable estate and adjusted taxable gifts)	═══
Compute	(11)	Tentative Tax (apply rates from page 97 to line 10) .... ____	
Minus	(12)	Gift Taxes Paid on Post-1976 Gifts .... ____	
Equals	(13)	Tax Payable before Credits	____
Minus	(14)	Tax Credits	

  (a) Unified credit   _____
  *(b) State death tax
      credit   _____ (b-1) _____ √
  (c) Credit for foreign   (State death
      death taxes   _____ tax payable)
  (d) Credit for tax on
      prior transfers   _____

		Total Reduction ═══	____
Equals	(15)	Net Federal Estate Tax Payable	═══ √
Plus	(16)	Total Cash Bequests	____ √
Equals	(17)	Total Cash Requirements (sum of 2, 3, state death tax payable, 16, and 17) ..	$ ═══

*See Maximum Credit Table for State Death Taxes, p. 99. Apply rates to Line 8 taxable estate.

Determination of Cash Requirements
(COMMUNITY PROPERTY STATES)

      (1) Gross Estate .... $ _____

Minus
      (2) Funeral and Administration Expenses
           (estimated as _____ % of _____) . _____ ✓

      (3) Debts and Taxes .... _____ ✓

      (4) Losses .... _____

                               Total Deductions .... $ ========== _____

Equals
      (5) Adjusted Gross Estate .... ==========

Minus
      (6) Marital Deduction .... _____

      (7) Charitable Deduction .... _____

                               Total Deductions .... $ ========== _____

Equals
      (8) Taxable Estate .... ==========

Plus
      (9) Adjusted Taxable Gifts (post-1976
           lifetime taxable transfers not
           included in gross estate) .... _____

Equals
    (10) Tentative Tax Base (total of taxable
           estate and adjusted taxable gifts) .... ==========

Compute
    (11) Tentative Tax (apply rates from page 97
           to line 10) .... _____

Minus
    (12) Gift Taxes Paid on Post-1976 Gifts .... _____

Equals
    (13) Federal Estate Tax Payable before Credits $ ==========

Minus
    (14) Tax Credits
           (a) Unified credit   _____
       *(b) State death tax
              credit   _____ (b-1) _____ ✓
                                                             (State death
           (c) Credit for foreign   tax payable)
              death taxes   _____
           (d) Credit for tax on
              prior transfers   _____

                     Total Reduction ==========   _____

Equals
    (15) Net Federal Estate Tax Payable ...... ========== ✓

Plus (In states where appropriate)
    (16) Total Cash Bequests .... _____ ✓
    (17) Spouse's Share of Community Expenses
           (a) Administration expenses
              (estimated as _____% of _____) _____

           (b) Debts and taxes .... _____
                                Total Costs .... _____ ✓

Equals
    (18) Total Cash Requirements (sum of 2, 3,
           state death tax payable, 16, 17, and 18) ==========

*See Maximum Credit Table for State Death Taxes, p. 99. Apply rates to Line 8 taxable estate.

Bank accounts, money market certificates and life insurance are good examples of "low cost," highly liquid assets. But if there's little cash and many assets and properties, all of which have to be valued or appraised, your estate expenses will be higher.

About attorney's fees

One hint for the person you've named as your executor: Shop around! There's no reason why you can't shop around for an attorney the same way you shop for any other service. It's extremely important that your executor(s) demand (and be satisfied with) a written *hourly* fee structure and a rough estimate of the number of hours involved. (Incidentally, if you are the executor of a will, the laws of most states allow you to choose the estate's attorney and pick anyone you want—regardless of who drew the will or who was specified in the will to be the estate's attorney.)

A guesstimate of these two categories of costs is $_____
(A minimum of $10,000 for this category is suggested.) Seven percent of Category 1 assets will give you a *rough* idea of the minimum cost you can expect.

A third category of deduction is allowed for "debts and taxes." This means your executor can deduct all your bona fide debts—including mortgages and liens that you owe when you die. So if you own a $100,000 home in your own name but your outstanding mortgage is $60,000, your executor will enter $100,000 in category 1 but will be allowed a $60,000 deduction here.

Deductible taxes include income, gift and property taxes you owe when you die.

A guesstimate of this third category of costs is..... $_____

The fourth category of deduction is casualty losses incurred while your estate is being administered. Few estates receive any deduction for this category, but from time to time an uninsured fire, theft or other loss creates a deduction.

Now total up all your estate's deductions........... $_____

Then subtract that amount from the figure you have guesstimated to be your gross estate. That figure is your "adjusted gross" estate.

As you will see from the estate tax computation form on page 93, we're now at Stage 2 (line 5). From the amount we've arrived at, we can subtract a marital deduction and perhaps a charitable deduction.

The "biggie" is the marital deduction. (Look at line 6.) It's the largest deduction most estates of married couples receive. It's typically allowed for property that's in your estate and will go to your surviving spouse either outright or in a manner that's tantamount to outright.

This deduction is (virtually) unlimited. You could actually leave your spouse your entire estate and the deduction would wipe out the federal estate tax entirely. Of course, it can't be more than the net value of what you leave your spouse. And you have to remember that if your spouse dies before you—even one minute before you—there is no marital deduction in your estate.

My marital deduction will be roughly .... $_____

Your estate will be entitled to a charitable deduction for anything you leave to charity at your death (line 7). Like the marital deduction, the charitable deduction is unlimited. Conceivably, you could leave your entire estate to charity and receive a deduction for the entire amount.

A guesstimate of my charitable deduction is .... $_____

Total deductions .... $_____

Subtracting the total deductions from the adjusted gross estate results in my taxable estate .... $_____

This brings us to Stage 3, the taxable estate. Actually, this is a misnomer because certain lifetime gifts you made, post-1976 taxable gifts that have not been included already in the computation, are added in here. List any post-1976 taxable gifts (so-called "adjusted taxable gifts") you didn't include already.

A guesstimate of adjusted taxable gifts .... $_____

The sum of your taxable estate and adjusted taxable gifts is the amount upon which the federal estate tax is based. It's called the *"tentative* tax base."

A guesstimate of my tentative tax base is .... $_____

Unified Rate Schedule for Estate and Gift Taxes

If the amount with which the tentative tax to be computed is:	The tentative tax is:
Not over $10,000	18% of such amount
Over $10,000 but not over $20,000	$1,800 plus 20% of the excess over $10,000
Over $20,000 but not over $40,000	$3,800 plus 22% of the excess over $20,000
Over $40,000 but not over $60,000	$8,200 plus 24% of the excess over $40,000
Over $60,000 but not over $80,000	$13,000 plus 26% of the excess over $60,000
Over $80,000 but not over $100,000	$18,200 plus 28% of the excess over $80,000
Over $100,000 but not over $150,000	$23,800 plus 30% of the excess over $100,000
Over $150,000 but not over $250,000	$38,800 plus 32% of the excess over $150,000
Over $250,000 but not over $500,000	$70,800 plus 34% of the excess over $250,000
Over $500,000 but not over $750,000	$155,800 plus 37% of the excess over $500,000
Over $750,000 but not over $1,000,000	$248,300 plus 39% of the excess over $750,000
Over $1,000,000 but not over $1,250,000	$345,800 plus 41% of the excess over $1,000,000
Over $1,250,000 but not over $1,500,000	$448,300 plus 43% of the excess over $1,250,000
Over $1,500,000 but not over $2,000,000	$555,800 plus 45% of the excess over $1,500,000
Over $2,000,000 but not over $2,500,000	$780,800 plus 49% of the excess over $2,000,000

For 1982 — *In the case of decedents dying and gifts made in 1982:*

Over $2,500,000 but not over $3,000,000	$1,025,800 plus 53% of the excess over $2,500,000
Over $3,000,000 but not over $3,500,000	$1,290,800 plus 57% of the excess over $3,000,000
Over $3,500,000 but not over $4,000,000	$1,575,800 plus 61% of the excess over $3,500,000
Over $4,000,000	$1,880,800 plus 65% of the excess over $4,000,000

For 1983 — *In the case of decedents dying and gifts made in 1983:*

Over $2,500,000 but not over $3,000,000	$1,025,800 plus 53% of the excess over $2,500,000
Over $3,000,000 but not over $3,500,000	$1,290,800 plus 57% of the excess over $3,000,000
Over $3,500,000	$1,575,800 plus 60% of the excess over $3,500,000

For 1984 — *In the case of decedents dying and gifts made in 1984:*

Over $2,500,000 but not over $3,000,000	$1,025,800 plus 53% of the excess over $2,500,000
Over $3,000,000	$1,290,800 plus 55% of the excess over $3,000,000

For 1985

Over $2,500,000	50%

The table shown here is the rate schedule you apply to the tentative tax base. For example, if your tentative tax base is $250,000, your tax would be $70,800.

Note that the rates are "progressive." The tax on a tentative base of $1,000 is $180. But the tax on 100 times that much, $100,000. is $23,800, much more than 100 times $180. The tax on $1,000,000 is much more than 1000 times $180—it's $345,800. (You are up to at least a 50 percent rate once your estate exceeds $2,500,000. That's another way of saying 50 cents of every additional dollar you earn and keep from that point on doesn't go to your heirs—it goes to the federal government.

A guesstimate of tentative tax .... $_____

As you can see by the form, there are reductions allowed even from this "tentative tax."

The most important of the remaining reductions are the tax credits (line 14). The key credits are the so-called "unified credit" and the "state death tax credit."

The unified credit is a dollar for dollar reduction against the federal estate tax otherwise payable by your executor. It's called a "unified credit" because it can be used as an offset against gift as well as estate taxes (or both but to the extent you use it while you are alive it's used up). It wouldn't be available again when you die.

Fortunately, the credit is large—and getting larger. Roughly, that means that your "tentative tax base" can be as large as $225,000 in 1982 before you pay one dime in federal estate tax.

The unified credit is being phased in as follows:

Year	1982	1983	1984	1985	1986	1987 and later
Estate Protected by the Credit	225,000	275,000	325,000	400,000	500,000	600,000
Actual Credit	62,800	79,300	96,300	121,800	155,800	192,800

The tax figure calculated above can be reduced by $_____
(Insert the actual credit for this year)

The second major credit is the one allowed for state death taxes. There's a table below that gives you the upper limit on this credit.

To figure your state death tax credit (this goes on line 14), find your taxable estate (line 8) and apply that amount to the table below. For instance, the credit for an individual who had a taxable estate of $200,000 is $1,200. That means your federal tax burden would be reduced by $1,200—if your executor paid at least that much in state death taxes.

The federal estate tax payable can be further reduced by a credit of .... $_____

If I were to die today, my federal estate tax liability would be roughly .... $_____

My estate's total "liquidity" (cash) needs are at least $_____*

*Sums of all lines with ✔. (This amount can be substantially higher if your will makes cash bequests or if you've made charitable gifts in cash. The trick is to provide—in your will—that your executor can satisfy gifts you make in your will, to friends, relatives or charities, in cash *or* in "kind." That way your executor could give them property and use cash to pay debts and taxes.)

Now you know what the feds get. It can be a lot—or a little. A lot depends on what you do—or don't do.

Remember, the federal estate tax is a *voluntary* tax. Your heirs won't have to pay much (or anything) when you die—if you take the time to plan—now!

Maximum Credit Table for State Death Taxes

The amount of any state death taxes paid may be subtracted from the federal estate tax as determined under the preceding table, provided, however, that the maximum to be subtracted may not exceed the maximum determined under the following table:*

If the taxable estate is:	*The maximum tax credit shall be:*
Not over $150,000	8/10ths of 1% of the amount by which the taxable estate exceeds $100,000
Over $150,000 but not over $200,000	$400 plus 1.6% of the excess over $150,000
Over $200,000 but not over $300,000	$1,200 plus 2.4% of the excess over $200,000
Over $300,000 but not over $500,000	$3,600 plus 3.2% of the excess over $300,000
Over $500,000 but not over $700,000	$10,000 plus 4% of the excess over $500,000
Over $700,000 but not over $900,000	$18,000 plus 4.8% of the excess over $700,000
Over $900,000 but not over $1,100,000	$27,600 plus 5.6% of the excess over $900,000
Over $1,100,000 but not over $1,600,000	$38,800 plus 6.4% of the excess over $1,100,000
Over $1,600,000 but not over $2,100,000	$70,800 plus 7.2% of the excess over $1,600,000
Over $2,100,000 but not over $2,600,000	$106,800 plus 8% of the excess over $2,100,000
Over $2,600,000 but not over $3,100,000	$146,800 plus 8.8% of the excess over $2,600,000
Over $3,100,000 but not over $3,600,000	$190,800 plus 9.6% of the excess over $3,100,000
Over $3,600,000 but not over $4,100,000	$238,800 plus 10.4% of the excess over $3,600,000
Over $4,100,000 but not over $5,100,000	$290,800 plus 11.2% of the excess over $4,100,000
Over $5,100,000 but not over $6,100,000	$402,800 plus 12% of the excess over $5,100,000
Over $6,100,000 but not over $7,100,000	$522,800 plus 12.8% of the excess over $6,100,000
Over $7,100,000 but not over $8,100,000	$650,800 plus 13.6% of the excess over $7,100,000
Over $8,100,000 but not over $9,100,000	$786,800 plus 14.4% of the excess over $8,100,000
Over $9,100,000 but not over $10,100,000	$930,800 plus 15.2% of the excess over $9,100,000
Over $10,100,000	$1,082,800 plus 16% of the excess over $10,100,000

*This table resembles the table contained in IRC Section 2011(b), but it is not the same. The table in the Code is based on the *adjusted taxable estate*, defined as the taxable estate reduced by $60,000. This table is based on the *taxable estate*. Note that the state death tax credit column in the computer printout, following, is likewise based on the *taxable estate*.

PART 2: THE STATE OF STATE DEATH TAXATION—WORSE THAN YOU WOULD THINK

Because of the liberalization in the federal estate tax laws, as discussed under Part 1 of this chapter, many people will not have to worry about the tax burdens of the federal estate tax at their deaths. However, the same cannot be said about state death taxes. In fact, the chances of your beneficiaries paying a state death tax at your death may be even greater than you'd think. Fortunately, there are many ways to avoid or reduce state death taxes, but before you can successfully attempt to reduce or eliminate these taxes, you must first know what they are and how they work.

What to expect—not 57 varieties

Actually, there are only three varieties of state death taxes, the state "inheritance" tax, the state "estate" tax, and the state "credit estate" tax.

The "inheritance" tax

An "inheritance" tax is a tax on your beneficiaries' right to receive your property. It's the type of tax found in most states.

The amount of inheritance tax payable depends on the value of property each of your beneficiaries receives—and their relationship to you. Typically, beneficiaries are divided into categories.

Those beneficiaries most closely related to you (such as your spouse) and your "lineal" relatives (essentially your children, grandchildren, parents and grandparents) will receive the largest exemptions and the lowest rates. Pennsylvania law is a good example. Real property held jointly between spouses with rights of survivorship is totally exempt from state death taxes. But the same property held in the same manner by brothers is subject to a 15 percent tax. Property left to a child is subject to a 6 percent tax. The same property left to a cousin or aunt or friend generates a 15 percent levy.

The "estate" tax

A state "estate" tax is imposed not on the right to receive your property but rather on your privilege of transferring it. In other words, a state estate tax is measured by the value of the property transferred. It's similar in that respect to the federal estate tax.

Some states impose both an inheritance and an estate tax.

The "credit" estate tax

A "credit" estate (often called a "gap") tax is designed to bridge the gap between the state's inheritance (or estate) tax and the maximum state death tax credit allowed under federal estate tax law.

Let's try an example to see how this works. Carl Reigle's taxable estate for federal estate tax purposes is $500,000. Using the table on page 99, you'll see that a credit of up to $10,000 is allowed against the federal estate tax for the taxes the executor pays to the state as death taxes.

But what if the state inheritance tax is only $8,000? If the federal law allows a $10,000 credit and the state imposes only an $8,000 inheritance tax, a second state tax, amounting to the $2,000 difference, i.e., the credit estate tax is imposed. That, of course, means that the total state death tax is increased to $10,000.

How to beat the system—or win by playing their game your way

Many factors will influence the amount of state death taxes your estate will have to pay. These include state exemptions and deductions, multiple state taxation and tax rates. Planning can lower your taxes considerably.

Double trouble

There's a famous case of Dr. Dorance, the scientist-businessman who maintained two large fully staffed homes only a few miles from each other, one in New Jersey and the other in Bryn Mawr, Pennsylvania. Seems the New Jersey residence was maintained for income and property tax reasons, while Dr. Dorance really lived in the socially prominent main line area outside Philadelphia of which Bryn Mawr is the hub.

When he died, both states claimed the right to tax Dr. Dorance. He hadn't helped his case much. He deliberately kept the lights on in his New Jersey home, kept a car out front, maintained his church membership, and even wrote in his will that he considered himself a domiciliary of New Jersey. So New Jersey levied a state death tax of about $17,000,000. Not to be outdone, Pennsylvania imposed a tax of almost the identical amount.

When the case went to the Supreme Court, it held that both sides had the right to tax. So they did. The total state taxes alone were over $34,000,000. That's in 1933 when a dollar was worth more than a dollar! Worse yet, this case is still on the books—it could affect *your* estate!

Dr. Dorance wasn't alone. Many people have both summer and winter homes or have land and other property in states other than where they live.

Typically, our property will only be taxed in one state—but in certain situations, an estate or its beneficiaries will be liable for the taxes of two—or more—states.

The right of a state to impose a death tax depends on the type of property involved. Here's how it typically works:

Your land and buildings are taxed only by the state in which that property is located. Attorneys call this the "situs" of the property.

"Tangible" (you can touch it) "personal" (non-real estate) property, such as your cars, boats and household goods, is taxed in the state where they are situated. A boat, for example, is taxed where it is permanently docked. Its registry and location for insurance purposes are examined in order to determine its legal location.

The big problem lies with intangible (you don't hold the actual property—only paper representing the underlying asset) personal property. Stocks, bonds, notes and other securities you own may be taxed, in the absence of interstate reciprocal agreement, by several states.

Generally, intangible personal property is taxed only by the state of your domicile (technically this is the place that you call home and—no matter where you are or for how long—intend to return to). Unfortunately, if you've established residences in more than one state or don't clearly establish which state you want to be treated as your domicile, two or more states can still impose death taxes on the same intangible personal property.

It's easy enough to beat it: Just remember your actions do speak louder than your words. Look at your driver's license, where you receive your mail, where you spend the bulk of your time, and where most of your home furnishings are. These are just a few of the things tax authorities examine. Don't split your time evenly. Spend more time (and plant more daisies) at your "home sweet home."

Rates rate

Rates rate consideration. Many wealthy individuals considering retirement shop around for the state that offers not only a warm sun but also a warm inheritance tax climate. It can make a big difference.

The rates at which transfers or receipts of property are taxed vary considerably from state to state. Some states have graduated or progressive rates similar to the federal estate tax. Others, such as Pennsylvania, have flat rates that do not grow progressively higher as the size of the estate increases.

Talk to your attorney—describe what type of property you own, how it's titled and who your beneficiaries are. Have your attorney or other tax advisor check to see which states would treat your estate most favorably.

Not all exemptions or deductions are created equal

Not all property is subject to state death taxation. Most states exempt property you leave to the federal government, to the state itself or to certain charitable organizations.

A few states exempt property passing to a surviving spouse, some totally or partially exempt life insurance. One word of caution: If you've named your estate or your creditors as the beneficiary of your life insurance, any exclusion you would have had is lost. For instance, a $100,000 life insurance policy is inheritance-tax free in Pennsylvania—if you've named a beneficiary other than your estate or your creditors. But if the same policy is paid to your estate and then to your brother under your will, a $15,000 tax will be imposed: $100,000 or $85,000—it depends on just a few minutes of planning with a knowledgeable advisor.

This chapter deals with the different types of state death taxes. However, every state does not have each type of tax, and the exemptions and rates vary from state to state. For specific information concerning the taxes in your state, write to the State Inheritance Tax Department in your state capitol.

11.
That's Life (Insurance)

Almost all estate planners agree that life insurance is one of the most important tools available to provide financial security after your death to those persons and organizations you love. This chapter is about what life insurance is, how it works, and how you can make it work for you.

What's it all about?

Life insurance is a legal contract. In return for a stipulated consideration (a premium) one party (the insurer) agrees to pay the other (the insured), or his/her beneficiary, a specified amount upon the occurrence of death or some other designated event. It's a contract that buys "time" in terms of dollars. In other words, it's an agreement under which economic protection is provided for your family against the risk that your income will stop at your death.

The term "life insurance" includes accidental death benefits under health insurance policies, "whole life," "term insurance," and "endowment" insurance policies. Life insurance is owned for both personal and business uses and includes the "group" coverage you have from your employer as well as individually purchased plans.

Who needs it?

Do I need life insurance? Can't I do without it? The straight answer is, *you* don't need life insurance at all! But others may—desperately. Life insurance is purchased to provide an income for family expenses such as food, clothing and shelter; family needs that continue long after the head of a household dies.

Life insurance can provide cash to pay college expenses, mortgage balances, or other large capital needs.

Estate planners recommend life insurance to provide cash for the payment of estate and inheritance taxes, debts, administrative costs, and other estate settlement expenses. Life insurance provides a way to pay federal estate taxes at a "discount." For example, if you were to purchase a $100,000 policy and die within the first year (say you've paid $2,000 in premiums) $100,000 worth of estate taxes and other expenses can be paid at a cost of only $2,000. The $98,000 difference can be considered a discount. Another way to look at it is that you obtain an "instant estate" of $100,000.

Life insurance can be thought of as a "transfer of capital," a means of transferring assets from your estate to your children or grandchildren in the most efficient manner possible. For example, properly arranged life insurance (owned by a third party who is also your beneficiary) can shift assets from you to that individual (or individuals) without probate costs, without inheritance or other state death taxes, without income taxes, without transfer fees, and without federal estate taxes.

Life insurance is used in businesses to indemnify the business for the loss of a key individual. This is called "keyman" or "key employee" life insurance. The proceeds of such coverage have protected the profits and sometimes the very existence of thousands of partnerships and corporations. Banks look favorably on a firm that has insured its most valuable assets, its key personnel.

Life insurance is also used to fund a "buy-sell." In other words it serves as a mechanism for providing the cash for one shareholder to purchase the stock of a deceased coshareholder.

Financial planners call life insurance the foundation upon which your financial house should be built.

Chocolate, vanilla or strawberry?

What are the various types of life insurance and which type is right for me? Probably the answer to that question is the same as which flavor ice cream is best. The answer is, it depends. It depends on your need and ability to pay.

Term insurance is "die to collect insurance." Under this type of coverage, you must die before the term expires. At the end of the "term," the coverage runs out. Because the insurance company's liability is limited and typically of short duration, the cash outlay for term insurance protection is relatively low. For instance, Chet Horst is thirty-five years old. Chet is interested in providing dollars to his wife, Cathy, and his children if he should die. At Chet's age the premium for $100,000 of insurance is less than $300 the first year (but of course this goes up every year). So term insurance is the coverage to buy if you're looking for maximum short-term protection for a minimum cash outlay.

Chet and Cathy asked their insurance agent, Ric Smith, if there was more than one type of term insurance. Ric replied that there are basically four types or features of term insurance. The first type of term insurance is "annual renewable" term (also called "yearly renewable" term or "YRT"). This type of policy is renewable each year regardless of your physical condition. However, premiums increase year by year (because the risk of death increases year by year) and are often quite difficult to afford at ages greater than fifty or fifty-five.

If you have group insurance at work, yearly renewable term is the type of insurance policy used. If you are young and paying for some of the group coverage, you may be able to save money. The difference between the group plan you have at work and the YRT you purchase on your own is that—if you are young and in good health you may be better off purchasing insurance on your own. If you're older or in poor health, you're probably better off with the group coverage. That's because with group insurance young and healthy employees, in essence, "subsidize" older and less healthy members of the group.

One other point: No matter what type of term policy you buy, you should demand the guaranteed renewable feature. On almost any term policy you can add this right to renew the policy for another year without passing an exam. Sure, it will boost the premium slightly, but if you come to the end of your term and you're seriously ill, wouldn't it be nice to be able to continue the term insurance? (The premium rate you'll pay when you renew will be based on the age you are at that time—not on your age when you bought the original policy.)

"Convertible" term is a contractual right to exchange your term policy for a "whole life" or "endowment" type of policy without evidence of insurability. This means that you don't have to prove you are physically (or otherwise) in a "standard" class of risks in order to stop the term from running out. You have until a specified age—such as sixty-five—to "convert" your term into "whole life" or "endowment" coverage at standard premium rates even if you have cancer.

This feature, which you should demand no matter what type of term you purchase, can be extremely important even if you don't become ill. Sooner or later, as you grow older, the rates for renewing your term policy will become prohibitive. (Ask your agent for the rates you'd have to pay to renew a policy when you reach ages fifty-five, sixty, sixty-five, and seventy. And check out the tables below showing—in five-year intervals—what happens to premium rates.)

RENEWABLE TERM INSURANCE PREMIUMS

Age	Annual Premium for $100,000 of Protection
55	$ 1,200
60	1,800
65	2,800
70	5,000
75	8,100
80	14,200
85	23,300
90	36,900
95	56,800
99	77,200

In many policies, at age sixty or sixty-five or seventy you can't renew your policy—for any amount of money.

You may be asking yourself, why will I need life insurance when I reach that age? The answer is, you may need life insurance no matter how your life turns out. If your other financial ventures *haven't* been successful, your life insurance may be the only significant financial asset to provide security for your family and pay the bills you've left behind. Conversely, let's say you've *been* successful, very successful, in real estate or stocks or in a business. Even if things have gone super-well financially, your assets may be "nonliquid"; they may not be available to pay death taxes or other estate settlement expenses (which must be paid in cash and generally within nine months of your death). If you have it, life insurance can satisfy that need.

The third type of term insurance coverage is called "decreasing term." You've probably heard of "mortgage" insurance. This is nothing more than decreasing term coverage that is used to pay off a mortgage. The death benefit decreases over the specified period of time (essentially at the same rate as your mortgage). The premium for decreasing term coverage generally remains level.

It is important that you name a member of your family and not a bank as the beneficiary of this coverage. If a bank is named as beneficiary, the mortgage will be paid off but your family may lose the right to a very favorable mortgage interest rate. You've protected the bank at your family's expense. On the other hand, if a family member is the recipient of the insurance proceeds at your death, that individual can choose to pay off the mortgage or decide to continue it at favorable rates and invest the insurance proceeds at a substantially higher interest rate.

Level term is the fourth type of term insurance coverage. Death benefits under a level term remain the same for the entire term of the policy. Generally, the premium also stays level. Level term policies are sold in one-year, five-year, ten-year or twenty-year terms. Some companies express the duration in terms of the age you'll be when the policy runs out—such as "term to age sixty-five."

Nothing is paid under this type of coverage unless you die during the term. If you survive the term or if you die one day after the term expires (just as is the case with any term policy), your beneficiaries receive nothing.

Chet has asked his agent, Ric Smith, if there is a term insurance policy that will never run out and in which premiums remain level for as long as Chet lives. Ric responded that "whole life" (permanent) insurance is "term to age one hundred." Ric explained that one of the major characteristics of whole life insurance is that the premium remains level throughout the life of the contract and that it can be kept for as long as Chet lives no matter how long he lives. The insurance company can never cancel the policy no matter how old Chet becomes or what his health or hobbies.

A whole life contract is, in essence, a "term for life" policy. To maintain a level premium as you grow older, the insurance company builds up a "reserve." It is the amount of money, together with the future premiums you'll pay and the interest that will be earned, that in later years will be used to keep the contract going when the level premiums you pay become insufficient.

This reserve that builds up in early years and is used up in later years can also serve another purpose: If you need money for an emergency or opportunity, you can borrow a guaranteed portion of this reserve (the "cash value") from the insurer. This policy loan can be made at extremely favorable rates. Alternatively, if you surrender the contract, since the company no longer has a potential liability, you can cash in ("surrender") the policy for its "cash value."

Obviously, to build a reserve requires that the premium for whole life be higher than the premium for term insurance (just as the premium for twenty-year term is higher than that for ten-year term). A $100,000 policy for a man Chet's age, for instance, is about $1,800 a year.

So should you buy term and invest the difference? Why not? Buy a lot of term—all the term insurance you honestly think your widow and surviving children will need. Then try, for one year, to invest the difference between the whole life premium and the term premium. If you did—and didn't touch the money you invested for the entire year (and your investment equals or exceeds your after-tax objective), do it again—and again until you find that you've forgotten to invest the difference or until the "difference" didn't grow as it was supposed to grow.

Keep one other thought in mind: If the "difference" you invest does grow and compound beyond your wildest dreams in the form of stocks or real estate or a business, how will your executor pay the estate and inheritance taxes? Probably your CPA or attorney will recommend you help your future executor to pay these costs by purchasing life insurance. So eventually, you'll probably end up converting your term to whole life.

Settling up

What if you can't afford to pay premiums but still need insurance protection? Should you cancel your policy? Before you do, remember you have "settlement options." These are guaranteed choices built right into your policy that can't be denied to you. For example, you can elect either "reduced paid-up" life insurance or "extended term" life insurance instead of cashing in your policy. When you elect "reduced paid-up" life insurance, the cash value that is in your contract will be used by the insurance company to buy as much permanent life insurance as possible on your life. It will be the same type as the original policy but it will be "paid-up." In other words, you will never have to put another nickel of premium into this contract and you'll be insured for as long as you live.

For example, if Chet purchases a $100,000 whole life policy at age thirty-five and keeps it for fifteen years, you'll see in the table below that the cash values at this time can be used to purchase a

Plan and Additional Benefits	Amount	Premium	Years Payable
Whole Life (Premiums payable to age 90)	$100,000	$2,000	55
Waiver of Premium (to age 65)		43	30
Accidental Death (to age 70)	100,000	78	35

(A premium is payable on the policy date and every 12 policy months thereafter. The first premium is $2,000.)

TABLE OF GUARANTEED VALUES

End of Policy Year	Cash or Loan Value	Paid-up Insurance	Extended Term Insurance	
			Years	Days
1	$ 140	$ 300	0	152
2	1,740	4,500	4	182
3	3,380	8,600	8	65
4	5,060	12,500	10	344
5	6,760	16,400	12	360
6	8,790	20,700	14	335
7	10,840	25,000	16	147
8	12,930	29,100	17	207
9	15,040	33,000	18	177
10	17,190	36,900	19	78
11	19,080	40,000	19	209
12	20,990	43,000	19	306
13	22,940	45,900	20	8
14	24,900	48,700	20	47
15	26,900	51,400	20	65
16	28,910	54,100	20	66
17	30,950	56,600	20	52
18	33,010	59,100	20	27
19	35,080	61,500	19	358
20	37,180	63,900	19	317
Age 60	46,200	72,000	18	111
Age 65	55,040	78,600	16	147

(Paid-up additions and dividend accumulations increase the cash values; indebtedness decreases them.)

	Direct Beneficiary:	Cathy Horst, wife of the insured	
	Owner:	Chet Horst, the insured	
	Insured:	Chet Horst	
Policy Date:	May 1, 1981	Age and Sex:	35 Male
Date of Issue:	May 1, 1981	Policy Number:	000/00

fully paid-up whole life policy with a face amount (death benefit) of $51,400. Although the death benefit payable to Chet's beneficiaries is smaller than if he'd continued to pay premiums, it still has a cash value as well as the continuing protection.

A "paid-up" option would be the right one to use where your need for insurance has decreased but there is still some need and it can be expected to continue for quite some time or is indefinite.

What if you can no longer afford to pay premiums and your life insurance needs have either stayed the same or actually increased? Here, the right choice may be what is known as "extended term" life insurance. In this case, the cash value would be used to buy an amount of level term insurance equal to the face amount of the original policy. However, it would not purchase a policy for as long as you live. Instead, it would purchase a policy that would last for a term of time. How long a term? Again, looking at the guaranteed value schedule, you'll see that if Chet purchased a $100,000 policy at age thirty-five and stopped paying premiums fifteen years later, at that time he could have the insurance company purchase a term insurance policy with a face amount of $100,000 that would last for a term of twenty years and sixty-five days.

This is a particularly good buy, since the premium rates that are applicable under these nonforfeiture options are lower than they would be if Chet purchased a new policy of the same type on his own. That's because the insurance company doesn't charge you with any underwriting or administrative expenses and there is no agent's commission to be paid.

Very interesting (loans)

In a preceding paragraph, you noticed a reference to policy loans. There are several differences between a loan you take out from a life insurance policy and a loan from a bank.

The first advantage of a policy loan is obvious: The interest rates are substantially lower (possibly eight to ten percentage points) than what you'd have to pay at a bank.

Second, you know in advance exactly how much you can borrow from your insurance policy, while banks provide no such guarantees. You can be sure the insurance company will make the loan, regardless of the condition of the economy or your own financial situation.

Third, you never really have to pay off a policy loan. This is because the insurance company treats that money—if you never pay it back—as an advance payment of the cash value that the policy must contain at age one hundred (a typical permanent life insurance policy obligates the insurance company to pay you the entire cash value, in an amount equal to the face amount of the policy, when you reach the end of your life expectancy—age one hundred). In other words, your loan will be subtracted from the death benefit if you do not pay off the principal before you die.

The reason you pay any interest at all is that the insurance company, in determining its premium rates and making its promises, has assumed that it would have the use of that money. So when you borrow it, you pay (a modest rate of) interest to the insurance company to make up for its loss of the investment income it presumed it would have.

If you look at your contract you'll see that the insurance company has guaranteed a specific rate of interest. Most new policies provide for an 8-percent policy loan interest rate.

In some states you'll pay a floating interest rate based on the prime if your policy is relatively new. This is one advantage of holding on to older policies. Another reason to keep the policy you have is that many older policies contain an astounding 5- or 6-percent policy loan interest rate.

Another interesting and important fact about the interest you pay on policy loans is that it may be deductible. In fact, the interest will usually be deductible for income tax purposes unless you enter into "a systematic plan of borrowing" in order to finance the purchase of the policy.

What's a "systematic plan of borrowing"? Probably, it's easier to explain how to avoid that tax trap. There is no systematic plan of borrowing (and therefore the interest you pay is deductible) if you pay at least four of the first seven annual premiums without borrowing (either from the policy or from some outside source).

You must be very careful, in the three years that you do make policy loans, not to borrow any more than you need for the premium payable in that year. The reason is, if you borrow an amount in one year that is greater than the annual premium for that year, that excess will be treated as if it were borrowed in a previous year. That may disqualify you in meeting the so-called "four out of seven" test.

Fortunately, once you've paid any four of the first seven annual premiums without borrowing, you are "home free." Starting in the eighth year you can borrow as much as you want (and the policy will allow) without worrying about the deductibility of interest you pay.

Why is the interest deduction so important? Very simple. If you do qualify under the "four out of seven" rule, you can "minimum deposit" the policy. That means that the bulk of the premium you need to pay each year can be obtained through a policy loan. So you may have no out-of-pocket outlay except for the interest on that loan and if the interest is deductible, you are really acquiring life insurance protection with an extremely low net after-tax cost. If you are in a 50-percent income tax bracket and pay $1,000 of tax-deductible interest, your cost is only $500.

The end result may be life insurance protection at a net after-tax cost far less than a comparable amount of term insurance. The higher the income tax bracket you're in, the more attractive this minimum deposit concept becomes.

Say grace

Every insurance policy must, by law, contain a safety device called "a grace period." This is a limited time during which a policy will remain in force even if you don't pay the premium when it is due. The grace period is one month. If you pay the premium at any time before the end of that grace period, the policy will not be cancelled. If you die during the grace period, the company will pay your beneficiaries just as if you had kept the insurance in full force. If you don't pay the premium by the end of the grace period, the policy will be cancelled. Of course, if it is a permanent policy and has a cash value, one of the nonforfeiture options described above can be selected.

Whole life insurance comes in two varieties. The first is known as "straight" life. The second is known as "limited payment" life. In a straight life policy you pay a level premium each year from the time you take the policy out until the time you either die or "surrender" it (cash it in). (But you can use policy dividends to pay up the policy much more quickly.)

With a "limited payment" life policy, premiums are "compressed," that is, they are payable over a shorter period of time. For example, Chet is thirty-five years old. If he purchased a $100,000 straight life policy, the face amount would be $100,000. If he purchased a $100,000, twenty-payment life policy at the same age, the death benefit would still be $100,000 and the protection would still be provided for as long as Chet wanted to keep the policy in force. But because premiums would be compressed into a much smaller period of time (twenty annual payments) they would be considerably higher under the limited payment type of plan than under the straight life plan.

You may have heard about several other types of whole life plans, such as "modified" life and "preferred risk" life. A modified life insurance policy typically provides a given amount of insurance at unusually low premium rates for an initial period (for example, the first three years) after issue, and then the premium is correspondingly higher for the remainder of the premium paying period. Modified plans generally have lower initial cash value than a corresponding face amount of typical straight life would have.

Preferred risk is the type of policy that generally requires that you be in above-average health. Typically, preferred risk plans are sold only to professionals or to others who are in a low-risk occupation, are in above-average health, or are nonsmokers. Also, preferred risk policies are generally sold only in higher amounts, such as $50,000 or $100,000.

But in return for being a "preferred risk," the premiums you pay under such a plan could be substantially less per $1,000 of protection than you would pay on a standard policy. It is definitely worth your while to qualify for a preferred risk plan if you can.

Not everyone is "well endowed." But almost everyone can purchase endowment insurance. Endowment insurance is the type of coverage that pays the face amount (for example, $100,000) at the sooner of the time of "endowment" (the maturity of the contract) or the death of the insured. Here's a contract that pays if you live (to a specified date or age) as well as if you die. Many of us went to college because our parents, when we were born, purchased a $2,000 endowment policy on our lives. That $2,000 may have taken you through your first year or two of school (the same amount will probably take your children through their first month or two of college).

Endowment policies are basically purchased to provide a means of forced savings, since the protection element is relatively minimal. Generally, in today's market, these plans are not recommended.

All life insurance, no matter what it is called or how it is marketed, is really one of these three types or a combination of two or more.

Universal life—something new under the sun?

A number of insurance companies are now offering a policy known as Universal Life. Universal Life was designed as a means of providing a better rate of return than is provided by the typical cash value permanent life insurance policy.

"Universal" or "adjustable" life permits the policyholder to change the amount and timing of premiums and the size of the death benefit automatically as the policyholder's needs change. These contracts sometimes allow a policyholder to invest a significant amount of cash without a related increase in the amount of pure insurance in the policy.

A universal life policy is—generally speaking—one in which the investment, expense, and mortality elements are separately and specifically defined. A contract owner selects a death benefit level. From the premium that is paid, the insurer then deducts a "load" for contractually defined expenses. The remaining premium is then credited toward the contract owner's cash values. Mortality charges are deducted. Interest earned on the remaining cash is then credited at rates based on current investment earnings. (Specific design features will vary from company to company depending on marketing policies and product objectives.) Under this configuration, increased interest rates result in higher cash value levels while increased expense loads and increased mortality charges result in lower cash values.

There is no such thing as a predetermined "standard" universal life plan; each contract owner selects the level of premium and death benefit desired as well as the length of premium paying period.

Significant flexibility in premium payments is possible. Usually a stated minimum premium must be paid the first policy year. But after that the contract owner can vary the amount, the payment date, or frequency of subsequent premiums. (Depending on the amount of the initial premium, additional premiums or premium increases may be limited to stated minimum or maximum levels.) "Stop and go" features allow the discontinuance as well as subsequent resumption of premium payments at any time. (It is not necessary to reinstate the policy to do this.)

As long as there is enough cash value to pay the expense (loading) charges and mortality costs, the policy will remain in force. If the cash value falls below that level, the policy will terminate. (Usually there is a 61-day grace period.)

Inflation seems to make Universal Life, with its relatively high rates of return, a very viable and appealing product. Certainly, it is an important alternative to low-outlay term insurance as well as competitively priced whole life insurance.

Ask your insurance agent to give you a list of the advantages and disadvantages of Universal Life in your personal situation. Insist, as you would with any other life insurance product, that he or she "shop around" and give you comparative illustrations.

How high is up (how much insurance)?

How much insurance do I need? That's one of the most difficult questions of all. You need information on your personal financial status, your company's employee benefits, and social security benefits. There are literally dozens of different charts, formulas, and computer programs to answer that question. And you'll go absolutely crazy trying to figure out which answer is the right answer.

There are a couple of easier ways. One is to have two or three insurance agents stop over and analyze your situation. You can pick the analysis that gives you the lowest insurance need. Alternatively, you can take the average of the insurance needs projected by the agents. If you choose to be conservative, you could use the highest amount. (You're probably best off picking the figure used by the agent who seems most professionally competent.)

Alternatively, you can forget that approach altogether and allocate a given number of dollars (such as 3 to 5 percent of your after-tax income) to life insurance and buy as much insurance as that amount of money will buy. Consider hiring an agent. Pay the agent for the time spent in making an analysis, with the stipulation that you wouldn't buy insurance from him/her in any event.

Regardless of what amount you finally settle on, or how you decide the amount of insurance to buy, remember this: "No widow ever complained that her husband carried too much insurance."

Left or right (your rights in your policy)?

There are a lot of rights that you have in an insurance policy, and the more you know about them the easier it is to exercise them. Let's look at some of the ownership provisions, dividend provisions, and various additional benefits (called "riders") such as the accidental death benefit, disability waiver of premium, and guaranteed insurability (often called insurance of insurability) option.

When Chet purchases his life insurance policy, regardless of whether it is term, whole life, or endowment, he will have the right to name and change the beneficiary. This is the first and most important right you have in a life insurance policy. It is extremely important that you always name a secondary beneficiary. That way, if the primary beneficiary you have named dies before you do or "disclaims" (refuses to take) his or her share, your estate won't inadvertently become your beneficiary.

What's wrong with naming your estate as beneficiary? A lot. Typically, if your estate becomes your beneficiary, the proceeds become subject to the claims of your creditors, or become subject to a disgruntled heir who attacks the validity of your will, and may be exposed needlessly to state death taxes. So with life insurance what's important is not only what you have, and how much you have, but what you do with what you have!

You've already seen the major distinction between term insurance and permanent insurance. Permanent insurance contains guaranteed cash values. These cash values are an outgrowth of the fact that in the early years of the contract, the annual premium you were charged is slightly higher than the actual cost needed to provide you with insurance protection. As noted previously, that excess money is necessary for the insurance company to make up the deficiency of the level premium in later years when the annual cost of providing you with insurance protection actually exceeds the level premium you are paying.

The cash values are the portion of the insurance company's reserve that is available to you. You can borrow this money from the insurance company at a favorable rate of interest (in some cases as little as 6 to 8 percent), or if you cash the policy in, since you are releasing the insurance company from its potential liability (the death benefit), you may keep all the cash value and have no liability to the insurance company.

The policy cash value increases year by year. In fact, if you'll look at your policy you'll find that there is a schedule that contains a guaranteed year-by-year increase in the cash values. (See the chart on p. 110.) The amount of this guaranteed annual increase in cash value will differ from company to company and policy to policy.

Most policies have relatively small annual cash value increases during the first year or two, but the increases will become greater as you keep the policy for a longer period of time. The reason there is little cash value in the early years of the policy is to protect the insurance company from the substantial loss it would incur if you cashed the policy in during the first year or two after it was purchased.

The right to borrow on your policy or cash it in is called a nonforfeiture option. You could take the guaranteed value in cash (see the Table of Guaranteed Values on p. 110), or elect to have it applied under one of the so-called nonforfeiture options.

Horseless riders

What is the advantage of adding a waiver of premium rider to term insurance? One obvious advantage is that if you become disabled the premium for the term insurance will be waived. But another advantage is the effect of disability on your right to convert to a permanent policy and keep the term coverage from running out.

Some term insurance policies with waiver of premium will not allow "conversion" (a contractual right to change) to a permanent policy if you have become totally disabled. Other contracts do allow conversion. When you are comparing term insurance policies, be sure to check which provision you'll have. If you become disabled, it's quite advantageous to have a contract that automatically converts your term to a permanent contract, since the policy will not only stay in force and have its future premiums waived, but also build cash values and dividends.

Some insurance agents recommend that, instead of purchasing waiver of premium on your whole life policy, you buy additional amounts of disability income insurance. Why buy the waiver of premiums through a totally separate disability income policy rather than through a life insurance policy?

First, the additional costs under your personally owned disability income insurance may be lower than the disability waiver of premiums under your basic life insurance policy.

Second, and probably more important, the definition of "total disability" is typically more liberal in a disability income policy than the definition in your life insurance policy. For instance, under a disability income policy you'll receive income benefits if you are unable to perform *your present* occupation. Only after two years will you have to demonstrate that you are unable to perform in *any* occupation for which you are reasonably fit by virtue of education, training, or experience in order to continue to receive benefits. The point is that it is possible to be classified as disabled under the disability income policy long before you will be considered disabled under the life insurance policy definition.

Here's an upper G.I. (Guaranteed insurability)

Another benefit that can be added to your basic policy and may be advisable when you are young is known as "G.I.," "guaranteed insurability" or "insurance of insurability." This benefit allows you to purchase additional life insurance at certain specified future dates without proving you are insurable. This new insurance can be obtained at standard rates. In other words, when a given option date arrives, you will have the right to purchase additional life insurance without proving you are insurable. On that option date you can exercise all, part, or none of the option to purchase additional insurance.

You should know that the options are noncumulative. Either you use them or you lose them. The rights when you exercise a guaranteed insurability option are those applicable to the age and the year in which you exercise the option. In other words, if you wait until you are thirty-five to exercise an option to purchase more insurance, you will pay standard rates for a thirty-five-year-old individual of your sex.

A typical guaranteed insurability rider allows you to purchase additional insurance three years after the date of your original insurance purchase and every three years thereafter until you reach age forty.

If you marry or have (or adopt) a child, some companies will allow you to move up a purchase date, and others will allow additional purchase dates, over and above those you already have.

Typically, these guaranteed insurability riders will allow you to purchase up to an amount equal to the face amount of the original policy (or some lower specified dollar amount). For example, if you purchased a $100,000 policy, the company may issue a guaranteed insurability rider enabling you to buy $25,000 of additional insurance every three years until your fortieth birthday.

When is this G.I. rider indicated? The guaranteed insurability rider is a good deal if your family has a history of serious illness (such as high blood pressure or kidney problems) prior to age forty. Since you will probably need more insurance in the future if you are below age forty, the guaranteed insurability option would be a good purchase, since it guarantees that you will be able to buy additional insurance at standard rates regardless of your physical condition or the hobbies you may acquire (such as sky diving or scuba diving) in the future.

Another extremely important advantage—with some companies—is that if you become disabled and you have waiver of premium under your original policy, not only will premiums be waived under that policy, but also the guaranteed insurability option will automatically be exercised to purchase new insurance. Premiums under the new insurance will automatically be waived. Obviously, when comparing policies, this feature is extremely important.

Getting it out and keeping it out (of your estate)

Many attorneys advise keeping insurance out of your estate. What's the best way to get life insurance out of your estate and keep it out? The easiest answer to that question is to never have it in in the first place. If at all possible, your beneficiary (such as your spouse) should own the policy right from the beginning. If your spouse (or child or trust for your spouse/child's benefit) purchases the policy and your spouse or child pays the premium personally, nothing will be includable in your estate.

Alternately, if you are assigning a policy to someone to get it out of your estate, make an absolute transfer—don't keep any right to the policy or the IRS will attempt to bring it back into your estate.

He (or she) who hesitates is lost. If you are going to give a policy on your life to someone else or to a trust to remove it from your estate, do it now. If you die within three years of a policy transfer, for tax purposes, it's in your estate. (The Economic Recovery Tax Act of 1981 didn't change this result.)

Beware of this tax trap: If your spouse purchases a policy on your life, he/she should be the beneficiary of the policy. If your wife names your children as the beneficiaries of a policy she owns on your life, at your death the IRS will claim that she is making a gift in the entire amount of the proceeds to your children. For instance, say your wife buys a $100,000 policy on your life and names your children as beneficiaries. If you predecease her, she will be deemed to be making a gift of $100,000 to your children.

What should be done? She should name herself the beneficiary. Then she should have your attorney provide in her will that at her death prior to yours, the policy should go to you (if that is what you want to happen) or it should go directly to your children. Alternately, your life insurance agent can provide for a contingent owner, an individual who'll become owner of the policy in the event your wife predeceases you. You can be that contingent owner or it can be your children or a guardian or trustee for your children's benefit.

Is "out" in?

Insurance proceeds from a policy you own on your own life payable to your spouse are in your gross estate. At best, until 1982 a portion of these proceeds was deductible under the "marital deduction" allowed for property left outright (or in a manner tantamount to outright) to a spouse. No deduction at all was allowed if your wife received only the income from the proceeds, with the balance going to your children.

Current federal tax law is very different. You can now name your spouse as beneficiary of an unlimited amount of life insurance. Not one dime of it will be taxed in your estate. You can even provide that your spouse is to receive only the income and that the balance is to go to your children. Your estate will still receive a marital deduction and no tax will be generated even if the proceeds total $10,000,000. The cost of this right to pick your children (or anyone else you want) as the ultimate recipient of the principal is that your executor must agree that when your spouse dies, the principal remaining at that time becomes taxable in your spouse's estate.

Formerly, an estate planner would almost always advise successful clients to divest themselves of life insurance and have their spouses, or a trust for their spouse's benefit, own the insurance. "Get the insurance out of the estate as soon as possible." But under current law, getting insurance out may not be "in" if the same tax result can be accomplished without giving up control of the policy and its valuable contractual rights. Talk to both your agent and your attorney about the best way to set up policy ownership.

This transfer is a one-way wrong-way ticket

Another tax trap to avoid is the "transfer for value" problem. Here's how it works: Typically, the proceeds of a life insurance policy will be federal income tax free. So if you die and your beneficiaries receive $100,000, the entire amount is income (but not federal estate) tax free. This is true even if you name your estate as beneficiary. (Estate planners generally recommend against naming your estate as beneficiary.)

The general rule exempting life insurance proceeds from income taxation is an extremely valuable one. The tax on $100,000—if the proceeds of the policy *did* become taxable—would be approximately $50,000 if your recipient was single.

The fly in the ointment is the insidious "transfer for value" rule. The best way to explain how this rule works is through an example. Let's assume you sold a policy on your life to your spouse or child. The transfer of that policy in return for valuable consideration (the money you received) would "taint" the insurance proceeds. The death benefit would lose its income tax free status. The entire amount received when you die would be subject to ordinary income tax (with the exception of the consideration paid for the policy plus any premiums the new owner pays after transfer). If you sold a $100,000 policy for $5,000 and the new owner paid two $2,500 premiums shortly before your death, $90,000 of the proceeds would be subject to ordinary income tax. That's tax disaster!

The transfer for value rule is highly technical. The important thing is to know that if you transfer any interest in a policy and receive any kind of valuable consideration (other than love and affection), you may be setting the trap. The solution is not to make any sales of insurance on your life to any family member or trust without checking first with your agent and counsel.

A.P.L.—apples, potatoes and lettuce?

A.P.L., remember those initials. A.P.L. stands for "automatic premium loan." This is a provision that is in every whole life policy. It is designed to prevent a permanent policy from being cancelled if the premium has not been paid within the grace period. Under the A.P.L. provision, if you don't pay a premium by the time the grace period expires (thirty-one days after the due date of the premium) the insurance company will pay the premium for you out of any policy loan value. This automatic loan is treated the same as any other policy loan. In other words, you are not required to pay the insurance company any money, but if you die, the loan can be taken by the insurance company from the death proceeds.

What's the advantage of A.P.L.? A.P.L. prevents a policy from "lapsing" (terminating) unintentionally. The nicest thing is that this provision is available at no additional cost. That means there is almost no reason why it shouldn't be elected in every policy. (Call your agent and make sure all your permanent policies have A.P.L.)

A.P.L. makes it possible to shop for life insurance using the "sixty-day umbrella." Many times you're not sure if the policy you are looking at is the "best buy," but you know you need insurance and you know you need it immediately. What should you do? Purchase the insurance even if you feel there may be another policy that you could purchase at a lower cost. This gives you not thirty days but (together with the thirty-one-day grace period) over sixty days to "look around." During that time, you are fully insured. If you decide the policy you have selected is the best around, pay off the premium that you should have paid during the grace period. But if you find a policy with a lower net cost (and its other features are comparable) have the new coverage begin on the fifty-ninth day (a little overlap is better than a lapse of even a few minutes). By using this method, you have the option of keeping or refusing the first policy and your family has been protected meanwhile.

Come again (reinstatement)?

Reinstatement is another privilege you have with every policy. If you allow a policy to lapse (either inadvertently or purposely) and your coverage is cancelled, you can still reinstate the policy if you meet certain conditions.

First, most policies contain a time limit, within which you must choose to reinstate the policy. Typically, this is three to five years from the date the policy is cancelled. Second, if you decide to reinstate a policy, you will usually have to present new evidence of insurability. That means that you may have to take a new physical exam or answer certain questions about your health, occupation, and avocations. Furthermore, you've got to pay any premiums (together with interest) that you would have paid had you not allowed the policy to lapse.

But why would anybody choose to pay back premiums (plus interest) to reinstate an old policy rather than simply buying a new one? One reason is that in the old policy you've already paid off high first-year costs that are involved in putting a new life insurance policy into force. That means that you are building up cash values and dividends (explained below) more quickly than if you started a brand-new policy.

Second, many older life insurance policies have a lower policy loan interest rate than policies currently being used. In the long range, this can save you hundreds or even thousands of dollars.

Third, if your age has changed, a new policy would require you to pay a higher annual premium. This higher annual premium would go on for as long as you live.

Be sure, before you do anything, to have your insurance agent show you—in writing—the pros and cons of reinstating the insurance you have allowed to lapse.

Can't argue with this one (incontestable clause)

It's incontestable that life insurance is unique among all legal contracts. One proof of that statement is that life insurance is the only contract that has incontestable clauses in it (this may be a reason for reinstating a lapsed life insurance policy rather than purchasing a new one).

An incontestable clause provides that after a life insurance contract has been in force for a stated period of time (two years in most contracts and one year in some contracts), the insurance company legally cannot deny a claim because of any error, concealment, or misstatement that you have made. In other words, a steel door closes on the insurance company. Once the contestable period has expired, there are very few grounds on which an insurance company could challenge a death claim. Obviously, this clause has substantial significance to a beneficiary after your death, since it almost eliminates any possibility that the insurance company will contest the claim.

Another extremely important provision in a life insurance policy is a suicide clause. This legal provision provides that if you commit suicide within a specified period of time after the purchase of a contract (generally two years, but in some policies only one year), the insurance company will pay your beneficiary an amount equal to the premiums you have paid (some companies also pay interest). Once your policy has been in effect for the stated period of time (for example two years), the insurance company must pay the full face amount even if your death is the result of suicide.

Life (insurance) is full of dividends

Knowing how to use policy dividends can make your life insurance much more effective.

Life insurance, either term or permanent, may be "participating" or "non-participating." "Participating" means that your policy shares or participates in the favorable investment, expense, and underwriting experience of the company. In other words, if the company earns more than it expected, the favorable position of the company will be shared with its policy owners. These refunds are called "policy dividends."

Technically, premiums from participating policies are set at a slightly higher rate than would normally be required in order to provide funds that might be needed by the insurance company in the event it has an unexpected emergency. But at the end of every year, the insurance company will refund (in the form of a policy dividend) an amount that reflects its favorable experience in investment income, operating expenses, and death claims.

It is important to note that the insurance company does not guarantee the amount of each policy dividend. This is particularly important in comparing or selecting an insurer (ask your agent to show you not only what the company "projects" but how well dividends in the past have matched its dividend projections). The amount you receive will be determined by the actual experience of the insurance company.

The larger insurance companies typically tend to be conservative in their estimates of future policy dividends. In many cases actual dividends are substantially higher than their projections. As mentioned above, if actual dividends have equaled or exceeded the estimated dividends in the past, you have some indication that the company's estimates are not highly inflated.

It's not what you've got but what you do with what you've got that counts (dividend options)

This is particularly true with respect to policy dividend options. You have a number of choices, and what you do is particularly important if your estate is small or medium-sized.

As the policy owner, you can elect to (1) take dividends in the form of cash, (2) use your dividends to reduce the premiums you would otherwise pay, (3) buy "paid-up" additional insurance (each dividend buys a small single premium policy in addition to your basic policy but no physical examination is required for this additional insurance and it is purchased without paying sales charges or other expenses), (4) leave the dividend with the insurance company to earn (taxable) interest (the dividend is not taxable but the interest is), (5) purchase one-year term insurance equal to the cash value of the policy, (6) use dividends to "pay off" the policy at an earlier date than expected, and (7) use some combination of the above dividend options.

Let's look at these options a little more carefully.

The first option needs no explanation. The insurance company will send you a check each year (typically starting at the end of the first or second year) and you cash the check.

The second option is that the insurance company automatically uses your dividend to reduce the next premium due on the policy. This is very much the same as if you had received the dividend and endorsed your check directly to the insurance company.

The third option involves using your dividend to purchase more life insurance. If you elect to buy "paid-up adds" as insurance agents call it, your dividend will be used as a single premium. They will buy an additional amount of completely paid-up life insurance. The policy you buy will be the same type as the policy you already own. This single premium purchases insurance based on your attained age. But it's a better deal than if you bought a new policy on your own. That's because there is no charge for underwriting expenses or commissions. This is a highly recommended option.

The fourth option is to leave your dividend with the insurance company to earn (taxable) interest. Here, the insurance company is more or less acting like a bank or savings and loan institution. Although the dividend you receive is not taxable (because it is treated as a return of your capital), the interest you earn on your dividend accumulations will be taxable as income to you in the year you earn it even if you choose not to take it in that year. Typically, the interest rate paid on dividend accumulations will be comparable to the rate you could earn in a local savings institution. However, be sure to check. Sometimes a company will pay even more (sometimes less) than you could earn if you invested a similar amount in a local bank or savings and loan.

The fifth option described above was the purchase of "one-year term insurance." This is often called the "fifth dividend" option. Your dividend, whatever its amount, can be used to purchase one-year term insurance. The premium will be based on your attained age. But the rates again are very low because you are not charged for underwriting expenses and you pay no commissions. Obviously this is such a good deal that the insurance company puts a limit on how much term insurance you can buy using your policy dividends. Typically, the maximum amount of one-year term insurance that your dividends will buy cannot exceed the cash value of the policy at the end of the prior year. But what happens if you have more dividends than you need? You have a right to select one of the other options for the balance of your dividend.

The sixth option is to use your dividends to pay off your policy faster than it would normally be paid off. Ask your agent how long it will take for you to "pay up" your policy if you use your dividends in this manner. You can actually pay up a whole life policy in twenty-four to twenty-eight years in most cases. This means you'll never have to pay another premium.

Not every policy is "participating." That means that some policies do not participate in the favorable underwriting, investment, or experience of the company. If you have purchased a nonparticipating policy (agents call these "non-par" policies), then regardless of how well the company has done, you won't receive any policy dividend. The premiums you will have paid for a non-par policy will be less than the gross premium for participating "par" policy of the same type and amount.

So should you buy a "par" or "non-par" policy? No one knows for sure which will be a better buy. It appears that inflation will continue, life expectancies will increase, and mortality costs will reduce. That should mean that future policy dividends on contracts purchased today will increase each year. But the ultimate question is, how long will your policy stay in force? Obviously, the longer you keep your policy, the lower your costs (because you receive more dividends).

Easy rider

You've already seen that you have the right to add a number of benefits to your life insurance policy. These additional benefits are called "riders." That's because they "ride" on top of your basic policy. Term insurance riders are popular on whole life plans. There are other features you can add to your basic policy. For example, for a small extra premium, you can add an accidental death benefit to your basic plan. Should you die by accident before a specified age, a large additional benefit will be paid to your beneficiaries.

The most popular form of accidental death benefit is known as "double indemnity" since the accidental death benefit is based on a multiple of the face amount of the underlying policy. If you purchased a $500,000 policy, the accidental death benefit would be equal to (or a multiple of) the face amount. This would double the indemnity paid to your beneficiary at your death to $1,000,000. Some insurance companies issue "triple indemnity," which pays the basic amount plus an accidental death benefit of twice that basic amount.

Should you have an accidental death benefit rider? Is it a ripoff? The answer is, death by accident is statistically infrequent. However, if you are between age twenty-five and age forty-five, the odds are that your death within that period of time will occur because of an accident. If you are over age forty-five, the likelihood is that your death will occur through some kind of illness.

The key point to remember is that whatever amount of money your family needs is not increased because you die by accident. As a matter of fact, just the reverse is often the case. If you die by accident, the financial impact is sudden but often short. Conversely, death through heart problems or cancer, or other sicknesses, is often long and drawn-out and therefore extremely expensive. Your family needs adequate coverage regardless of when or how you die, and that should be your major concern.

Some taxing questions

How is the policy taxed during my lifetime?

Premiums you pay for life insurance are not deductible. Premiums are considered nondeductible personal expenses. There are two very isolated cases where the outlay for premiums is deductible: The first is where the premium payment is considered alimony. The second is the premium you pay on a policy you have assigned (transferred absolutely) to a charity. The rules to gain deductibility in either of these two cases are highly technical and the tests are easily flunked. Be sure to talk to both your insurance agent and your tax advisor before taking action in this area.

Dividends you receive on "participating" policies are not taxable income. That's because life insurance policy dividends are considered to be a partial return of your premiums rather than payments of profits from the insurance company.

If you leave your dividends on deposit with the insurance company to accumulate interest, any interest on that accumulated dividend is taxable just as if you had earned the interest in a bank. But dividends that are used to purchase paid-up additional insurance or one-year term insurance create no income tax liability. The IRS treats such dividends as if you have received them in cash (a return of your capital) and then used them to buy single premium insurance.

How are you taxed when you cash in (surrender) a policy? If you cash a policy in and receive more back than you paid, the difference will be considered ordinary income. It is taxable in the year you surrender the policy. What you paid (your cost) is measured by the total premiums you paid (excluding premiums paid for accidental death benefits or waiver of premium). If you have received your dividends in cash or used them to reduce your premiums, it is only your net premiums (gross premiums less dividends received in cash or applied to reduce policy premiums) that determine your costs on the contract. For instance, if you paid in $10,000 but received $2,000 of dividends back, the cost would be $8,000. If you cashed the policy in for $12,000 you would have a $4,000 gain taxable at ordinary income tax rates.

If you do realize a substantial income tax gain in a given tax year, you may be able to income average.

How are you taxed if you take the money over a period of years rather than in a lump sum? Many people do choose to take living benefits of a life insurance policy under "a settlement option." A settlement option is a way you can take money other than in a lump sum. Proceeds that an insurance company places under a settlement option are taxed under the "annuity rules." Basically, annuity rules are designed so that you will not be taxed on the portion you receive that is considered to be a return of your cost. In other words, a portion of each payment you receive will be a nontaxable return of your cost. The other portion of each payment will be taxable income.

Your insurance agent can work with you and your tax advisor to determine what portion of each payment will be taxable and what portion will be income tax free.

Which way to pay?

How you pay insurance premiums can make all the difference. Insurance companies will calculate premium rates on the assumption that you will pay the entire premium at the beginning of the policy year. Under that assumption, the insurance company will be able to invest your premium dollars for the entire year.

But if you pay premiums semi-annually, quarterly, or monthly instead of annually at the beginning of each year, the insurance company has lost the use of money it has planned on. To make up for that loss, it will levy an additional charge. Furthermore, it has the extra administrative expense involved with collecting premiums more often than once a year. The question is, how can you beat these surcharges?

One answer is through a bank authorization. Most companies will allow you to make premium payments directly from your bank account. You authorize your bank to pay the insurance company monthly with funds from your account. Because of the savings involved in computer-to-computer transactions, the surcharge is reduced to approximately what it would be if you paid premiums semi-annually. Another way of accomplishing the same objective is through a payroll deduction plan. Many insurance companies will allow you to pay the same surcharge that would be levied on a semi-annual basis even though you are actually having salary withdrawals on a monthly basis. Of course, your employer has to be willing to assist the insurance company and typically there must be at least ten employees participating in the payroll reduction plan.

Combatting the ultimate certainty—change

Our needs change over our lifetime. As our needs change, the amount and type of insurance we own should probably change too. In recognition of that fact, a number of companies have created "adjustable" life insurance.

An adjustable life insurance policy, as its name implies, allows you to start with term and change to permanent, or start with permanent and change to term, or apportion your premium dollars periodically between the two types of coverage in accordance with your needs. Not only can you change the type of coverage; you can also change the amount of coverage. You can decrease the amount of insurance coverage you have without cancelling your policy (you can do this with a typical life insurance policy by splitting the policy into two or more smaller ones and then cancelling one of the smaller contracts).

How does adjustable life work?

You tell your agent how much you can afford each year for insurance premiums and together you determine how much life insurance protection you need. This information is given to the insurance company's computer, which then tells you whether the amount of money you have committed will purchase all the protection you need using the lowest-cost premium plan available. If the premium you have committed is not sufficient, the computer program will illustrate an insurance package with less protection and the lowest premium policy available will be purchased.

But if the amount of money you are willing to pay each year is greater than the cost of the protection you want using the lowest premium policy, your coverage will be adjusted automatically to a combination of term insurance and permanent insurance. As long as you continue to pay an amount at least equal to the premium needed to buy your desired insurance coverage using the lowest premium policy, you will be fully protected. If more money than the lowest efficient amount is needed, some or all of your protection will be in the form of permanent insurance.

There is an alternative approach: You can change the amount of the premium you are willing to pay and thereby purchase a different amount of term and permanent combination.

What are the drawbacks of adjustable life? Basically, the net cost under these contracts may not be as favorable as it would under similar non-adjustable contracts (assuming no change in coverage). Furthermore, the adjustable life contract cannot match certain "pure" type policies such as the annual renewable term life policy. This is an extremely low-outlay type of coverage (at least in early policy years) but it cannot be selected under the adjustable life type contract.

The adjustable life contract is most popular for relatively young individuals who currently need substantial amounts of insurance protection but who have minimal ability to pay. The flexibility of adjustable life is extremely important because of the changing needs and changing circumstances of such an individual.

How to fight the unfightable (inflation)

Inflation is an enemy that every financial planner is struggling to defeat. Inflation has a particularly significant effect on the death benefit payable from your life insurance policy. If we assume a 10 percent annual inflation rate and death occurs twenty years from the time the policy is purchased, the purchasing power of the dollars paid will be substantially less than those same dollars purchased at today's prices. For instance, assuming a 10 percent annual inflation rate and a $50,000 policy, the $50,000 would purchase only $7,430 worth of goods twenty years from now—compared to $50,000 worth of goods and services if death occurs immediately. Stated in a different way, it will take $350,000 of life insurance twenty years from now to provide you with the purchasing power $50,000 will give you today.

Fortunately, inflation is a two-edged sword. Since the premiums you pay are level, the cost of paying premiums reduces year by year. For instance, if you assume the $50,000 policy requires an annual premium of $1,250, you will have paid approximately $25,000 in premiums. But the "buying power," that is, the cost of these premiums, is only a little bit greater than $10,000.

Another factor that should be considered is what you do with policy dividends. If you receive them in cash or use them to reduce your premium payments, they will of course reduce your cost substantially. If you use them to purchase additional one-year term insurance, you'll have much more than $50,000 of coverage.

Many insurance companies have developed other tools to fight inflation. One of these is known as "the adjustable premium" policy. Under this arrangement, the initial premium is guaranteed for the first two policy years. After that time, the premium can increase but only to a specified maximum. The premium can be reduced, perhaps even below the initial premium, if the actual experience of the company is better than that upon which the guaranteed maximum is based. Savings that result from better-than-expected experience under this contract are automatically applied to reduce the premium you would pay.

Another type of contract to fight inflation is the "automatically increasing" whole life insurance policy. Under this arrangement the face amount of the policy automatically increases at a given rate each year. One whole life policy grows at a compound rate of 3.5 percent annually for the first twenty years. Naturally, the premium must increase as well. Every five years the premium increases in an amount equal to 25 percent of the original premium. The last increase would occur after the fifteenth year and the premium would remain level from then on. Obviously, to the extent inflation exceeds 3.5 percent compounded annually (which it has done with a vengeance in the last few years), this policy will only partially offset inflation.

Perhaps the best way to fight inflation is to purchase more insurance than you need initially. One way to do that is through the use of as much term insurance as possible. Dividends on a whole life policy, as described above, can be used to purchase one-year term insurance at extremely low cost.

12.
More Taxpayers Mean Less Taxes

Cheaper by the dozen

This chapter introduces you to some very interesting tax saving devices. Some of them, like the corporation, may be familiar. Others, like the "short-term trust" or "sale or gift leaseback" might be new concepts. But the reason why these tax savings ideas can work wonders for you is easy to understand. More taxpayers do mean less taxes.

If you have any doubt about that statement, make this simple test. Turn in the Appendix to the income tax rates for years beginning with 1982, and you will see that married taxpayers filing joint returns will pay a tax of approximately $3,200 on taxable income of $20,000. You will also see that a single taxpayer earning $60,000 will pay a tax of almost $20,000. Therefore, a single taxpayer earning $60,000 pays $10,000 more (about twice as much) in taxes than three taxpayers each earning $20,000.

How to use the "more means less" concept to increase spendable income for you and your family is what this chapter is all about. A "short-term trust" can enable you to reduce your income tax bracket by transferring property in trust to one or more of your children, or to another person, such as a parent, to whom you are providing money on a regular basis. If you have the type of property that is suitable for a short-term trust, and your income warrants it, considerable tax savings can be realized. The "sale or gift and leaseback" arrangement is a sophisticated way in which property can be given away and then leased back with excellent tax advantages.

When you form a corporation, you have created a separate taxable entity. As an employee of the corporation that you have created, you are now entitled to the same type of fringe benefits as an employee of General Motors—with the same tax advantages. At the same time that you can avail yourself of the tax savings consequences of incorporating, you are also in a position to realize the other advantages of incorporating, such as the ease of transferring your ownership interest by giving away or selling shares of stock.

If you want some of the advantages of incorporating, and still want corporate income taxed directly to you, then a "subchapter S corporation" might be just what the doctor ordered. And last, if you are really in the chips, consider setting up a "personal holding company."

Not all of these ideas apply to everyone, but if any one is suited to your situation, the tax savings that result can be thousands and thousands of dollars.

The long and the short of it (short-term trusts)

What's short and long at the same time? Give up? A short-term (some people call it a "Clifford") trust. It's short because typically it lasts only ten years and one day, but it's long on tax savings. A short-term trust can provide the cash to send your child to college through tax savings. The best thing is, after you've used it for your child's benefit, the property you put into it to make it work comes back to you.

Who cares?

Do you care enough to want to send a child to college? Do you have a widowed aunt or other relative you're supporting?

Are you in a high income tax bracket and do you want to use your bond or stock income more efficiently to help you provide financial assistance for someone other than your spouse?

If you've said yes to any of these questions, read on: The short-term trust may be your solution. (Be sure to read about low- and no-interest loans in Chapter 15, as an alternative.)

Here's how

Say you're earning a good income and you've managed to accumulate $100,000 worth of income-producing assets. You are married, in a 50-percent state and federal income tax bracket and in your early forties.

You figure you will need the $100,000 (which, you hope, will have grown considerably) by the time you retire. Yet you are frustrated when it costs you half of every dollar the $100,000 earns in taxes. Let's assume those assets are producing $10,000 a year, which means you net $5,000. Here's how you could make your money work harder for you—and use tax savings to pay for a good bit of your children's college education or your relative's support:

First, your attorney drafts a short-term trust. This is a trust that will last ten years and one day (most attorneys suggest you make it ten years and one month to be safe). The trust could be set up for longer than that or could be set up to last the shorter of (a) ten years and one month, or (b) until your beneficiary dies (assuming your beneficiary's life expectancy is longer than ten years).

Second, you put the $100,000 in the trust (you can set up a short-term trust with a lot more or a lot less than $100,000). That capital will produce a stream of income for your child lasting the length of the trust.

Third, your trustee pays out income to your child. The income can go directly to your child or it can go into a second trust (see the discussion of Section 2503(c) Trusts in Chapter 19) or it can be paid directly to a Uniform Gifts to Minors Act account (see Chapter 19) for your child. At the appropriate time the accumulated income can be used to purchase school books or pay tuition, or for other expenses.

Fourth, when the term of the trust is up, the trust terminates and the property in the trust is returned to you. You can now use it for whatever purpose you'd like—including retirement.

In essence, from your viewpoint the short-term trust is like owning a non-interest-bearing note payable ten years from the date you put the income-producing assets into the trust. If you need to, you could use your right to recover the $100,000 as collateral. As time goes on and you get closer and closer to getting the $100,000 back, the value of that collateral becomes greater.

Tax-I?

Who pays the tax? Not you, if you've set up the trust right. Let's work the tax implications by the numbers.

First, when you put the $100,000 into the trust you are making a gift. The gift is not the $100,000, since you'll get that back. Actually, you are giving your beneficiary a stream of income, which is valued according to extremely favorable (would you believe these figures are based on a 6-percent return) federal government tables. So if you put $100,000 into a trust that will last shortly over ten years, your gift of income is valued at about 44 percent of that $100,000—$44,100.

Here's a table to help you figure out the value of your gift based on putting $100,000 into the trust:

Number of years the trust will run	Gift tax value of income interest
10	$44,161
11	47,321
12	50,303
13	53,116
14	55,769
15	58,274
16	60,635
17	62,864
18	64,966
19	66,949
20	68,819

Will you have to pay gift tax? That depends. If you've required the trustee to pay out all the income every year, you and your spouse can each take a one-time $10,000 gift tax exclusion. In other words, at the time you create the beneficiary's stream of income you could exclude a total of $20,000 of the $44,161 gift in the year it's made. Only $24,161 ($44,161 − $20,000) would be subject to the gift tax after the exclusions. The tax on that entire $24,161 amount could be wiped out by your "unified gift tax credit" (equal to an exclusion of $275,000 as of 1983 and growing even larger in each consecutive year). If you are married, this $275,000 unified credit equivalent means you could put more than $550,000 as a couple into a ten-year-and-one-month short-term trust (even before your $20,000 annual exclusions) and not pay one nickel's worth of gift taxes—assuming you haven't made any substantial gifts in the past.

How about income taxes? How about income tax savings? Say you just put $100,000 into the trust. You're in a 50-percent income tax bracket, which means you lose $5,000 in taxes for every $10,000 your assets earn. If you have three non-wage-earning children, they'll each receive $3,333 a year and pay about $300 a year in taxes—a total of less than $1,000 a year. That's a $4,000-a-year difference each year for at least ten years, approximately $40,000 in total savings. Stated another way, you would have paid $50,000 in taxes, but after you set up short-term trusts, as a family unit you actually paid less than $10,000.

Put or call?

What do you put into a short-term trust? Anything you'd like. Practically any type of property can be placed into a short-term trust, although the best property to put in is high-yield (over 6 percent) income-producing property that you are not likely to want to sell for some time.

We advise against using mortgaged property or assets that you've depreciated. That leaves high-grade corporate bonds, preferred stock, and cash as the three typically best types of property to contribute to a short-term trust.

Sidestepping a tax trap

The law says that if the income from a short-term trust is used to pay for your child's necessaries (in other words used to satisfy your support obligations) you'll be taxed on that income just as if you received it directly. How do we get around that rule?

Simple. Require the trustee to use the money for your child's benefit but not pay for necessaries. The trust income could be used to purchase a car for your child, pay for travel, music or art lessons, or many other non-support expenses.

An alternative is for the trust to accumulate income until your child is no longer your legal responsibility. In many states a child becomes an adult at age eighteen. That means you have no support duties and therefore trust income can be used directly to provide tuition, books, room and board, and even food or clothing.

Once your child receives money from the trust, he or she could even use it to purchase life insurance on his or her life, on your life or your spouse's life, or on the life of a relative. That in turn would provide even more financial security in the event of your death. (The insurance should not be purchased by the trustee if it is to be on your life or your spouse's life, since that would make income used to pay premiums taxable to you.) Your child should personally own and be the beneficiary of the insurance.

Sales in your sunset (sale—or gift—leaseback)

Doctors do it—all the time. What do doctors do for pain in the upper tax? They set up sale leasebacks—or gift leasebacks—

to shift the burden of income taxes to children in lower brackets. If doctors do, maybe you can too!

A sale leaseback involves one party selling property to another party—and then leasing back the same property. A gift leaseback is similar except that you give—rather than sell—the property you intend to leaseback.

Why, oh why?

Why would anyone sell or give property away and then turn around and lease it right back? In a nutshell the answer is that there are big income and estate tax advantages.

Neil Herman is the sole shareholder of a corporation that is "rich" in assets but "poor" in cash. A sale of carefully selected machinery, equipment, land, or a building could generate sorely needed cash that will help the firm enter more profitable markets. The immediate leaseback assures Neil that his firm wouldn't lose the use of the asset—even for a day.

Herb Cheezeman, a physician, is in a 50-percent income tax bracket. He's looking for a way to have income taxed to his sons Mark and Steven, who are about to go to college. Herb makes a gift of cash to a trust set up for each of the boys. The trustee, Herb's accountant, Frank Valle, uses the money to purchase sophisticated medical equipment, which Herb then leases from the trust. Herb deducts his lease payments at his 50-percent bracket and the income is split between the trusts and Herb's two sons at much lower brackets. The annual savings are accumulated for the boys' education.

Phyllis Friedman is a real estate investor who purchased property in Chattanooga that is appreciating rapidly. She doesn't want the property taxed in her estate and would like the appreciation to occur in the hands of her twenty-five-year-old niece, Laura. Phyllis, however, would like to build on the land and so she gives the land to Laura but then immediately leases it back. All the appreciation will occur in Laura's hands and Phyllis's estate will not pay any tax on the land.

What's it take?

Since the savings potential is big (the IRS views it as a loss of revenue), everything has to be done just right. But just what is "everything"?

To avoid a fight with the IRS (which can be done if you do it by the numbers) you must: (1) actually make a sale, or gift; (2) enter into a legitimate enforceable lease with the new owner (or the trustee or custodian for the new owner); (3) arrive at the terms of the lease in an arm's-length manner (this means the rent and all the other terms of the lease must be reasonable—the best test is to ask what terms the parties would have come to if they were not related in any way, but both had knowledge of the relevant facts); and (4) if a trust is involved, be sure that the trustee is an independent party.

What does the IRS look at to see if these requirements are met?

Simple, they check to see if you've followed the provisions of the lease and made payments on schedule. They check the "market" to see if the rent is reasonable. They check the trust to see if you control—or if you let go of the controls—of the trust. They check to see if you really need the property to run your business or practice your profession—or whether the whole deal is just a sham to shift the tax burden.

Tie tax

Obviously, in the case of a sale leaseback, if you sell an asset that has already appreciated in value, you have to pay tax on your gain—just as you would in the case of any other sale.

But then, just as in the case of any business rental, your firm may take a tax deduction for the payments you make each month. So the rental fees paid by the seller for the use of previously owned property are deductible as an ordinary and necessary business expense.

In the case of a gift leaseback, if the gift exceeds or does not qualify for the gift tax annual exclusion of $10,000 per donee ($20,000 if you are married and your spouse agrees to "split" the gift), the gift will be subject to the gift tax. Of course, you can (each) use your gift tax credit to shield up to $275,000 of otherwise taxable gifts (as of 1983). That figure rises each year until it levels off at $600,000 for each spouse by 1987. (See page 78 for the tax-free "exemption equivalent" amounts each year.)

What about the recipients of the income? The new owners of the sale or gift property—how are they taxed? When rental income is paid to an adult child or other relative, that person is considered to be receiving ordinary income as the payments are made. If the income is paid to a trust on behalf of your beneficiaries, it will be taxed to the trust—to the extent it is accumulated, or to the trust's beneficiaries if and when it is paid out.

How much savings can you expect each year? You can make a *rough* guesstimate by multiplying the amount of the rental income you are paying times your top tax bracket—and then subtract the result of multiplying that same income times your beneficiary's top bracket. For instance, assume you are in the 50-percent income tax bracket. After your gift (or sale) your daughter becomes the owner of the property your sole proprietorship or corporation would like to lease. If a fair annual lease is $12,000, you can deduct $12,000—a $6,000 savings—at your 50-percent tax bracket ($12,000 times 50 percent). Your daughter must enter the $12,000 rental payment into her income. Since she's in a 20-percent bracket she'll pay (roughly) $2,000 in tax. This means there's at least a $4,000 savings within your family unit. (Your after-deduction cost was $6,000. Her tax cost was approximately $2,000, a total of $8,000. She receives $12,000, so there's a "gain" within the family of $4,000.)

How about estate tax savings? The answer is—if you are selling property to a child or to a trust for your children—the cash you receive (and don't use up or give away) is in your estate, but the property itself and all the appreciation grows outside your estate. This is an example of the technique estate planning experts call estate "freezing." At the very least you are doing more than swapping dollars if the asset your children now own grows in value at a faster rate than the money you have received or will receive.

If you have given the property to your child or to an irrevocable trust for your child's benefit, the property itself will not be in your estate—even if you die within three years of the transfer. This means that all the appreciation in the property—as well as all the income the property produces—is out of your estate and avoids tax when you die. If your gift is so large that you have to pay a gift tax, even that tax isn't brought back into your estate if you live more than three years after the gift.

Will there be gift taxes to pay on the transfer? Yes, if the gift is large enough, but most individuals can give a significant amount of property to loved ones without paying any gift tax. (See Chapter 9 on gift giving.)

If you are selling the property and leasing it back, be sure to have it appraised first. If the sales price is less than the fair market value, the difference is a gift. Also, check with your attorney and accountant about state gift and income tax implications.

Divide and conquer (incorporation)

You may never have thought about it like this, but a corporation is a super tax shelter. Sam Davis, a west Texas widower whose business is raising horses, is looking for a more effective way to accumulate, conserve and distribute his assets. Here's what he gets by incorporation:

1. As an employee of his own corporation, he will be entitled to a number of fringe benefits—most of which are tax deductible by the corporation and not taxable to Sam. These include: (a) pension/profit sharing plans; (b) group life insurance; (c) group health insurance; (d) disability income coverage; and (e) medical reimbursement plans.

2. Sam's liability is, to some extent, limited. A creditor of the corporation can't proceed against the corporation's shareholders (unless Sam personally signed as guarantor or agreed to be personally responsible).

3. Before he incorporated, Sam had no ability to "time" or divide income; it was all taxed to him just as soon as he earned it, and it was taxed to him personally at his 50-percent income tax bracket.

But after incorporation, Sam personally will pay tax only if—and as—he receives salary, which can be timed within limits to avoid "bunching" too much income into any single tax year. Furthermore, the salary paid to Sam is deductible by the corporation. A great deal of the remaining corporate income can be siphoned off into tax deductible (by the corporation) and tax free (to Sam) fringe benefits.

After incorporation, instead of Sam's paying tax at a maximum personal income tax rate of 50 percent, the maximum rate to which corporate income is subjected is 46 percent. Better yet, the lowest corporate rates are very low (only 15 percent on the first $25,000 of corporate taxable income in 1983). It's likely that most of the corporation's taxable income will be subject to these lower levels.

4. Incorporating gives Sam a relatively simple and inexpensive way to transfer the ownership of his business. All he has to do to make gifts is to endorse shares of stock over to his donees and record the transactions in his company's books. Sam can make gifts to friends, nieces, nephews, and charities quickly and easily.

5. Through gifts of stock, Sam can give family members an interest in the family business without giving up control (Sam "calls

Simplified Schematic of Corporate Taxation

GROSS INCOME

minus

Ordinary deductions from gross income

minus

Special deductions allowed only to corporations such as the "85 percent dividends received deduction"

equals

TAXABLE INCOME

A 15-percent rate is applied to the first $25,000 of taxable income.
An 18-percent rate is applied to the next $25,000 of taxable income.
A 30-percent rate applies to the next $25,000 of taxable income.
A 40-percent rate applies to the next $25,000 of taxable income.
A 46-percent rate applies to all taxable income in excess of $100,000.

the shots" as long as he keeps at least 51 percent of the company's stock). He also shifts the growth of the business to his children and by dividing shares among several family members he shifts a portion of his estate to the children's lower estate tax brackets.

6. Sam maintains privacy. The transfer of stock in a closely held corporation is not public information. Sam can therefore keep his business's and family's financial affairs from public scrutiny.

7. Legally, Sam's business can continue without him. This "continuity of operation" is one of the major advantages of incorporation. Within limits, the corporation may continue its business when Sam dies with little or no hindrance from the probate court. The corporation's other officers could continue to make business decisions without the necessity or delay of the judicial process.

Now you see it—now you don't

To some extent, a corporation is like a magician's magic money box. Dollars that would be taxable to anyone else are tax free or almost tax free to the corporation.

For instance, say you received a $1,000 dividend on stock you owned and you are in a 50-percent income tax bracket. You'd pay $500 in tax and have $500 left to invest or use for your personal needs.

Now assume you formed a corporation and transferred the stock to it. Suppose your corporation owned the same stock and received the same $1,000 dividend. A corporation is entitled to a special deduction known as a "dividends received" deduction. This deduction reduces the corporation's gross income by 85 percent of the dividends it receives from certain other corporations. In other words, your corporation pays tax on only 15 percent (100 percent − 85 percent) of the dividend it receives. In our example, that's $150 ($1,000 × .15). Since the maximum corporate tax rate is 46 percent, the most tax the corporation could possibly pay (it doesn't reach the 46-percent level until it has over $100,000 of taxable income) on the $150 exposed to tax is $69—46 percent of $150. That means the corporation would have $931 (instead of $500) to invest or use for its needs (including payment of tax-deductible fringe benefits).

This seems too good to be true, but it is—true, that is. There is a limit to how much money, securities, or other investments a corporation can shelter at its lower tax brackets. But current law allows accumulations of up to $250,000 for most business corporations ($150,000 for most professional corporations) even if you form or use the corporation to avoid personal income tax by allowing earnings and profits to accumulate at favorable corporate rates.

Sophisticated shuffles

Once you incorporate, you can shuffle the corporate structure at various times to help you accomplish your "people" and tax planning objectives. In other words, your attorney, accountant, and other financial advisors might suggest that you "recapitalize" the corporation (exchange one type of stock for another type of stock, exchange one type of security for another type or change voting or dividend provisions).

Why would a nice person like you want to do a thing like that?

Because, through a recapitalization of an existing corporation you could:

1. Give younger, more active employee/shareholders a larger share of the business, encouraging them to work harder and stay with the business; or
2. Shift control from you to a family member; or
3. Provide more active shareholders with greater voting rights; or
4. Transfer control to a family member working in the business and at the same time provide income for your retirement; or
5. Provide a key employee with a voice in management; or
6. Help "freeze" the value of your stock for federal and state death tax purposes and shift growth to the family member of your choice; or
7. Make it easier for a coshareholder to buy you out; or
8. Prevent nonworking, minority shareholders from voting on important business matters; or
9. Provide retirement income for you and at the same time shift the growth in your business to your children who are working in it.

One way it can work is like this: Larry and Dorothy own all the shares of common voting stock of the LD Corporation. Larry wants his son to eventually become the owner and key employee of the business. Larry wants to encourage his son to stay with the firm and have the benefit of what he expects to be rapid appreciation in the business's value.

Larry and Dorothy could exchange all their voting common stock (say it was worth $1,000,000) for a combination of voting stock (worth say $100,000) and preferred stock (assume this worth $900,000). The preferred stock will be worth about 90 percent of what the stock they exchanged was worth. That means that the common stock (which carries both the growth and voting rights) would be worth 10 percent of the value of the stock surrendered.

Larry and Dorothy could give that common stock to their son, as they see fit, over a period of time. This means control could be shifted as slowly or as quickly as they felt appropriate. Because of its currently low value, Larry and Dorothy would pay little, if any, gift tax on the transfers of the common stock.

Larry and Dorothy would keep the preferred stock. They could receive dividends on the preferred stock to help provide retirement security.

The "recap" has provided retirement income for Larry and Dorothy, and at the same time provided them with a way to shift the future growth of the corporation from themselves to their son.

Getting high on a sub (subchapter S corporations)

Many accountants and attorneys are high on a subchapter S corporation (these are now called "S" corporations) for certain of their clients. Why?

You might ask Rodger Schambacker, president of Rugged Steel Foundries. When he founded the steel company, Rodger knew he and his associates would be putting hundreds of thousands of dollars into a high-risk business that was subject to wide market swings and profit volatility. His accountant told Rodger that the company might show losses in the first few years of business. Rodger wanted the legal protection against creditors offered by corporate status but also wanted to be able to deduct what he expected would be several years' losses against his outside income (he knew the business itself wouldn't have enough income to take advantage of the losses).

By electing S corporation status, it became possible to pass through corporate losses to Rodger's personal tax return (to the extent of the capital investment and loans he had made). That way, Rodger could use corporate losses to reduce his personal income tax liability.

When the business turns the corner and begins to make a profit, Rodger and the other shareholders will terminate the "sub S" election. That would make the corporation's profits taxable to the corporation—at its initially relatively low tax brackets. Future profits will all be taxed to the business.

As long as the subchapter S election is in effect, Rodger and his fellow shareholders can enjoy the typical fringe benefits and other advantages of a corporation. At the same time—if he is in a low tax bracket—he might want corporate income taxed directly to him. This is very different from regular corporate taxation, where income earned by the business is taxed once to the corporation and then is taxed a second time when paid out as a dividend. A sub S election, therefore, provides a way to beat the double tax.

Why else might Rodger's advisors recommend S corporation treatment?

Perhaps the biggest reason many S corporations are formed is that they have the potential for shifting income (and therefore spreading taxes) within a family unit. That's because the income earned by an S corporation is taxed by percentage ownership to the parties who own stock at the end of the corporation's tax year. So (assuming Rodger was taking a reasonable salary) if each of his three children owned 30 percent of the stock (a total of 90 percent) and Rodger owned 10 percent, he'd be taxed on only 10 percent of the corporation's net income—while they would each report 30 percent. If the corporation earned $100,000, $10,000 would be taxed—in addition to Rodger's salary—to him. But the remaining $90,000 would be taxed to his three children in their lower brackets.

By gifting (or selling) stock to family members, it is possible to shift the corporation's income to a larger number of relatively low tax bracket individuals. The result is income tax savings that go on—year after year.

Putting the S on solid ground

Looking at the S corporation from a non-tax standpoint, it's a regular garden-variety corporation. It looks (and is) different only because it has elected to be taxed differently from other corporations. That difference makes all the difference.

True, an S corporation computes its taxable income in much the same way as a non-electing corporation. It receives a deduction for salaries it pays to its employees (including shareholder-employees). It receives a deduction for contributions it makes to group life and health insurance plans and to pension or profit-sharing plans. So what's different about an S corporation?

Lots of things. The big difference, as you've probably guessed, is that once taxable income is computed it is not subject to the regular tax imposed on the taxable income of a corporation. (See page 141 of this chapter.) Instead, taxable income is charged directly to the corporation's shareholders as it is earned (even taxable income that is not actually paid out is taxed on a pro-rata basis to parties who own stock on the last day of the corporation's taxable year).

That leads to one of the biggest planning techniques of all—the "year end" gift. If you own 100 percent of the S corporation stock but give it away—say 10 percent of it—to your child or another relative before the corporation's year ends, that person must report

10 percent of the corporation's income. This makes substantial last-minute intra-family income tax shifts possible. At the last minute you can shift income to any family member you choose. Of course, your gift of stock is an irrevocable gift and if it is large enough there may be gift taxes to pay. But probably, they will be far outweighed by the year after year income tax savings.

Furthermore, since both the value of the stock you've given away and the after-tax income is in your child's estate rather than yours, significant estate tax savings can be realized.

Personal holding company

Harris Gary has an estate worth 7 million dollars. Five million dollars worth of Gary's estate consists of highly appreciated and readily marketable securities. He wants to reduce the federal estate taxes attributable to those assets. Gary currently reports income from dividends from the securities in the tax year he receives that income. He would like to achieve a more advantageous method of timing income. He would like to achieve all these things and at the same time retain substantial economic control and flexibility in making investment decisions. The solution to his planning goals may be the personal holding company.

Hold on

Most accountants think of a personal holding company as something to avoid. That's because there is a tax, separate from and in addition to the existing corporate tax, on the undistributed income of the personal holding company. The tax is 70 percent. That means the total of the special personal holding company tax and the corporate tax can be as much as 100 percent (or more) of the corporation's income. So a personal holding company is a bad—not a good—thing? No. If it is used properly, a "PHC" can be a very good thing.

Let's go back to the case of Harris Gary, the wealthy investor described above. Gary purchased shares of Computer-a-go Company many years ago. These Computer-a-go Company shares are now publicly traded and worth one hundred times what he paid for them. They are also continuing to grow rapidly. If Gary retains the stock, the shares will be includable in his estate. If he gives them away, he will incur a sizable gift tax. Furthermore, the gifts will be considered "adjusted taxable gifts." That means they will increase the rate at which his taxable estate will be taxed. Another reason Gary doesn't want to make gifts of his stock is that some of his beneficiaries are minor children and he doesn't want to make outright gifts. But he does not want to use a trust because of certain administrative problems associated with a trust.

Gary could form a corporation. He could retain 100 percent of its stock. He could then transfer a million dollars' worth of the publicly listed Computer-a-go Company stock to the newly formed personal holding corporation.

The new "PHC" would have a two-part capital structure. Part one would consist of $900,000 worth of voting dividend-paying preferred stock. He would also receive part two of the new capital structure, $200,000 worth of voting common stock. (This breakdown is arbitrary and can be varied as to the appropriate mix.)

Since one of Gary's main planning objectives is to limit future appreciation in the value of his estate, he would retain the voting dividend-paying preferred stock. But simultaneously he would begin a gifting program with the voting common. He and his wife, Anne, could give $20,000 worth of voting common to each of his five children and grandchildren. This would enable him to direct and control the investment program. The beauty of this arrangement is that because the common stock has a relatively low current value, its gift tax cost is minimal. If the gifts are made outright or in trust in a manner that enables them to be presently enjoyed by the recipients, the annual exclusion would eliminate the gift tax entirely. And because the common stock carries with it most or all of the financial growth of the business, all future appreciation occurs in the hands of the donees rather than in the hands of its original owner, Harris Gary. So if the underlying assets double in value after the common stock is given away, that appreciation will be realized in the children's hands rather than in Gary's hands.

There are other alternatives. Gary could sell rather than give the common stock to his children. They could pay him for the stock by issuing serially maturing notes. These notes would have a total face value equaling the fair market value of the stock Gary's children receive, $200,000. Gary could forgive all or a portion of each note as it matures. This would enable Gary to make gifts with minimal (or no) gift tax cost and delay the impact of the gift tax at his whim.

The two techniques described above are called estate "freezing" devices. This is because they enable Gary to give away the future appreciation in his marketable securities through the common stock mechanism. This siphoning device "freezes" assets at their present value for estate tax purposes with minimal gift tax implications.

The courts have consistently allowed federal estate and gift tax discounts of 15 percent or more (in one case as much as 55 percent) on the theory that stock of a personal holding company is less attractive to an investor than a similar stock invested on an exchange with ready access to the investing public.

For example, if Gary makes a gift of 100 shares of Xerox stock, that gift is worth more than a gift of a 10-percent interest in a personal holding company—which has as its only asset 1,000 shares of Xerox. Why? It would seem that 100 shares of Xerox are worth the same as a 10-percent interest in a corporation whose only asset is 1,000 shares of the same stock. But the truth is that an investment in a personal holding company is less desirable than an investment in the underlying Xerox shares. That's because the underlying assets (the Xerox shares in this example) can easily be traded in the stock market. Shares in the personal holding company cannot. This is why there is a discount from the net asset value of the underlying shares for federal estate and gift tax purposes. In the example above, Gary's million-dollar portfolio may be valued at less than the one million dollars that the underlying assets are worth. Of course, the result of a lower value is lower gift or estate taxation. Furthermore, if the stock Gary gave away is a minority interest, a further discount could be allowed to his estate because of the lack of voting control. A 10-percent interest would not be enough to allow the owner of the personal holding company's stock to control or even have a major influence on what the company did or did not do.

What more could you ask?

The substantial estate and gift tax savings possible through a personal holding company have already been described. But there are other advantages to a properly arranged personal holding company. One is what is known as the "85-percent dividend-received" deduction. Ordinary income can be substantially or totally avoided by a personal holding company through the 85-percent dividend-received deduction. This is a deduction allowed to a corporation that owns stock in another domestic corporation. In essence it allows 85 percent of any dividends it receives to be excluded from income taxation. Only the remaining 15 percent is subject to tax. For example, a corporation could receive a $10,000 dividend, exclude $8,500 of it, and pay tax on only $1,500. In the worst possible situation the corporation would pay tax in the 46-percent bracket, which would result in a $690 tax. That would leave $9,310 to invest. If the owner of the personal company had received that $10,000 dividend personally and he was in a 50-percent income tax bracket, there would only be $5,000 left for him to invest. Since this is a year-after-year difference of over $4,300, over a period of ten years the savings are substantial.

To the extent the individual forming a personal holding company actually performs bona fide services for it, he/she is entitled to receive a salary. Assuming the salary paid is reasonable, an individual would be taxed at a 50-percent bracket, and the corporation will be able to deduct the entire payment. (Compensation above a "reasonable level" is subject to taxes at the corporate level and again subject to tax at the individual level. In other words, no deduction is allowed for that portion of salary paid which is deemed to be "unreasonable.")

The taxable income of a personal holding company can be lowered even further by providing a working stockholder and working members of his/her family with various fringe benefits (the cost of which would be tax deductible by the corporation). In other words, Gary could work for the corporation and by performing reasonable services become entitled to be covered under the corporation's tax deductible qualified pension and/or profit-sharing plan.

If properly arranged, qualified fringe benefit plans could provide substantial estate tax free payments to specified beneficiaries. This would mean that even greater amounts could be shifted from Gary's generation to his children and even grandchildren estate tax free. In fact, all the advantages of incorporation are possible if the estate owner performs meaningful and active services for a corporation after placing his investment portfolio in it.

To have fish for dinner, there must be a catch

Most accountants are fearful of personal holding company status because if it is not properly handled there is a potential for a very onerous 70-percent personal holding company tax. But this is only on the income that is not expensed or paid out by the corporation. In many cases all or most of the corporation's income can legitimately be siphoned off through salaries and various fringe benefits.

There is also potential for double taxation, once when the corporation sells the securities it holds and again when the shareholder receives the proceeds or other property as a dividend or on the liquidation of the corporation. But this potential for double taxation can be minimized or eliminated altogether by carefully controlling the type of investments made and the type of expenses incurred.

One other problem is the imposition of state capital stock or franchise taxes on the value of the personal holding company stock or on the net income remaining in the corporation each year.

The problems inherent in a personal holding company can be solved—and should be solved—in advance. It is necessary to understand that the personal holding company concept is difficult for many accountants and attorneys to understand. Therefore it should be attempted only with the advice of seasoned and knowledgeable estate planning tax oriented practitioners, and used only after a careful study is made of the pros and cons.

13.
A Tax Shelter for Everyone

Those ever-loving deductions

The pages in this chapter should be colored green, because the ideas on these pages are as good as, if not better than, money in the bank for you and your family. Now, since the passage of ERTA, The Economic Recovery Tax Act of 1981, everyone is entitled to a genuine tax sheltered retirement plan, courtesy of your Uncle Sam. TEFRA, the Tax Equity and Fiscal Responsibility Act of 1982, increased these benefits for many individuals. It doesn't matter whether you're a big corporation, a little corporation, in business for yourself, in a large or small partnership, or an employee of any sized employer—you can now put money aside for your retirement and get a big fat tax deduction when you file your income tax return.

A pension or profit-sharing plan can be the ultimate tax shelter if the situation is right. "HR-10" plans permit an unincorporated business to set aside money for its employees' retirement on a tax favored basis. The new tax laws now permit everyone to have his own individual retirement accounts. Regardless of what other retirement plans you have, you should read the section on IRA's thoroughly; it could mean money in the bank for you. If you are self-employed, the S.E.P.P., a "Simplified Employee Pension Plan," might be the way you want to go.

Not only are you entitled to receive tax deductions when you pay money into these plans, but the interest on your investment can accumulate income tax free, be paid to you on a favorable tax basis, and, if set up properly, be received by your family all or substantially free of federal estate tax at your death.

Some deductions you are permitted to take (like medical expenses or automobile repairs when our cars are used for business) help at tax time, but the money spent is gone forever. How much

A Tax Shelter for Everyone

more pleasant to be able to take a deduction for money to be used to provide a more secure future for your family and yourself.

Pension and profit-sharing plans—the ultimate tax shelter

Imagine a tax shelter that allows your corporation to make large tax deductible contributions to a special fund that will provide security for your retirement.

Assume, no matter how much interest these funds earn, not one penny will be taxed until you begin receiving benefits. Even if the fund sells an asset and realizes a whopping gain, you pay no current tax.

Picture taking the money at retirement under special tax rules that allow you super-favorable ten-year (five years is normal) income averaging if you take a lump-sum or special annuity reporting that enables you to spread your tax over your entire retirement lifetime.

Consider that if you die, up to $100,000 of death benefit can be federal (and in many cases state) estate tax free.

If you are an employee of a corporation—even if you are a stockholder/employee—you are eligible for all of these tax benefits through a "qualified" pension or profit-sharing plan.

Not for everyone

For you to obtain the benefits of a pension or profit-sharing plan, the plan must be "qualified." That is, it must meet a number of requirements. These include:

1. The exclusive benefit rule: The plan must be for the exclusive benefit of employees. Shareholders who are not employees cannot participate.

2. The primary purpose of a pension plan must be to offer employees a retirement benefit. A profit-sharing plan must provide employees with a share in the company's profits.

3. The plan cannot favor officers, stockholders, or highly compensated employees. That doesn't mean these people can't participate. It doesn't mean they cannot receive larger benefits than other employees. It means that certain guidelines must be followed in order to obtain the substantial benefits described above.

4. The plan has to be in writing and employees must be given information about how the plan works, the benefits it provides, and how and when they'll enjoy those benefits.

5. The plan must be permanent. This means the plan must contain no set ending date.

What's available

You shouldn't attempt to set up a pension or profit-sharing plan yourself; it should be a joint project attempted only after you've had your accountant, attorney, and employee benefit planner study its feasibility, direct tax implications, and the indirect effects it has on other employee benefit plans. An employee benefits consultant can provide you with a number of plan designs with varying cost-benefit ratios from which to choose.

To make the right decision, you should know something about the various types of plans available.

Essentially, there are two types of pension plans—the "defined benefit" and the "money purchase" plan.

A defined benefit plan is one in which you start with a promise that a specified benefit (for example, $3,000 a month for life) will be paid when you reach normal retirement age. A predetermined formula is used to define the benefit each participant will receive. Your corporation then makes an annual contribution large enough so that at retirement the plan can provide that benefit. In other words, the corporation's contribution is based on the actuarial determination of the cost of benefits promised. This type of plan generally favors an older employee with relatively few years until retirement.

A money purchase (some people call these a defined contribution) plan is the second type of pension plan. This arrangement bases the retirement benefit upon an employer's commitment to make an annual contribution. Benefits are dependent on how long you participate in the plan and how much money has been contributed on your behalf each year. Your benefit also grows in relation to the earnings and appreciation of the money contributed. This type of plan generally favors a younger employee with a number of years until retirement.

There are specifically designed hybrids of these two called "target benefit" plans. A target plan starts with a defined benefit plan. You figure out what you'd like to end up with. Then you figure out how much is needed to get there. But instead of giving you just the promised amount, the target plan then turns into a money purchase plan. That way you contribute what the corporation should have contributed each year under a defined benefit plan, but you end up with what you would end up with if the plan was a money purchase plan. In other words, if the plan's interest assumptions are exactly met, it's like a defined benefit plan. But if earnings and other assumptions were conservative and the plan does better than expected, all plan participants share in the gains. (Of course, if the plan does less favorably than anticipated, plan participants receive less at retirement.)

In a profit-sharing plan, your corporation shares a portion of its profits. It's a type of defined contribution plan. A profit-sharing plan doesn't have to have a set formula for determining how much profit will be shared—your board of directors can decide that on a year-to-year basis. But once that decision is made, there must be a definite formula for dividing these profits among the participants. Furthermore, if there is no definite formula for deciding what contribution will be made each year, the corporation must make recurring and substantial contributions. That means that you can't make contributions in one year and then arbitrarily, without regard for profits, skip contributions until your corporation feels like making more.

Your firm doesn't necessarily have to choose between these types of plans; it can set up more than one. Many firms superimpose a profit-sharing plan on top of a modest pension plan so participants will have both growth possibilities and guaranteed income at retirement.

How (income) taxing is it?

Dr. Jonathan Frank owns 100 percent of the stock in the J. F. Professional Corporation. His corporation has established a pension plan for its employees, Jon and his two nurses.

Contributions made by the pension toward each of the three employees' retirements will be fully deductible from the corporation's income.

As the money is invested within the plan for the covered employees, it grows income tax free. This of course boosts the pre-retirement yield considerably.

Neither Jonathan nor either of the two nurses have to include the corporation's contribution on his or her behalf in their income, even if their rights to benefits in the plan can't be forfeited. (Tax practitioners refer to complete nonforfeitability as a "fully vested benefit.") Jonathan pays no tax until he actually receives a benefit payment.

If the plan includes life insurance protection, Jonathan will be treated as if he had received a taxable distribution each year (tax people call this a "current economic benefit"). That "distribution" is essentially the employer's contributions or trust earnings that have been applied during the year to provide "pure insurance" (term insurance only) on the employee's life. Jonathan would enter this cost into other income on his tax return just as if he had received a bonus of that amount.

Jon may choose to take his pension money at retirement in a lump sum or as an annuity. If he takes the money in a "lump sum" (essentially this means taking whatever he's entitled to at retirement—and taking that money within one taxable year), the distribution will be entitled to favorable ten-year income averaging.

What if Jon chooses to receive payments as an annuity, that is, in the form of an income for life that he can never outlive? In that case, Jon would be taxed under the "annuity" rules. These rules tax payments as ordinary income when received.

If he made a contribution to the plan, but he will be able to recover an amount equal to or greater than his contributions within three years of the time payments begin, he can recover his cost tax free before reporting any payments. For example, if he contributed $6,000 and will receive $4,000 a year for life, he will not report any income for the first year and six months.

If Jon can't recover his cost within three years, a portion of each payment will be income tax free and a portion will be taxable. For instance, if Jon contributed $20,000 in the example above, and would receive retirement payments at the rate of $4,000 a year, he could not recover his cost in the first three years. This would mean a portion of every payment he receives is tax free while the remainder is taxable.

Death and taxes

At Jon's death, there are (at least) two taxes to consider—the federal estate tax and the federal income tax. (There may also be state income and inheritance taxes.)

The first $100,000 of death benefits generated by the corporation's contributions is federal estate tax free, as long as (1) it isn't paid to Jon's estate; (2) Jon's beneficiary takes it in a form other than a lump sum; or (3) Jon's beneficiary takes a lump sum and makes an irrevocable election not to take ten-year special income averaging.

Even though the balance of the death benefit is in Jon's estate, it wouldn't generate any federal estate tax—no matter how large it is—if it is payable to Jon's surviving spouse. This is because of the federal estate tax unlimited marital deduction. Even if the marital deduction is unavailable, if Jon's estate—including the estate tax includable portion of the pension distribution—is under the "exemption equivalent" ($600,000 in 1987 and later years), his beneficiary should elect special income tax averaging. That's because the federal law allows each of us to pass an amount of property equal to the "exemption equivalent" to any beneficiary we choose and pay no federal estate taxes.

There are income taxes to be paid by a beneficiary receiving death benefits from a qualified pension or profit-sharing plan.

The entire amount attributable to employer contributions is subject to income tax (that's because you never paid tax on that amount). That tax will be paid by the beneficiary who receives the payments.

If the plan's death benefit was financed through life insurance, the "net amount at risk" (this is the "pure insurance" amount, the amount in excess of the life insurance policy cash values) is entirely tax free. Only the balance is (with certain exceptions) subject to income tax. This is one of many reasons why you should consider purchasing some life insurance in your plan.

The right way to borrow

Your company's pension plan can provide for loans to participants. The loan must be made in accordance to specific plan provisions allowing loans. A reasonable charge must be made for the use of plan assets, and the borrower must give adequate security for the money borrowed. Loans must be available to all participants on a reasonably equivalent basis. With the exception of loans to buy or build a principal residence, all loans must be repaid within five years.

Where there's life (insurance)

Are there non-tax advantages to putting life insurance inside the plan? The answer is that life insurance could serve a number of valuable functions.

First, insurance provides protection against the premature death of a participant. If Jon died in the early years of the plan, his survivors would receive a large benefit (the life insurance) instead of a small benefit (either nothing or what the plan had grown to by that date).

Second, the purchase of life insurance assures a participant of the right to use guaranteed annuity rates when he retires. So no matter how long people are living when Jon reaches retirement age or how much it costs to buy a contract to purchase a life-long income, Jon is guaranteed the right to purchase an annuity at today's favorable rates.

Third, if a plan participant wanted to purchase the insurance on his life from the plan, the policy rates would be those in effect when the policy was purchased by the plan. So Jon can be assured that he can buy the policy on his life when he retires or terminates employment.

Buy the numbers (HR-10 plans)

What a nest egg you could accumulate if you could set aside up to $30,000 a year, take a tax deduction from your highest marginal tax bracket, have the money accumulate income tax free, and take it at retirement under favorable tax conditions. You can. Legitimately.

Just remember the letters and numbers HR-10. HR-10, Keogh Plan, Self-Employed Retirement Plan, they're all the same. And it may just be the buy of your lifetime.

There's no question that you can't rely on social security alone to provide retirement income. If you're a self-employed individual, a sole proprietor or partner who owns 10 percent or more of a partnership, you are allowed to take a tax deduction for money you put aside for your retirement (as well as a tax deduction for dollars you put aside for the retirement of your employees—including a spouse or child who works for you).

THE AMOUNT AN ANNUAL CONTRIBUTION WILL BE WORTH ASSUMING A 10-PERCENT RATE OF INTEREST

	$ 1,000	$ 2,000	$ 10,000	$ 15,000	$ 30,000
10 years	$ 15,937	$ 31,874	$ 159,374	$ 239,061	$ 478,122
15 years	31,772	63,545	317,724	476,587	953,174
20 years	57,275	114,550	572,749	859,124	1,718,249
25 years	98,347	196,694	983,470	1,475,205	2,950,411
30 years	164,494	328,988	1,644,940	2,467,410	4,934,820
35 years	271,024	542,048	2,710,243	4,065,365	8,130,731
40 years	442,592	885,185	4,425,925	6,638,888	13,277,776

An HR-10 makes sense, and dollars, because it defers paying money that would currently go in taxes to the federal government—and allows you to put these dollars to work—tax free for your retirement. That means you can couple the power of compounding interest with the advantage of tax free growth. The chart on page 158 shows you just how impressive this can be. A 10-percent interest rate has been assumed.

Paying the price

If you're covered by an HR-10 plan as an employee, you've got a free ride. Sit back and enjoy. But if you are an "owner/employee" (a sole proprietor who owns 100 percent of the business or profession, or a partner who owns more than 10 percent of either the capital interest or profit interest of the partnership), and your business employs other people full-time, they've got to be included in the plan too. You can exclude full-time employees who have worked for you less than three years and seasonal or part-time employees (one who works less than 1,000 hours during a twelve-month period).

Putting it in and taking it out

The maximum annual deductible contribution to a "defined contribution" HR-10 plan (one in which the amount you get at retirement depends on how much you've put in and how fast and long it grows) is the same as a corporate pension plan, up to the lower of (a) 25 percent of your earned income, or (b) $30,000 a year. So Sam Glick, a self-employed salesman with an income of $60,000 a year, could contribute and deduct $15,000 a year, the lower of (a) 25 percent of his $60,000 income, or (b) $30,000. His retirement fund at age sixty-five would depend on the amount to which his contributions grew, together with the interest.

A second type of HR-10 plan is the so-called "defined benefit" plan. This type of HR-10 plan starts with a given level of retirement benefits and works backwards. In other words, Sam's contributions would be based on actuarial calculations designed to accumulate enough of a reserve to pay the benefits promised by the plan. The maximum annual benefit that can be funded is $90,000. It may pay to have your tax advisor investigate this type of plan since your deductible contribution can, in some cases, be as much as 70 percent higher than the allowable limits under a defined contribution plan.

Generally, a defined contribution plan will favor younger individuals while older "late starters" will obtain greater financial security through a defined benefit plan. (It makes sense to consider both types and have a comparison made.)

Once contributions have been made, the funds can be invested in life insurance contracts, mutual funds, savings accounts, variable annuities, government bonds, or a combination of these funding vehicles.

If you die prior to retirement, the amount in the plan can be paid (in most cases probate free) to the person(s) you have specified. Since you never paid tax on either the contributions or the income that money earned, your beneficiary must report the amounts he/she receives as ordinary income. If the plan was partially financed through a life insurance policy, to the extent the death benefit represents "pure" life insurance (amounts in excess of the cash value of the policy at the date of your death) it will be income tax free.

Regardless of how much is payable when you die or how it is taken, none of the money in your HR-10 will cause a federal estate tax problem if it is paid to your spouse. That's because of the unlimited federal estate tax marital deduction. Up to $100,000 can also be federal estate tax free even if someone other than your spouse is the recipient. The only catch in that case is that it's got to be taken by your beneficiary as an annuity or over two or more taxable years (or if it is taken in a lump sum, the recipient must sign an election to forgo special ten-year income tax averaging in return for allowing the death benefit to pass through your estate federal estate tax free).

In most smaller estates, a beneficiary who is someone other than the spouse should elect special (favorable) income averaging, since there wouldn't be much estate tax to pay in the self-employed person's estate. For example, Steve Roberts died in 1983. His estate was worth about $125,000. He also had $100,000 benefits under an HR-10 plan payable to his twenty-eight-year-old son, David. Because of the estate tax credit allowed to every taxpayer—equivalent to a $275,000 exemption in 1983—there would be no federal estate tax in Steve's estate no matter which choice David made.

If Steve lives until retirement, he reports the amounts he receives as ordinary income (since he never reported either his contributions or the plan's earnings as income).

A not so tender trap
Congress wanted to discourage individuals from "raiding"

their HR-10 plans prior to retirement years. It also wanted to encourage owner/employees to continue making payments to the plan. So the tax laws provide that an HR-10 plan that includes an owner/employee must require that no payments can be made to the owner/employee before he or she reaches age 59½ (except where death or permanent disability occurs).

Severe tax penalties are imposed if a withdrawal is made by an owner/employee before age 59½ or if no withdrawals are started before age 70½.

The people's pension (individual retirement account—IRA)

The prestigious legal counselors' tax advisor, *U.S. Tax Week,* says that an IRA is "the most basic tax shelter existing today." It goes on to say, "it may also be the safest and the wisest."

Why? Because an IRA allows you to defer your otherwise reportable earned income, invest it (income tax free), and enjoy the rewards later when you'll probably be in a lower income tax bracket.

At a 10-percent compound interest rate, money put in this year will double itself in about seven years. At 12 percent, it will double over six years. If you were twenty-five years old and put $2,000 a year into an IRA each year until you were sixty-five, you'd retire with $1,700,000.

Almost everyone can now take advantage of "the people's pension." You can use an IRA even if you already participate in your employer's pension or profit-sharing plan, or if you are a sole proprietor or partner and have your own pension plan. You can even have an IRA if you are an employee of a nonprofit organization and are saving for retirement through a tax deferred annuity plan.

What's up?

The amount you can set aside and deduct is higher than ever. Current law allows you to deduct the lower of (a) $2,000 a year, or (b) 100 percent of your compensation. That means that if you earned only $2,000, you could contribute and deduct the entire amount. This rule makes it possible to shelter all or a large part of your family's second income.

Naturally, if you have a working spouse, another $2,000 can be contributed and deducted. That boosts your family's limit to $4,000 a year. It wouldn't take long at that rate to build a sizable nest egg—as the chart on page 162 illustrates.

THE AMOUNT AN ANNUAL CONTRIBUTION WILL BE WORTH ASSUMING A 10-PERCENT RATE OF INTEREST

	$1,000	*$2,000*
10 years	$ 15,937	$ 31,874
15 years	31,772	63,545
20 years	57,275	114,550
25 years	98,347	196,694
30 years	164,494	328,988
35 years	271,024	542,048
40 years	442,592	885,185

If you both work and you earned, say $20,000, and your spouse earned only $1,000, you could deduct a total of $3,000.

If you are working, but your spouse is not, you are entitled to "spice up" your IRA into a "SPIRA," a spousal IRA. In a nutshell, that means you can set aside and deduct up to $2,250 (instead of just $2,000) even if your spouse has no employment income.

It ain't necessarily so

As good as an IRA is, it is, of course, not for everyone. You should take a careful look at the pros and cons of an IRA and the alternatives.

Unless you die or become disabled, you can't take your money out before you are 59½—without (a) paying the normal income tax rates on the money you've taken, and (b) paying a 10-percent penalty tax. For example, if you take $5,000 out of your IRA at age fifty (a so-called "premature distribution"), you have to pay a $500 penalty tax in addition to the normal tax on the $5,000 itself. That's a technical way of saying that you are in essence tying your money up until at least 59½. (That forced savings may be a big advantage if you have trouble putting money away—and keeping away from it once you've put it away.)

You must begin to take the money by age 70½ (and who wouldn't?).

Consider, if you own your own business, whether you'd be better off with an HR-10 plan. If you are self-employed, you can have both an IRA and an HR-10, or if you are incorporated, a qualified pension plan may generate a large income at retirement. (Again, you can be a covered employee who participates in both his employer's corporate pension plan and your own personal IRA.)

Where does it all go?

If you've decided an IRA is the way to go, your next decision is what type of IRA to set up. Your IRA contribution can go to one (or more) of a number of places. Talk to your insurance agent, your banker and your stockbroker. Compare each according to the ability of the product to meet your needs, the quality of the service offered, and the knowledge level provided. This last point pertains to the question of whether you are dealing through the mail or over the counter with an under-informed clerk or with a highly trained and well-schooled financial planning professional. The advice you receive can save you considerable aggravation as well as tax dollars.

Rolling over into clover

Say you've made an investment and you later find it wasn't the wisest of all decisions. IRA law allows you to "rollover" your IRA investment as often as once a year into a new IRA investment medium. That can help minimize the cost of an investment error.

If you can use the same bank, insurer, broker or mutual fund manager to change your investment (say from one type of mutual fund account to another), it can be done tax free and the exchange wouldn't count as a rollover.

It's all in the timing

You have until the time you have to file your income tax return to set up and contribute to your IRA. That gives most taxpayers until April fifteenth of next year to take a deduction for this year's income.

A super IRA (simplified employee pension plan—S.E.P.P.)

A S.E.P.P. is a "super IRA," a retirement savings program with most of the same rules but higher limits than a regular IRA. Unlike its smaller brother, the S.E.P.P. is available only to employees (including yourself if you are self-employed).

Just as in the case of an IRA, contributions to a S.E.P.P. are currently deductible, earnings grow income tax free, and you pay no tax until you begin to receive benefits.

How high is up?

How much can you contribute to a S.E.P.P.? The answer is 15 percent of your compensation or $15,000, whichever is less. Starting in 1984, the 15 percent limit jumps to 25 percent and the $15,000 amount becomes $30,000.

So if your income is:	In 1983 you can contribute and deduct up to:	In 1984 you can contribute and deduct up to:
$ 20,000	$ 3,000	$ 5,000
30,000	4,500	7,000
40,000	6,000	10,000
50,000	7,500	12,000
60,000	9,000	15,000
70,000	10,500	17,000
80,000	12,000	20,000
90,000	13,500	22,000
100,000	15,000	25,000
150,000	15,000	30,000

No free lunch

Just as is the case with much of the tax law, there is no free lunch when it comes to S.E.P.P.'s. The cost of the substantial boost in deductible limits is that to have a S.E.P.P. there must be:

1. An employer (can be a corporation, partnership or sole proprietorship).

2. That employer must make a contribution to the S.E.P.P. on behalf of each employee who is twenty-five or older and who has worked for the employer during three of the last five years.

3. That employer's contribution can't discriminate in favor of employees who are "highly compensated." That means contributions, as a percentage of pay, can't be more (can't be a higher percentage) for officers, shareholders (who own more than 10 percent of the value of the corporation's stock), self-employed individuals, or "highly compensated" employees than for others. For example, if Sue Goldman, the owner of Skyfly Travel Agency, a sole proprietorship, wanted to set up an S.E.P.P. for herself, she would also have to include any of her employees who have three or more years of service. If she had no other employees, she could set up the S.E.P.P. just for herself.

A Tax Shelter for Everyone 165

4. The S.E.P.P. must be in writing and it must spell out any requirements for participation and how each employee's share is determined.

These rules make an S.E.P.P. an almost perfect retirement plan for the typical family or "Ma and Pa" business.

It all comes back to me now

The plans described in this chapter all have one thing in common. They involve the systematic process of setting monies aside that can be tax deductible, if you pay them, or not reportable as income, if an employer provides the annual consideration. The plans have to be "qualified," which means approved by the federal government in accordance with the criteria established for each plan. But deductions, however sweet they may be, are not an end in themselves. The real beauty of the tax shelters described in this chapter is that, when you are ready to stop working and realize the benefits you have in your plan, there is indeed a pot of gold at the end of the rainbow. You will then be able to receive and enjoy the benefits derived from the deductions you so eagerly took during your working years.

14.
Pay Later and Save Money

When a payout pays

One of the most common preconceived ideas about buying and selling property of any kind is that the parties to the transaction, or at least the seller, would be better off if the full price were paid in a lump-sum cash payment. While this method might be the best when buying something relatively inexpensive, there are more sophisticated ways that you should consider when selling property of significant value.

The "private annuity" offers amazing income tax and estate tax advantages, especially applicable to family transactions like transferring a home, undeveloped real estate, stocks, or a business interest. One of the all-time most popular tax planning tools is the "installment sale." One of the principal reasons for its success is that it offers tax advantages to both the buyer and seller. The seller can spread his gain on the sale of the property over the years in which the installments are paid, and of course it's much easier on the buyer's pocketbook to be able to spread payments out over a period of years, as opposed to coming up with a lump-sum initial payment.

Under Section 6166 of the Internal Revenue Code, your estate can obtain relief against the problems caused by the fact that federal estate taxes must be paid nine months after death. It gives estates in which a business interest constitutes a substantial asset an extremely liberal means of stretching out the payments of the federal estate tax.

Each specific method of payment described in this Chapter has its own rules and regulations. If properly utilized, they can greatly reduce taxes.

A public idea? (the private annuity)

A private annuity is an arrangement between two parties in which one, the transferor, conveys complete ownership of property to the other, the transferee. In return the transferee promises to make periodic payments to the transferor for some period of time—usually for the transferor's life or for the life of the transferor and his/her spouse.

Dr. Lew Savar used a private annuity. He bought land in West Chester, Pennsylvania, several years ago for $10,000. It's now worth $100,000. Lew wants to sell this property but would like to avoid a large capital gains tax. Lew is in the 50-percent income tax bracket. The private annuity will enable him to defer his gain and spread the tax over his entire lifetime. (In this respect the private annuity is similar to the installment sale discussed in this chapter.)

Milt Brown would like to retire and shift control of his business, M. S. Brown Jewelers, to one of his employees, Michael Stevens. He would like to sell the business to Michael and have him take over. But Milt is concerned about adequate income upon his retirement. Unfortunately, Michael can't afford to buy Milt's stock for a lump sum. But Milt could sell Michael his stock in return for Michael's promise to pay him an income he can never outlive no matter how long he lives. In fact, the arrangement could provide that the income will last for Milt's life and then for as long as his wife Sylvia lives. This "creates" a market for the business where there might not otherwise be one.

Sam Rabinowitz owns a large parcel of land in Bryn Mawr. It is appreciating rapidly and will probably be developed in the near future. Sam could sell the parcel to his married daughters in return for their agreement to pay him an income for life. This arrangement not only will provide Sam with an income but also will remove the value of the land from his estate at no gift tax cost. When Sam dies, the payments stop and nothing but the payments he's already received will be in Sam's estate.

Liz Browning is a widow who owns a large parcel of non-income-producing property left to her by her husband. She wants to increase her spendable income and reduce her dependence on her son, Frank, who is currently giving her $700 a month. Because of the choice location of the real estate, it is increasing substantially in value. Over the next ten years, it will probably double or triple in value. Frank could stop making gifts. Liz could transfer the real estate to him in return for his promise to pay her a monthly lifetime income. This removes the property from Liz's estate and therefore reduces estate taxes at her death. At the same time, it gives Liz financial independence (and frees the dollars she was using to pay real estate taxes on the property). Frank becomes the immediate owner of the real estate and all the growth in value for tax purposes occurs in his hands.

Dr. Lew Savar used the private annuity to reduce overall income taxes. Milt Brown used it to help an employee purchase his business interest. Sam Rabinowitz used the private annuity to remove property from his estate. Liz Browning used the private annuity to give her independence and make non-income-producing property productive (while keeping family land within the family). You might want to use a private annuity—for any or all of these purposes.

What will it take?

What kind of property should you have to make the private annuity idea work? Although it is possible to use any type of property, the best types of property for this purpose will be income-producing, non-depreciable, and not subject to indebtedness. Many people have transferred a home, undeveloped real estate, stocks, or a business interest in return for a private annuity.

More important than anything is the ability and the willingness of the transferee to make payments to the transferor. If the transferee has little or no income, then the property in question should be income-producing, or at least be a type that can easily be sold or used as collateral for a loan.

Down on the farm

At age sixty-five, Ed Stoeber felt that he had worked hard—and long enough. He owned farmland in Chester County worth $100,000, which he had bought thirty years ago for $10,000.

Ed wants his son Eric to have the land. Ed does not want to pay any gift taxes on the transfer. He would like to remove the farm from his estate.

Ed asked his attorney to draft a private annuity agreement. The agreement states that the farmland is sold to Ed's son, Eric, in return for his promise to pay Ed an income for life that he can never outlive. (It might also provide that the annuity was to continue for the life of Ed's wife, Joyce.)

Pay Later and Save Money

At age sixty-five, Ed's life expectancy is fifteen years. (See following table.)

The promise made by Eric to purchase property worth $100,000 in return for a lifetime annual payment would result in an obligation to pay his father $12,445 a year. Ed will be able to exclude a portion of that $12,445 from income each year. This is because he invested $10,000 in the property and he is entitled to recover his $10,000 cost, income tax free. The amount he can recover income tax free is found by dividing his $10,000 cost by his life expectancy, as shown by the following government table. A male age sixty-five is expected to live fifteen years. $10,000 ÷ 15 = $666. So out of each $12,445 that Ed receives, he can exclude $666 from income.

ORDINARY LIFE ANNUITIES—ONE LIFE— EXPECTED RETURN MULTIPLES

Ages Male	Female	Multiples	Ages Male	Female	Multiples
6	11	65.0	31	36	41.9
7	12	64.1	32	37	41.0
8	13	63.2	33	38	40.0
9	14	62.3	34	39	39.1
10	15	61.4	35	40	38.2
11	16	60.4	36	41	37.3
12	17	59.5	37	42	36.5
13	18	58.6	38	43	35.6
14	19	57.7	39	44	34.7
15	20	56.7	40	45	33.8
16	21	55.8	41	46	33.0
17	22	54.9	42	47	32.1
18	23	53.9	43	48	31.2
19	24	53.0	44	49	30.4
20	25	52.1	45	50	29.6
21	26	51.1	46	51	28.7
22	27	50.2	47	52	27.9
23	28	49.3	48	53	27.1
24	29	48.3	49	54	26.3
25	30	47.4	50	55	25.5
26	31	46.5	51	56	24.7
27	32	45.6	52	57	24.0
28	33	44.6	53	58	23.2
29	34	43.7	54	59	22.4
30	35	42.8	55	60	21.7

Ages		Multiples	Ages		Multiples
Male	Female		Male	Female	
56	61	21.0	84	89	6.0
57	62	20.3	85	90	5.7
58	63	19.6	86	91	5.4
59	64	18.9	87	92	5.1
60	65	18.2	88	93	4.8
61	66	17.5	89	94	4.5
62	67	16.9	90	95	4.2
63	68	16.2	91	96	4.0
64	69	15.6	92	97	3.7
65	70	15.0	93	98	3.5
66	71	14.4	94	99	3.3
67	72	13.8	95	100	3.1
68	73	13.2	96	101	2.9
69	74	12.6	97	102	2.7
70	75	12.1	98	103	2.5
71	76	11.6	99	104	2.3
72	77	11.0	100	105	2.1
73	78	10.5	101	106	1.9
74	79	10.1	102	107	1.7
75	80	9.6	103	108	1.5
76	81	9.1	104	109	1.3
77	82	8.7	105	110	1.2
78	83	8.3	106	111	1.0
79	84	7.8	107	112	.8
80	85	7.5	108	113	.7
81	86	7.1	109	114	.6
82	87	6.7	110	115	.5
83	88	6.3	111	116	.0

Ed must also pay capital gains tax on a portion of each payment he receives. Since he would have had a $90,000 capital gain had he sold the property for $100,000 ($100,000 minus $10,000 cost = $90,000 gain), he is allowed to apportion that capital gain over the fifteen-year life expectancy period—$90,000 ÷ 15 = $6,000. This means $6,000 of each year's payment will be long-term capital gain. If Ed lives longer than his fifteen-year life expectancy, the $6,000 becomes taxable as ordinary income.

The balance of each annual payment ($12,445 − $6,666) will be considered ordinary income ($5,779).

What's in and what's out

The big advantage of a private annuity is that it receives the property transferred from your estate immediately. This means that Ed, in the example above, has removed $100,000 of property and had no gift tax cost. If he dies the very next day, not one nickel of the $100,000 will be in his estate. Likewise, since his son, Eric, promised to pay to him as long as he lives—and only as long as he lives—Eric's obligation to continue the payments stops at his father's death. Therefore, nothing is in his estate because of this promise.

I never promised you a rose garden

There is a big disadvantage: The promise made to Ed by Eric can't be secured. Once the deal is made, Eric is the outright and absolute owner of the property. Ed becomes a general creditor and has to rely on Eric to make the payments he's said he'll make. For this and other reasons, the private annuity will be the "right" tool in very few estate planning situations (but where it is "right," it is very right!).

Why take your lumps? (installment sale)

Bob Cooper is a real estate investor who is about to retire. Bob just sold some land he's held for many years. His gain on the sale is $100,000, and he's in the 50-percent income tax bracket. On a long-term capital gain, tax is figured by first deducting 60 percent of the gain (here $60,000) and adding the balance ($40,000 in this example) to any other taxable income. At worst, that would expose $40,000 to a maximum 50-percent income tax rate. That means Bob will pay $20,000 in tax and have only $80,000 to use or invest. Bob has taken his lumps because he received a lump-sum payment all in one tax year.

Divide and conquer

Bob could have beaten the tax by dividing the gain and deferring part of it into more than one tax year. In other words, he could have taken the sales proceeds in installments. If he takes $50,000 of the gain this year and $50,000 the first week of next year, he'll only pay $10,000 in tax this year on the sale ($30,000, 60 percent of the $50,000 gain, is deductible; that means only $20,000 is exposed to tax at the 50% rate). Since, technically, Bob doesn't have to report the remaining $50,000 of gain until April fifteenth of the year after next, even if his tax liability is $10,000, he'll have that $10,000 to invest for more than a year before he has to pay it. If his income has dropped, the rate at which the other $50,000 of gain will be taxed also falls. For instance, if Bob is in the 30-percent tax bracket, before adding in the gain from the sale, the tax will be $6,000 ($50,000 gain − $30,000 deduction = $20,000, which is added to income and taxed at 30 percent: This results in a $6,000, not $10,000, tax, a savings of $4,000).

Who a payout pays

Many people should consider the installment sale. Essentially, the major ingredient is that the seller agrees to accept the purchase price in installments over a period of years (or agrees to accept no payment in the year of the sale and one or more payments in later years).

Who might find the installment sale concept advantageous?

(1) A person (or business) who wants to sell property to someone who may not have enough capital to buy the property overnight. Calvin Koolhedge was looking for a way to buy out his employer, Gene Arnold. Calvin couldn't pay Gene a lump sum, but in return for a higher price for his business Gene was willing to accept a long-term payout. In this respect, the installment sale can help create a market for property where none previously existed.

(2) Someone in a high income tax bracket who holds substantially appreciated securities or real estate can spread ordinary income or capital gains over the period of installments. That pro-rates the tax due and the seller (for instance, Bob Cooper in the example above) pays tax only as actual payments from the sale are received. This can make it possible to shift most of the reportable profit from a high-income (high tax) year to a year (or years) when the seller is in a lower bracket.

(3) Installment sales between family members provide a way to remove rapidly appreciating assets from the seller's estate. All the growth from the date of the sale is shifted to the family member who buys the asset.

Just how good is it?

Of all the tax planning tools discussed by attorneys and accountants, the installment sale is probably the most heavily and effectively used. Here's why:

The amount the seller receives in the year of the sale is entirely up to the seller and the buyer. Payments could be as little as nothing in the year of the sale or as much as everything but one dollar. This flexibility means that the seller of property can agree to accept payments at a time when it is more advantageous (or least disadvantageous). It's even possible for the parties to agree, for example, that the entire purchase price of a $10,000,000 parcel of land will be paid ten years after the sale, and that ten payments of interest will be made until then.

You don't have to elect installment sale treatment; it's automatic if you've agreed to accept at least one payment in a taxable year after the year in which the sale occurred.

Try the numbers

Monroe Berger sells property for $100,000. He paid $10,000 for it five years ago. He agrees to accept payments from the buyer, Hope Mitchell, in installments rather than in a lump sum. He'll receive payments of principal and interest spread out equally over a ten-year period. The sales agreement specifies that the buyer must pay 9 percent interest on the unpaid balance.

How do we figure how much Monroe (a) will receive each year, (b) can recover income tax free, (c) reports as long-term capital gain, and (d) declares as ordinary income?

The first step is to use the government table on page 174 and find the present value of a dollar payable once a year for ten years assuming a 9-percent return (6.90030).

(The parties to the agreement must provide for at least a 9-percent rate of return on the unpaid balance. Otherwise, the IRS will impute a 10-percent rate in computing the seller's income tax liability.)

By dividing 6.90030 into $100,000 (the assumed fair market value of the property being sold), you find the amount that Monroe will receive each year—$14,492.

How much can Monroe recover each year as a return on his $10,000 investment? To find the tax-free portion of each year's payment, the cost of the property sold is divided by the number of years of installments. The answer is $1,000 a year.

The potential gain ($90,000) is divided by the number of years of installments (ten). The capital gain—if the property had been sold for a lump-sum $100,000 payment—would have been $90,000 ($100,000 amount realized minus $10,000 cost). Since the install-

**PRESENT VALUE OF ANNUITY CERTAIN:
$1.00 EVERY 12 MONTHS**
(Applicable to Contracts Entered into
on or after September 29, 1980)

Number of years final payment deferred	Column A Present value at 9% simple interest	Column B Present value at 10% compounded semiannually
1	0.91743	0.90703
2	1.76489	1.72973
3	2.55229	2.47595
4	3.28758	3.15279
5	3.97724	3.76670
6	4.62659	4.32354
7	5.24009	4.82861
8	5.82149	5.28672
9	6.37398	5.70224
10	6.90030	6.07913
11	7.40281	6.42098
12	7.88358	6.73104
13	8.34441	7.01229
14	8.78689	7.26738
15	9.21242	7.49876
16	9.62226	7.70862
17	10.01752	7.89898
18	10.39920	8.07163

ment sale rules allow pro-rata reporting of gain, the $90,000 gain can be spread over ten years also. This means $9,000 a year is capital gain.

The total payment received less the sum of the tax-free recovery of capital and the capital gains portion is ordinary income. Since Monroe receives $14,490, recovers $1,000 a year tax free, and reports $9,000 of capital gain, only the difference, $4,492, is interest (reportable as ordinary income).

A word of warning

As is the case with every planning tool, the installment sale should be utilized only after consultation with both accounting and legal counsel. This caveat is particularly appropriate where the sale is to a related party, where the property is depreciable, where the buyer is a related party who plans to dispose of the property before completing the installment payouts, and where the property in question is mortgaged. All of these solutions may result in additional and unexpected adverse tax consequences.

An alternative to the installment sale as an income and estate tax savings device is the private annuity (previously discussed in this chapter).

Good as gold—or better? (installment payments of estate tax—Section 6166)

Let's say you've been financially successful beyond your wildest dreams. The little business you started so many years ago with a few thousand dollars of borrowed money is now a multi-million-dollar operation. Your children are rapidly learning the business and are enthusiastic about working with you.

There's only one problem. Your accountant or attorney or other financial advisor has shown you that at your death if the business is left to those children, substantial federal estate taxes would be payable. That's a big problem because you have little liquidity; there's just no cash to pay taxes—it's all been invested in the business.

"Don't worry" says one of your golf buddies. "I just heard that there's a section in the tax law that enables you to borrow money from the federal government to pay estate taxes. It's called Section 6166 and it can solve all your problems."

Is he right? The answer is yes—and no.

Yes, there is a Code Section 6166 and it does provide for installment payments of estate tax. No, Virginia, there is no Santa Claus in the tax law. All that glitters is not gelt.

6166 by the numbers

Section 6166 of the Internal Revenue Code provides relief against the general requirement that the federal estate tax must be paid in full (payment must be made in cash—no credit cards, stock certificates, or real estate deeds are acceptable) within nine months of death.

Under 6166, your executor—at his/her discretion—could elect to pay the federal estate tax attributable to your interest in a closely held business (sole proprietorship, partnership or corporation) in installments.

In fact, your executor doesn't pay any tax for the first four years after the tax becomes payable—just interest on the unpaid balance. For up to ten additional years, principal and interest are payable. That does stretch out the payments. But, there are requirements that must be met to qualify for this favorable treatment. They are: (1) the business must be included in your gross estate; (2) the value of your business interest must compose *more* than 35 percent of your adjusted gross estate.

If these tests are met, your executor can pay all or a portion of the estate tax in installments. The formula for determining how much can be paid in installments is:

$$\text{Net Federal Estate Tax Payable} \times \frac{\text{Value of Your Business Interest}}{\text{Adjusted Gross Estate}}$$

For instance, Ann Rigney's business is worth $600,000. Her estate—after adjusting for (subtracting) debts and expenses—is $1,000,000. Since her $600,000 business interest exceeds $350,000, 35 percent of her $1,000,000 adjusted gross estate, her executor is entitled to elect to pay estate taxes in installments.

Ann is single. She's leaving her entire estate to her friend, Barbara Kiley. Since the federal estate tax totals $236,000, Ann's executor could elect to pay $141,600 (60 percent of the $236,000) of federal estate taxes in installments:

$$\$236{,}000 \times \frac{\$600{,}000}{\$1{,}000{,}000} = \$141{,}600$$

Fool's gold

It is tempting to assume that the existence of Section 6166 means you don't need to plan and don't need to assure estate liquidity. It is true that Section 6166 is an excellent post-death tool that an estate's attorney should use if it applies and makes sense to use.

But it is foolish for you to think that Section 6166 makes it wise to ignore the need your estate will have for cash. Here's why:

First, Section 6166 only applies to active businesses. It doesn't apply to investments, no matter how profitable they may be. The income source you consider a business may be classified as an "asset holding company" rather than a trade or business. For instance, a one-hundred-room apartment house or $10,000,000 office building may not be treated as a business if you are merely supervising your capital, rather than performing substantial managerial services.

Second, your business may be worth 35 percent or less of your estate. In other words, your estate may flunk the mathematical "more than 35 percent" test.

Third, your estate may just barely meet the "more than 35 percent" test. Your business might constitute just slightly over 35 percent of your adjusted gross estate. Since 6166 only provides for installment payments of federal estate tax attributable to your business, 64 percent of the federal estate tax may have to be paid immediately. Section 6166 does not allow a deferral of the rest of the federal tax. That must be paid in cash—nine months after your death.

Fourth, only the federal estate tax is deferred; 6166 doesn't allow a deferral of state death taxes. Your executor will also need cash to pay funeral costs, debts, administration expenses and specific cash bequests to relatives, friends or charities.

Fifth, your estate has to remain open until the tax is paid. That's a nice way of saying that your beneficiaries can't be paid their full shares of your estate for many years. Can they do without? Will they want to wait? (Incidentally, the person you've named as executor is fully and personally liable for the tax while it is unpaid. Would you want to have that personal liability for over fourteen years?) Don't forget, if your business does not succeed without you and it has to be sold for an amount less than the unpaid tax, your executor may have to pay these taxes out of his own money.

Sixth, 6166 doesn't provide a source of funds; it merely delays the time payment is due. So you should ask yourself these questions: Where will your executor obtain the cash to pay both the tax and the interest? Will the corporation pay the estate (your estate will be the shareholder of your stock) dividends? Why isn't it paying dividends now? (Will a corporation that's just lost its key profit maker and is struggling to survive in the worst economic environment since the great Depression be able to pay dividends?) Can a portion of the business be sold by your executor? (If more than 50 percent of the business is sold, the unpaid tax becomes due and payable immediately.) Who would buy less than a controlling interest? What price would a minority interest bring? Would that be enough for your family? Would some other asset have to be sold to pay the tax and other immediately payable expenses?

Paradise lost?

Section 6166 is quite valuable in spite of the problems it poses. The trick is to have enough estate tax free life insurance (it could be owned by an irrevocable life insurance trust so that it wouldn't be taxed in your estate) so that when you die, the trustee of that trust can buy assets from your estate with the insurance proceeds. That gives your executor cash and shifts your assets to the trust for your children.

Your executor could pay taxes in installments under Section 6166 and invest the life insurance received from the sale of estate assets (there's no requirement that your executor has to "need" to use 6166).

To some extent, a very favorable 4-percent rate applies to the unpaid tax. But the amount of unpaid tax eligible for the 4-percent rate diminishes year by year as follows:

1982	1983	1984	1985	1986	1987
$283,000	$266,500	$249,500	$224,000	$190,000	$153,000

If the federal estate tax exceeds these amounts, a significantly higher interest rate is due on the unpaid balance. That rate will be the average bank prime rate (redetermined twice a year).

But there's a kicker! Interest on the unpaid tax is compounded daily. At a minimal rate of 15 percent, thanks to daily compounding, taxes and interest you owe the IRS can double in 4.6 years and triple in 7.3 years. The IRS will have "a financial time bomb" ticking away for it if there's a large sum of money involved.

The idea is to have income on the estate's investments exceed the interest and principal payments on the unpaid tax. This is possible if you purchase adequate amounts of life insurance, arrange it so that it will be estate tax free, and select an executor with investment expertise.

15.
Everybody Likes a Bargain

Here are a couple of ideas that are almost guaranteed money savers. "Interest free loans and low interest loans" are easy to set up, and each can reduce taxes. If you have children in college, be sure to read the section on "college bound through the reserve loan."

Flower Bonds are government bonds that enable you to discount your federal death taxes. It's a good section to read and keep in mind, for that time in the future when it might be indicated.

Why all the interest in interest free (and low interest) loans?

An interest free loan is nothing more complex than a loan of money to a party who is required to pay no interest on it. A low interest loan, as its name implies, is merely a loan to a party who will be charged much less than the "going rate" for similar loans from commercial institutions.

Interest free and low interest loans are commonly made by a corporation to an employee (check your state's law to see if an employee/shareholder is eligible) or from a parent to a child or between other family members.

Aside from the obvious economic advantage of such a loan, that is, the borrower's ability to use either the funds or the interest from the funds, interest free loans have substantial income, gift and estate tax advantages.

Is it good for you?

Who might want to use the interest free loan?

Sam Corey might make loans to his children and grandchildren to limit the growth of his cash assets and shift the income (which otherwise would have been subject to estate tax in his estate) to his children.

Kasey Reisman might use interest free loans in her corporation, Teddy Bear International, as an employee fringe benefit and incentive. Kasey's corporation could make low- or no-interest loans to executives and other key employees in order to help them buy a home, send a child to school, help pay extraordinary medical bills or even buy stock in the corporation.

Kelly Reisman, Kasey's sister and the president of the corporation, might use the corporation's interest free loan policy to help young Mel Green, the firm's comptroller, set up a significant life insurance plan. Interest free loans would be made by the corporation to Mel for three years. The loans would be enough for Mel to pay the net premiums on a policy for three years. During the next four years, the corporation would pay Mel an extra bonus sufficient (after he pays taxes on it) to pay premiums. In the eighth year, Mel could borrow enough money from the policy he owned to pay back the loan to the corporation. If he wanted to, Mel could then borrow—year after year—enough money from the policy's increasing cash values to pay premiums until he retires. So his only out-of-pocket cost would be interest payments on the policy loans, and they would be tax deductible.

Sonia Young, a highly successful insurance agent who is known throughout the South as the Purple Lady (she always wears purple), is in a 50-percent income tax bracket. She was looking for a way to send her daughter, Melanie, to college. By making an interest free loan to Melanie—say $100,000—Sonia shifted the income (and therefore the taxation) to Melanie's lower bracket. The $100,000 will earn $15,000 in either person's hands. But since the $15,000 would have been taxed on a 50-percent level in Sonia's hands ($7,500 tax), and in fact will be taxed at a much lower level in Melanie's hands (about $2,000 in tax), the family unit saves around $5,500 a year.

How do you do?

If you decide an intra-family interest free loan makes sense (and dollars), then:

1. The loan you make should be in writing.
2. You should maintain careful records of the debt as well as payments received.
3. You'll probably want to make the note a "demand" obligation so that you can call the note and recover your loan at any time.

4. If you've made a no-interest loan, the debt instrument should specify that no interest is payable.

5. A schedule of repayment should be established. The lender should demand repayment before the statute of limitations runs out (some states have time limits on the collection of a demand note). If the note is not demanded within that time, the "lender" may be making a taxable gift to the "borrower."

Where the loan is from a corporation:

1. There should be written evidence of the debt.
2. There should be a reasonable repayment schedule.
3. If the loan is to a shareholder, the terms of the loan should be strictly followed and repayments made on schedule to avoid an IRS claim that the loan was really a dividend in disguise and that the employee has currently taxable income in the amount of the loan.
4. The corporation should not borrow money to make the loan.
5. A resolution should be adopted by the corporation's board of directors authorizing the loan.
6. Security for the loan (other than a life insurance policy) should be signed.

Interesting yes—but taxing?

Courts have consistently stated that "if the lending or borrowing of an interest free loan is to become a taxable event, it is for Congress and not the courts to make it such." So if the transaction is in fact a loan and it is the intent that no interest be charged:

1. No gift is made by the lender since the gift law taxes only transfers of property. Interest free loans do not constitute taxable gifts. (The interest free use of money is not a transfer of property.)
2. The lender does not have reportable income (a taxpayer has no duty to earn a profit).
3. The borrower does not have taxable income (based on the "wash transaction" rationale that even if the taxpayer had borrowed money from some other source at a given interest rate, the interest would have been deductible when paid).
4. As income is earned by the funds, it is taxable to the borrower.

College bound through the reserve loan

Borrow money from your children. Pay them a high but

reasonable rate of interest. You can deduct the interest payments you make at your high bracket, and the interest you pay will be taxable to them at their relatively lower bracket.

Your children don't have any money? Make gifts to them. Then borrow the money.

For example, Sander Kurtz gives his daughter, Stacey, $100,000. He uses the annual exclusion ($10,000) to eliminate the gift tax on $10,000 of the $100,000. Because his wife, Arlene, splits the gift with him, Sander can give Stacey another $10,000 gift tax free. Even the $80,000 gift remaining (treated by the IRS as if it were $40,000 from Sander and $40,000 from Arlene) does not generate any tax since both spouses can use a portion of the unified gift/estate tax credit to offset the gifts.

Sander then borrows $100,000 back at 20 percent interest. He pays his daughter $20,000 in interest each year. At his 50-percent income tax bracket, that saves him $10,000 in income taxes. Stacey must report the $20,000 as income. Since she has little or no outside income, she'll only pay about $4,000 in tax.

To recapitulate, it cost Sander $10,000 in after tax income to pay the interest and it cost Stacey about $4,000 in income taxes to receive it. In total, the cost to shift $20,000 of income each year to Stacey is lowered to $14,000. That's a $6,000 a year income tax savings! In ten years, $60,000 is saved.

You are probably thinking that there's just one catch; you don't have $100,000. Borrow it! Go to a bank and borrow it. Give it to your donee (file a gift tax return). Then borrow it back. Repay the bank loan. Now your loan is from your children. A secondary benefit of this arrangement is that when you pay off the loan from your children (which you must do), you are removing assets from your estate and avoiding both estate and gift taxes. Both the interest and the payoff of the loan are in essence gift tax free gifts.

A word of caution

If you are making either gifts or loans to minors, the transfer should be made to a trust you have established for the child's benefit. This is because a minor cannot be legally bound to carry out the provisions of a contract entered into prior to majority. If you don't use a trust or custodial account (see Chapter 19 on the 2503[c] Trust and on Uniform Gifts to Minors Accounts), the IRS might consider the transaction a gift rather than a valid loan.

Demand a sample

Here's a sample of what a demand note for an interest free loan looks like. Keep in mind that, like any other important document, the actual instrument should be drafted by your attorney.

DEMAND NOTE FOR INTEREST-FREE LOAN

The undersigned, _____ as Trustee under the _____ minor's trust, dated _____ in consideration of a loan, for the amount of _____ ($_____) and bearing no interest charge, made by _____ to
          (GRANTOR)

_____ on _____ unconditionally
  (TRUSTEE)   (DATE)

agrees to repay the amount of _____ ($_____) to

_____ on demand.
  (GRANTOR)

                              _____
                                  TRUSTEE

A rose by any other name (Flower Bonds)

There are two ways to pay federal estate taxes at a discount. One way is through life insurance. That's *the* way to go if you are insurable. But if you are not insurable (most of us are), "Flower" Bonds are your answer.

Flower Bonds are called Flower Bonds because they "blossom." They are traded and can be bought at a deep discount (would you believe about seventy cents on the dollar?). The federal government will redeem them—buy them back—at one dollar on the dollar in payment of the federal estate tax.

Soft-peddling

You can buy Flower Bonds, which are actually U.S. government bonds, through bank trust departments. Flower Bonds are also available from stockbrokers.

The only requirements are that they must be bought while you are alive, and they must be owned by you at death. They must be purchased by you, or at your direction pursuant to an effective power of attorney (see Chapter 19). They can actually be bought at a discount on your deathbed.

There are thorns

John Dunn was riding westward when he became quite ill. He was told he had a fatal disease and had only a few months to live. His attorney told him that at his death a federal estate tax of about $200,000 would be due.

John quickly purchased a 3.5-percent 1990 series Flower Bond. The price he paid was 73.26; that is, he paid $732.60 for each $1,000. So he had to pay $146,520 (73.26 × 2,000) for $200,000 worth of bonds (redemption value).

At first glance, it appears that the "discount" is the difference between the $200,000 of taxes the federal government will accept the bonds in payment of and the $146,520 John paid. In other words, it seems as if John's estate has "made" $53,480 on the deal.

The catch (there is no free lunch in the tax law) is that the bonds are included in John's estate at their par value ($200,000 in this case) even though the day before John bought the bonds only $146,520 was in his estate. Since he's in a 37-percent estate tax bracket, 37 percent of $146,520, or $19,787 of the "discount," is lost. To add insult to tax injury, whether or not the bonds are actually used to pay the federal estate tax, to the extent they *could* be used to pay taxes, they must be included in John's estate at their par, and not their market, value.

Another cost is that the bonds generate a very low interest rate (3.5 percent in this example). This makes these bonds a foolish investment for any reason except the payment of federal estate taxes by someone who has a short time to live.

Stem too stern?

Not everyone has had—or has taken—the opportunity to do all the planning or purchase all the life insurance necessary for liquidity purposes.

Flower Bonds are the last-ditch tool, which should not be overlooked by the uninsurable.

16.
Specific Techniques for Eliminating or Reducing Taxes

This chapter covers in detail three specific ways that you can greatly reduce, and in some cases eliminate, taxes—mostly death taxes that will be imposed by the federal government at your death. The new tax law has changed the nature of the "marital deduction" by permitting a person to leave his/her entire estate to his/her spouse and pay no tax. But is this always the best course to take, and when, if ever, do you eventually have to pay the piper? How the marital deduction trust works is a very important chapter for anyone whose total estate, including the proceeds of life insurance, fringe benefits, and all other property, will exceed $270,000.

Are you interested in keeping all of the proceeds of insurance on your life, as well as other assets, completely estate tax free to your children when you and your spouse both die? If so, the inter vivos living trust, or "super" trust, should be of interest to you. In the section on "disclaimers," you can learn how sometimes it's best to refuse to accept property that has been left to you by someone else. It may be hard to believe, but the mere act of refusing to accept property (if done properly) can in itself constitute estate planning.

Last of the red-hot bargains (the marital deduction trust)

Of all the deductions allowed by the estate tax law, the single most important allowed to a married couple is the "marital deduction." This is a deduction you are allowed on the net value (gross value less indebtedness) of property you leave to your spouse. This deduction is unlimited. That means you could leave up to your entire estate to your spouse and pay no federal estate tax.

To take an extreme example, Barry Kohn could leave his wife,

Alice, his entire $50,000,000 estate. Because of the unlimited marital deduction, no federal estate tax will be due at Barry's death. (Most states do not have a marital deduction so there probably would be a state death tax to pay). If Barry's estate did not qualify for a federal estate tax marital deduction and had to pay tax on the $50,000,000, the tax would be almost $25,000,000.

There is no free lunch in the tax law, of course. Sooner or later the feds will come to collect. If Alice doesn't give the money away (she'll pay gift taxes on larger gifts) or use it up (perhaps in some cases the best estate planning of all), the $50,000,000 will be taxed in Alice's estate. The point is that the marital deduction does not, per se, eliminate the estate tax. But it does delay it until the surviving spouse dies. The longer your surviving spouse lives, the longer the tax is delayed (and the greater her opportunity to give property away tax free using the annual $10,000 per donee gift tax exclusion).

Not everyone has an estate of $50,000,000. But almost everyone can benefit a surviving spouse by delaying the impact of the federal estate tax through the marital deduction. The use of the tax dollars otherwise payable can provide significant financial security.

There is one very important factor you should know about the unlimited marital deduction. Many wills drawn before September 13, 1981, will not allow your estate to qualify. If your will is one of those, your estate's deduction may be limited to the greater of (a) $250,000 or (b) half your adjusted gross estate. Because thousands of estate tax dollars may be at stake, it makes sense to have your attorney make an immediate review of your will and trust.

There are many ways to qualify for the marital deduction. Most of them involve leaving property to your spouse outright or in a manner tantamount to outright.

For instance, if Don Wilson names his wife as the sole beneficiary of a $100,000 life insurance policy on his life, his executor can deduct the entire $100,000 and pay no federal estate tax on it. Bob Krauss and his wife, Arlene, own their $300,000 home jointly. The estate tax law requires $150,000 of that to be included in Bob's estate if he dies first. But since Arlene becomes the sole owner at Bob's death, and therefore owns the house outright, Bob's executor can take a marital deduction for the includable $150,000 and pay no estate tax on the house.

Why trust a trust?

Bob's wife, Arlene, in the example above, may not want,

Specific Techniques for Eliminating or Reducing Taxes

or be able to handle large sums of money. So Bob would like to have his probate estate, the assets that will pass under his will, go into a trust that will provide management and investment expertise for Arlene. Yet Bob would like to qualify those assets for the marital deduction. How does he do it?

There are several ways Bob can obtain the investment and management benefits of a trust and at the same time pass assets to Arlene federal estate tax free. The most commonly used is the "marital deduction" trust, a trust designed specifically to obtain the federal estate tax marital deduction.

Actually, most attorneys will probably draft at least two trusts, a marital deduction trust and a "nonmarital" trust. Assets that go into the marital trust will be in the surviving spouse's estate when she dies, while assets that go into the nonmarital trust will not be taxed when the surviving spouse dies. Here's a diagram of how it looks.

ESTATE OWNER'S ASSETS

"Nonmarital Trust"	*"Marital Trust"*
"My spouse is to receive all the income from this trust, but at her death, all the assets to go to my children."	"My spouse is to receive all the income from this trust. Additionally, she can take all the trust assets whenever she desires or leave all the assets to anyone she names in her will."
Assets in this trust are not in the surviving spouse's estate and therefore are not taxed when the spouse dies.	Assets in this trust *are* taxed when the surviving spouse dies.

You may be wondering why a "nonmarital" trust is needed or what goes into it if you can leave your entire estate to your spouse and pay no estate tax. The answer has to do with the credit that every person's estate is allowed.

This so-called "unified" credit allows each of us to leave substantial assets to anyone we'd like and pay no federal estate tax. In 1987, the credit will be equivalent to an exemption of $600,000. So what?

Let's say you die in 1987 and your estate, after paying expenses and debts, totals $800,000. Let's say your spouse has assets of

$50,000. If you leave everything to your spouse, there will be no tax on your estate because of the unlimited marital deduction. But when your spouse dies, your $800,000 will be added to her $50,000 (a total taxable estate of $850,000). Fortunately, since your spouse is allowed a credit that is equivalent to a $600,000 exemption (assuming she dies in 1987 or in a later year), only $250,000 will be taxed ($850,000 less $600,000). The tax on $250,000 is $70,800. But by not using *your* credit, you wasted it.

Assume, instead of leaving everything to your spouse, you set aside $600,000 and put that into the nonmarital trust. Estate planners call this a "zero tax" marital deduction because an amount equal to the credit equivalent in the year of your death is held back, and will not be taxed at your spouse's death. The rest of your estate, $200,000, goes to your spouse. The objective is to reduce total taxes in both estates to zero—or as close to zero as possible. (Remember, this nonmarital trust is the trust that bypasses taxation in your spouse's estate.) Since the $600,000 is not going to your spouse, it doesn't qualify for the marital deduction. So it's technically taxable. But the entire $600,000 is then exempted from tax because of the credit. You pay no tax on this amount. The remaining $200,000 goes to the marital trust for your spouse. There's no tax to be paid at your death on that $200,000 because of the marital deduction.

When your spouse dies, that $200,000 plus the $50,000 of his or her assets is exposed to tax. But now his or her $600,000 exemption shields that entire $250,000 amount. There's no tax at the death of your spouse.

The Bottom Line?

	"All to Spouse"	"Zero Tax" Formula
Tax at first spouse's death	—0—	—0—
Tax at second spouse's death	$70,800	—0—
Total Tax	$70,800	$ —0—

Savings with the "Zero Tax" Formula
$70,800

This potential saving is another reason you may want to have your attorney review your will. Wills and trusts drawn prior to September 13, 1981, are unlikely to have a "Zero Tax" marital deduction formula.

P.O.A. versus Q.T.I.P.—what's it mean?

A third reason to discuss estate planning with your attorney if your will was drawn before September 13, 1981, is the "Q.T.I.P." trust.

Before we explain what a Q.T.I.P. trust is, let's go back and examine how the marital trust generally works:

Tax law allows property you leave in trust to qualify for the marital deduction—if (and only if) the trust meets certain requirements. The key ingredients for success are:

1. Your spouse must be entitled to all of the income produced by trust assets; and

2. Your spouse must be given a "general power of appointment." What that means is that your spouse must have the right to take everything in the trust (if you've given her a lifetime "power of appointment"—that is, the right during her lifetime to name anyone she wants as the recipient of trust assets, including herself or her creditors) or to name in her will the ultimate recipient of whatever property you've placed into the trust (if you've given her a "testamentary power of appointment").

A trust that meets these requirements is called a General Power of Appointment (GPOA) trust.

There's one big problem with the GPOA trust; if your spouse remarries, her second husband (and eventually his children) may end up with the assets you've left to this trust (possibly to the exclusion of your own children).

How? First, your wife could give him or leave him that property. She has the right to do so. But even if she doesn't, he—or his children—may end up with it anyway. The reason is that most state laws give a surviving spouse a "right of election," a right to take a specified portion of your estate regardless of what your will says. Say your wife left all her property—including the property you left her in the marital trust—to your three children. A second husband could elect against that will and end up (in most states) with at least the amount he'd have received if she died "intestate," that is, without a valid will.

That's where the Q.T.I.P. (Qualified Terminable Interest Property) trust comes in. Prior to 1982, if you left property to your spouse for life and then to your children, you'd get no marital deduction unless you also gave your spouse a general power of appointment. You had a Hobson's choice—you could be sure your children would get the property by saying that your wife was to get the income from the trust property, but at her death the principal was to go to your children. But you'd lose the marital deduction. In other words, a large amount of federal tax would be payable when you died. Alternatively, you could be sure of getting the marital deduction by adding a power for your wife to appoint (direct who gets) trust principal—but then you couldn't be sure it would go to your children.

Current tax law provides a way to meet both objectives—obtain the marital deduction and be sure your children will receive your assets. This way is through the Q.T.I.P. trust.

How does the Q.T.I.P. trust work? Actually, it's essentially the same as the nonmarital trust described above that gives your spouse income for as long as she lives and then passes trust assets to your children (or whoever else you pick). The big difference is, if it's a Q.T.I.P. trust, your executor can then elect to have this trust qualify for the marital deduction.

Where's the catch? It all seems too simple. Well, there is a cost. Your executor has to agree to have the Q.T.I.P. trust property taxed in your wife's estate when she dies—even though she doesn't get the property—or have the right to say who gets it when she dies. But it may be well worth the cost since your spouse may live and enjoy trust income (and principal) for many years. You can be sure that at your spouse's death whatever is left after taxes are paid will go to your children or other parties you have specified.

Options—old and new

The two illustrations opposite compare marital deduction planning strategy before and after January 1, 1982.

Pre-1982 planning typically assumed that life insurance, death benefits from qualified retirement plans, cash, any business interest not subject to a buy/sell agreement, and securities would pass by will (after payment of expenses and taxes) to a revocable trust.

The revocable trust may have been established during lifetime (an "inter vivos" trust) or may be a "testamentary" trust (one created by an individual's will).

Assets would be apportioned according to a formula that would pass one-half of the estate owner's property (after taking into account jointly owned and other property automatically passing to the surviving spouse) to the so-called "marital" trust. Because of the marital deduction, assets passing to this trust would not be subject

PRE-1982 PLANNING. (50–50 or ½ + ½)

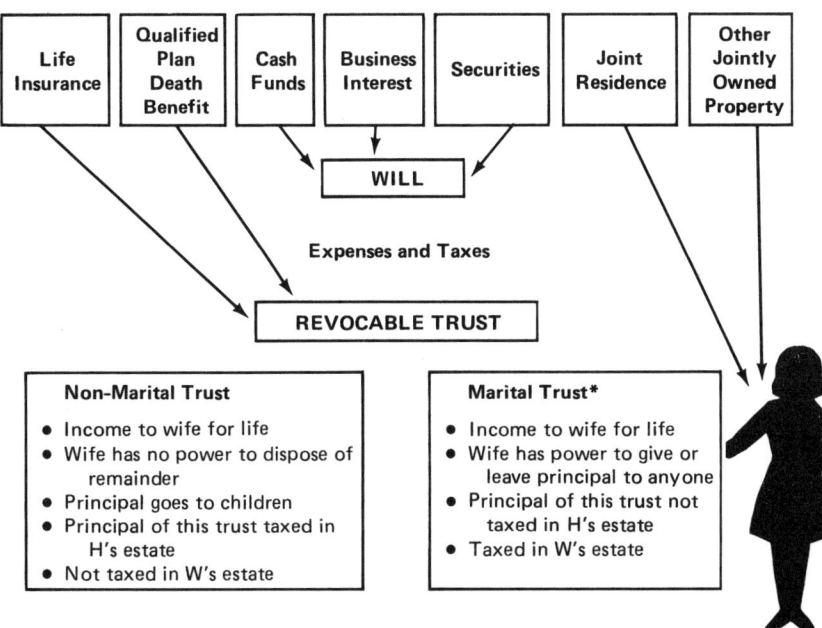

Advantages:
1. Management and investment provided for spouse.
2. Best tax planning prior to January 1, 1982.

Disadvantages:
1. Surviving spouse might leave one-half of estate to a future husband, to children of a different marriage, or to a favorite charity. Problem for remarrieds.

*If wife predeceases husband, the marital deduction is lost.

PLANNING OPTIONS AVAILABLE ON OR AFTER JANUARY 1, 1982

The marital deduction bequest to the spouse can now be:

A	B	C	D
	Traditional		Non-qualified
Outright	Marital Trust	Q.T.I.P. Trust	Trust
via	• Income to wife for life	• Income to wife for life	• Income to wife for life
• Simple Will	• Wife has power to dispose of principal during lifetime or at her death to anyone	• Remainder to children (or other party specified by husband)	• Remainder to children
• Joint Ownership		• Wife has no power to dispose of principal at her death	• Wife has no power to dispose of principal at her death
• Direct Beneficiary			

to federal estate tax in the estate owner's estate, but would be subject to tax when the surviving spouse died. The reason was that the wife would be given a "general power of appointment" over assets in the trust. In other words, she could take the assets herself at her whim or give or leave them to anyone she desired (almost as if she had outright ownership of those assets). This marital deduction trust was often called an "A" trust because the first provision in the trust document established it.

The second trust, the "B" or "non-marital" trust, also provided the surviving spouse with income for life, but gave the spouse no power to decide who would receive the principal at her death. The "remainderman" of the non-marital trust was selected by the estate owner. Assets going into the non-marital trust at the surviving spouse's death will be taxed when the estate owner dies (because assets passing into this type of trust will not qualify for the marital deduction), but are not taxed when the surviving spouse dies. For this reason, the non-marital trust was often called the "bypass" trust, since assets in it would bypass taxation in the surviving spouse's estate.

This "50–50" arrangement provided investment and management expertise for the surviving spouse and at the same time was the best tax planning available prior to January of 1982.

Unfortunately, assets in the marital trust were subject to the survivor's absolute power of disposal. That meant that property the estate owner might have wanted to go to his children could (and often would) go to children of the next marriage partner of the surviving spouse, or to a friend or favorite charity of the surviving spouse. There was no way the estate owner could be sure his (or her) dispositive desires would be met.

On or after January 1, 1982, there is much greater flexibility. It is now possible to leave tax free *any* percentage of your estate to your surviving spouse. Depending on your objectives and the size of your estate, you could leave your spouse everything, nothing, half, an amount designed to minimize or eliminate the tax in both your estate and your spouse's (the so-called "zero tax" marital deduction formula), or you could leave your estate in any other proportion you desire. All or most of it can pass tax free if you are married at the time of your death.

Better yet, you can still qualify for that zero-percent to 100-percent marital deduction by leaving property to your spouse outright (by will, joint ownership or as the beneficiary of life insur-

Specific Techniques for Eliminating or Reducing Taxes

ance), under the traditional marital deduction trust, or through the new Q.T.I.P. trust (deductible when you die—taxable at your spouse's death even though you pick the eventual recipients of this trust's property).

You could—to any extent you choose—decide to pay an "upfront" tax. That is, you could decide to take no marital deduction (and therefore pay tax) when you die in return for being certain the property will go to the party you have selected at your spouse's death and the assurance that the assets in this trust will bypass taxation in your survivor's estate.

Which course of action you select will depend on a number of factors your attorney, accountant and other financial advisors should discuss with you.

The inter vivos (living) trust

Barney Able was looking for a method that would help him provide for his wife, Aileen, and their children, yet reduce his estate and income tax as much as possible. His lawyer, Charles Bass, told him he could accomplish all he wanted to do if he would set up an irrevocable living trust.

Why would anyone want to set up a trust that couldn't be changed—that was irrevocable? Because, with an irrevocable trust, you can do many of the things a revocable trust can do but you can also make very significant income or estate tax savings possible.

Barney's beneficiary, the person for whose benefit the trust was created and who will receive the benefit of trust income or principal, is his wife.

In many trusts, there are two types of beneficiary; an income beneficiary and a remainderman. For instance, Barney could have named his wife, Aileen, as income beneficiary. The trust could provide that she was to receive the income from trust property for her life or for a fixed period of years or until a given event occurred.

Another type of beneficiary is the "remainderman." Barney could have provided that his son, Brad, and daughter, Allison, were to ultimately receive the assets in the trust at Barney's wife's death. They would receive what remains at Aileen's death.

Life or death?

Barney could put the trust into effect during his lifetime, in which case it would be called a "living" (inter vivos) trust. Alternatively, the trust could take effect at his death. In that case, his will would create the trust relationship and it would be called a "testamentary" trust.

String along

Barney could decide to keep a string on his trust so that at his whim he could revoke it, change its terms or regain ownership of the property in the trust. In that case, Barney has created a "revocable" trust. Most trusts are revocable so that the grantor can change both his mind and the terms—or beneficiaries—of the trust. Alternatively, Barney could set up the trust without retaining the ability to alter, amend, revoke or terminate it. He might decide to make a revocable trust irrevocable by cutting these strings.

It's super

Some estate planners have nicknamed the irrevocable trust the "supertrust," it's that good. Here's why.

No matter what's in the trust, it wouldn't be in Barney's estate—if he's willing to give up the right to:

1. any income provided by trust assets;
2. use or enjoy the trust property;
3. name new trust beneficiaries, or change the ones he's already named;
4. get trust property back;
5. alter, amend, revoke or terminate the trust.

That means that even if the trust holds a $1,000,000 policy on his life, none of the insurance—or any other trust assets—will be taxed in Barney's estate when he dies. This "supertrust" can even be set up so that there's no tax when Barney's wife, Aileen, dies. That way the insurance proceeds and other assets avoid federal and state tax in two estates and pass to Barney's children intact.

Perhaps an even better advantage of this "supertrust" is that the income produced by any property placed in the trust wouldn't be taxed to Barney as long as he doesn't retain the power to say who will enjoy trust principal or income; and trust income:

1. isn't paid to Barney or his wife; or
2. wouldn't be accumulated for later distribution to Barney or his wife; or
3. can't be used to pay premiums for a policy on Barney's life or on his wife's life; or
4. isn't used to support someone Barney is legally obligated to support; or

Specific Techniques for Eliminating or Reducing Taxes

5. isn't used to discharge Barney's legal obligations.

So who is taxed on trust income if Barney isn't? Simple. If a beneficiary receives (or has the right to receive) income, that person is taxed on it. If the trust accumulates income, it's taxed on it. Eventually, when that accumulated income is distributed to the beneficiary, that person is taxed on it but receives credit for the taxes the trust paid.

No free lunch

One of the primary laws of tax planning is "there's no free lunch in the tax law." This is true even when using the "supertrust."

When Barney puts mutual funds, cash, life insurance, or other property into a supertrust, because he's giving up dominion and control over these assets, he's making a gift for tax purposes.

If the gift is large enough Barney will have to pay a gift tax. Fortunately, the supertrust can be drafted in such a way that all or most of the gift is excluded from the federal gift tax. Estate planners call this a trust with a "Crummey power."

No, Crummey doesn't mean "bad." Just the opposite. It's named after the Clifford Crummey case, in which an annual gift tax exclusion was allowed to a taxpayer for gifts to a trust that allowed the beneficiary to make limited withdrawals each year. Barney can give his beneficiary the right to take out the greater of $5,000 or 5 percent of the assets in the trust each year. But it's a "use it or lose it" right; it's non-cumulative, so if the beneficiary never exercises the right to make withdrawals and lets his right go (which is what you are counting on), money Barney puts into the trust can be used to pay premiums on a life insurance policy on Barney's or his wife's life. Since the money being used is capital and not income, there are no income tax problems.

One last tax implication; if Barney transfers appreciated property to an irrevocable trust and that property is sold by the trust within two years, the trust pays the tax on it—but at Barney's bracket. For instance, if Barney bought land in Wildwood for $1,000 an acre and transferred it to the trust when it was worth $10,000 an acre, he doesn't pay tax on any gain. But if the trust sells the land within the next two years, any gain it realizes is taxed to it at the same rates it would have been taxed at if Barney personally had sold it. If Barney is in a 50-percent tax bracket and the trust is in a much lower bracket it might pay to wait until more than two years have passed before the trust sells the land.

What happens next?

Does this irrevocable supertrust help in estate planning? Absolutely. Not only does it save income and estate taxes but it also can be used to provide estate liquidity to help pay estate settlement costs.

The simplest way is for the trust, once it receives the insurance proceeds on Barney's life, to use those dollars to purchase assets (such as stock or land) in Barney's estate from Barney's executor. That gives the estate cash to pay taxes and other expenses and keeps key assets inside the trust for the benefit of Barney's children (but outside of Barney's estate).

An alternative is for the trustee to lend Barney's executor enough cash to pay immediate expenses.

Learning to say no (disclaimers)

A disclaimer is a refusal to accept property that has been left to you by someone else. It's a renunciation of your right as a beneficiary to take cash or other assets. Now who would do a thing like that—and why?

Let's say you were the first in a succession of heirs under your uncle Charlie's will.

You might say "no" to money or property you could otherwise have if you were a person with more than adequate income, a modest standard of living, and a large estate of your own. If you knew accepting the property would mean these assets would be added to the ones you already have and therefore compound your potential estate tax problems, you might disclaim the bequest so that by default your daughter, the next recipient under Uncle Charlie's will, would receive the property. That way the asset would go directly from Uncle Charlie's estate to your daughter and at your death the property wouldn't be taxed in your estate.

You might say "no" if you were in a high income tax bracket and you wanted your son in college to have both income and financial security, and he was next in line after you in Uncle Charlie's will.

Or you might say "no" if your father left property to you instead of to your mother, who was named as the residual (take everything that's left) beneficiary under his will. By disclaiming your interest, not only do you shift the property to your mother—gift tax free—but you also enable your father's estate to qualify for the federal estate tax marital deduction. That might wipe out the federal tax entirely. Your mother could then make a substantial gift to you—gift tax free, and the amount you'd retain would be enhanced with the significant estate tax savings.

What you have to do to disclaim

There are five major requirements that must be met for a disclaimer to be effective for tax purposes. You have to:

1. Make an irrevocable and unqualified refusal to accept the property;
2. Make that refusal in writing;
3. Have the refusal in the hands of your benefactor's executor or other legal representative within nine months of the date on which you reach age twenty-one, or if later, within nine months of your benefactor's death (or if you are receiving the gift under a trust set up during your benefactor's lifetime, within nine months of the time the property is placed into the trust for your benefit);
4. Make your disclaimer before accepting the property or income produced by it; and
5. The property must pass to the next person without any direction on your part (you can't say who is to receive the property when you disclaim).

Tax-imp-lications

Burke Christenson, a highly successful business owner, has four children. Under the terms of Burke's late Aunt Katherine's will, he is to receive her entire estate if he survives her. If he does not, her will provides that Burke's four children are to receive the estate in equal shares. By making an effective disclaimer, Burke will be treated for tax purposes as if he had predeceased his aunt. That would result in her estate being divided into four equal shares and distributed to Burke's children. Knowing that his children were financially secure, Burke could spend and enjoy his own fortune more freely.

Burke's disclaimer is not treated as a gift for gift tax purposes. The property he had refused to accept will not be in his estate for federal estate tax purposes. Once Aunt Katherine's property has been disclaimed, any income produced by it is taxed to Burke's low-bracket children rather than to Burke himself at his high income tax bracket.

17.
If You Work for a Living

Keep up with the fringes

If you work for a living, that is, work for someone else, then you may not have the opportunity to form your own corporation, set up your own pension plan, HR-10 plan, or group life insurance and health plan. That's too bad. However, chances are that you have a compensation package where you work that may include a pension or profit sharing plan, group life insurance, health insurance and other benefits—and that's terrific. In fact, your company benefits can help to provide a substantial part of your future financial security.

The fact is that the small employer or self-employed individual is, by utilizing the various programs discussed in this book, only trying to equalize his or her position with that of the employee who is already receiving these benefits from his employer. And while the employee of a large corporation does not have the flexibility to tailor plans specifically to his/her own needs, neither does he/she have the financial responsibility to make certain that these plans are properly funded.

Why are some of these plans so beneficial? In part, because they force you to do what you might not otherwise do. They put you on your own payroll by allocating part of the remuneration you might otherwise receive for your work, in the form of a contribution to a pension or profit-sharing plan, which money will accumulate tax-free for you—or by buying life insurance for you, or by asking you to save money in a plan in which they agree to match your contribution dollar for dollar up to a certain level.

Would you like it with, or without?

Shirley Simpson got started on her career a little late in life. After raising two children and obtaining a divorce from her husband of fifteen years, she went back to college in order to get a better job. Now in her late thirties, she has several job offers to consider. Because of her personal situation, Shirley is extremely interested in obtaining the best overall compensation package available. Although money for day-to-day expenses must be her top priority, she is also concerned about her future security. Shirley has two offers that she is seriously considering. The first is with Barney Ringle, a very successful manufacturer's representative, who feels that Shirley's credentials will make her valuable to him as an administrative assistant. Barney represents several quality toy manufacturers and has offered Shirley an excellent starting salary. Shirley likes Barney, and especially likes the money she can make working for him. But she is concerned because Barney has no benefits to offer her, and also because Barney has only been in business for two years.

Her other employment offer was from a medium-sized corporation, which would like Shirley to be the administrative assistant in one of its departments. The company has a long and stable history, and good prospects to continue to do well in the future. That corporation has offered Shirley a starting salary that is several thousand dollars less than the one offered by Barney, but the complete compensation package that Shirley will receive in addition to the salary includes a pension plan and group life, health and disability benefits. Confused as to which offer to accept, Shirley talks to her friend and accountant, Marty Spivak. Marty reviews with Shirley the information on the pension plan that the company supplied to her. Marty explains that this is a non-contributory plan, which means that Shirley does not have to contribute any of her salary to the plan. She also does not have to report as income on her tax returns the monies that the company puts into the pension plan for her. Marty estimates for Shirley the amount she could receive at age sixty-five, if she chose to retire, based on her present salary and also assuming that she receives periodic raises. Of course, these figures aren't exact, but they give an indication of the value of the plan to Shirley. Marty explains the "vesting" provisions of the plan to Shirley. Companies have different vesting schedules, subject to the limitations of federal law. These schedules indicate how much of the assets in

Shirley's plan she has the absolute right to take if she leaves the company. Shirley's plan schedule indicates that Shirley has to work ten years to have the right to keep all of the monies in the plan, regardless of whether she is still working for the company at retirement age. If Shirley leaves the company before ten years, then only a certain percentage of the monies deposited each year by the company will be available to Shirley, either to take at the time she leaves the company (subject to taxation), or to hold until retirement. The plan also contains a life insurance feature, and if Shirley dies these insurance benefits will be available to her children. Marty explains that the interest earned on the monies set aside for her are not taxed until she begins receiving benefits. Marty also explains the special tax rules (explained in Chapter 13—Pensions, Profit-Sharing Plans) that Shirley can use at retirement to spread the tax out. Marty estimates that the plan is worth at least $950 a year to Shirley.

Marty also reviews with Shirley the insurance package. Shirley must have medical insurance on herself and her children, which would cost an estimated $600 a year. This is provided for Shirley by the company, in a group plan that is more comprehensive than the one Shirley could buy as an individual. The group life insurance offered by the plan permits Shirley to buy extra insurance if she wants to, and the total cost to Shirley is less than if she were to purchase it on her own. In addition, the plan provides disability coverage for Shirley that would continue her income if she became disabled. Shirley would like this coverage, but if it were not offered by her employer she feels she could not otherwise afford it.

Shirley's decision, after her discussion with Marty, was that the company benefits plus the salary were equal to the salary offered by Barney Ringle, but in addition provided her with the security that she wanted for her own future, and also for her children in the event of her death.

Dollar for dollar
Some companies offer thrift plans or qualified savings plans to their employees. Employees authorize the company to deduct a certain percentage of their salary to be placed in a qualified savings type plan. The amount put into the plan can be placed in various investments such as common stock or life insurance annuities, or in a fixed plan with a guaranteed interest rate. As an employee, you may often be able to choose the type of investment

you prefer, depending on whether you wish a guaranteed return or the flexibility of an equity type (hedge against inflation) investment. After determining the percentage of your salary to be put into the plan, the corporation agrees to match your contribution, dollar for dollar, up to a given percentage. The same rules apply for vesting, in regard to the contributions made by the company only. You are always permitted to get back any contribution you make to any qualified plan when you leave your employer, regardless of the reasons for terminating your employment.

Steve Parker works for the Acme Computer Company, which has a qualified savings plan. Steve elects to have the maximum amount available deducted from his salary, which under his plan is 10 percent. From his salary of $30,000, the company pays $3,000 a year into the plan, rather than to Steve in the form of salary. The plan provides that the company will match Steve's contribution to the plan dollar for dollar, up to 3 percent. Therefore, on Steve's salary of $30,000 the company contributed $900 to the plan. Not only is Steve investing $3,000 in the plan, with interest on his savings accumulating tax free, but in addition he immediately receives a "bonus" of $900 from the company—an added feature that makes this a very worthwhile investment.

All of us together

Many large companies offer group insurance to their employees in the form of life, health and disability. The group life insurance usually takes the form of term insurance, and is purchased by the employer on a group basis from an insurance company. Premiums for the insurance are determined on an overall basis by the age composition of the employee group in the plan, with factors being added if the work performed is considered by the insurance company to be more or less risky than usual. Is this group insurance a good deal? In most cases, yes, but there are exceptions. For the younger employees it might be cheaper and safer in the long run to obtain their own coverage because group rates are averaged out. If your plan requires you to contribute toward the cost of the insurance, you should check with your own agent to see if it would be better for you to purchase the insurance on your own. That way you would always own the policy, and whether or not you terminated your employment, the insurance protection would remain. Group life policies are usually convertible within thirty days if you terminate your employment, but they are convertible at the age you are when you leave the company and usually only to a whole life policy. The cost may therefore be quite high at that time because of your age.

Of course, if you do not have to contribute toward the cost of the coverage, you should take all you can get. Or, if you feel it advisable to purchase your own insurance and also keep the group insurance, this might be the best solution.

An option worth thinking about

One fringe benefit not always available to all employees, but a popular one, is the stock option. A stock option is a right to buy stock in the company you work for within a certain period of time, and at a fixed price, regardless of what the stock is selling for at the time the option can be exercised. In the past, there were many restrictions imposed by the government in regard to these stock options, but the Economic Recovery Tax Act of 1981 has restored more favorable tax treatment to them. However, the details of each plan must be carefully reviewed with your tax advisor before you make a decision to exercise the option.

Specifically, the new tax law introduces the "incentive stock option." It works like this—Amy is an executive of a large chemical company. She is granted an incentive option to purchase ten shares of the company stock at $10 per share on March 15, 1984. If she exercises her option and buys the stock on March 15 when its value is $12 a share, and sells the stock when it is worth $15 a share, the gain will be long-term capital gain if she sells the stock at least a year after it was transferred to her.

Social security

One of the fringe benefits that almost everybody has is social security. While social security cannot provide you and your family with a completely secure financial future, it can provide a floor of protection upon which to build for economic independence. Since you are paying for it, you should know what benefits you and your family can expect to receive, or at least hope to receive if the system remains financially sound.

You pay social security taxes during your working years, which are pooled into special trust funds, but not earmarked specifically for you and your family. Benefits are then paid on your retirement, at your death, or in the event of disability. Part of the contributions you make go into a separate hospital insurance trust fund to provide coverage for hospital bills, which we know more familiarly by the name "Medicare."

Social security, even more emphatically than your other insurance benefits, forces you to accept its benefits by its non-voluntary nature. If you work in a covered employment, you must participate and pay your social security (FICA) taxes. You cannot "borrow" against your future benefits, so that you can be certain that, if the system survives, it will provide retirement benefits to you for the rest of your life. These benefits will begin with the date you elect to retire (which depends, of course, on the date on which the plan will permit you to retire).

The basic retirement benefits will provide a monthly income starting at age sixty-five (or whatever age is elected and then in effect) for the rest of your life. The amount of the monthly benefits will be determined by a formula based on your average monthly wage over your working years. The amount of benefits you will receive from social security and the contributions you make to the plan are constantly changing. Updated schedules can be obtained from the social security office, or your insurance representative.

Wives are also entitled to benefits equal to a percentage of their husband's income depending on their age—or a "mother's benefit" if the wife has dependent and unmarried children under age eighteen. Unmarried children under age eighteen, or under twenty-two if a full-time student, are entitled to benefits equal to 50 percent of retirement benefits. In certain cases, husbands of working women drawing primary retirement benefits are also eligible on the same basis as the wife would be. There are specific rules as to the amount of time you must have worked and contributed to social security before you and your family are eligible for the various types of benefits. To receive retirement benefits for yourself and your family, you must be fully insured.

A good life policy

You probably haven't thought of your social security as life insurance. However, at your death, social security can provide your family with survivorship benefits equal to a life insurance policy worth several hundred thousand dollars. How much will be paid, and who will receive the survivorship benefits, depends on the status of your family at the time of your death. Survivors' benefits will be paid to your family if, at the time of your death, you have survivors who would fit into the following categories.

1. A husband or wife at the then accepted retirement age (now sixty-five, but can retire at sixty-three or sixty-four at reduced benefits);
2. A surviving divorced wife who meets the above age requirements and who was married for at least ten years;
3. A disabled husband or wife fifty years or older;
4. A husband, wife or surviving divorced wife, who is caring for your child who is under age sixteen, or is disabled and entitled to benefits;
5. Your surviving children under age eighteen;
6. Surviving children who are presently disabled, and whose disability commenced prior to age twenty-two; and
7. Dependent parents age sixty-two or over.

There may also be a lump-sum death benefit.

You should be aware that social security benefits for survivors were recently, and quietly, reduced. These reductions could be substantial and may mean your children's college education years' security has been seriously undermined. Check with your insurance agent to see if you have suffered a shortfall of security.

Social security also provides disability benefits. You are eligible to receive those benefits if you have a physical or mental impairment that is so severe that you are unable to engage in any substantially gainful work or employment. The disability must last five months before benefits are paid, and at that time, benefits are payable if the disability can be expected to last for at least twelve months from when it began, or will result in death, or if it has already actually lasted twelve months. In the event that you qualify for disability benefits, then for the purpose of determining your future retirement or survivor benefits, your wage position is "frozen," so that you will not be penalized for that period of time when you are out of work because of disability.

Lastly, part of your social security taxes go to fund the health insurance plan of social security, known as "Medicare." Nearly everyone over sixty-five is eligible for Medicare, which provides benefits for in-patient hospital care and other medical expenses. There are many private hospital insurance plans that are designed to supplement Medicare payments, and because the Medicare benefits will

If You Work for a Living

be used to pay the bills first, and the additional insurance will be supplementary, the premiums for this other insurance are usually quite reasonable and therefore recommended.

How secure is it?

We have purposely avoided using specific amounts in discussing social security. Because of the size of the group (almost all "Americans"), the changes in the tax contributions, and the continual adjustments in the amount of benefits paid, any specific figures would be quickly outdated. Regardless of the specific amounts to which you or your family would be entitled under one of the categories of payments, the amount paid would be subject to a "maximum family benefit." That amount is now in excess of $1,000, but is again dependent on age and the period of time of full coverage.

We think the system is definitely going to survive regardless of any change in funding or benefit payments (although some people are calling the system "social insecurity"). But our assurance is tempered with this word of warning. Don't rely on social security to solve your future financial problems. Regardless of what happens to you and your family, it's hard if not impossible to imagine that social security can provide you with the material things and the intangible peace of mind that you are looking for. At the very best, it will provide minimum protection for you and your family—and you wouldn't be reading this book if you would settle for that.

Veterans' benefits

If you were on active duty in the U.S. armed forces and did not receive a dishonorable discharge, then you and your family may be entitled to VA benefits. Benefits include burial in a National Cemetery or a cash burial expense allowance and eligibility for a headstone.

Widows or widowers, and dependent children under eighteen of deceased veterans who died as the result of service-connected disabilities, are eligible for medical care under the Veterans Administration. There is a pension benefit available to widows or widowers of nearly all deceased veterans, which benefits are restricted according to income.

There are legal benefits provided for widows and widowers and children of veterans who died while serving in the armed forces.

These benefits include a death gratuity and monthly pension benefits. You might also have life insurance coverage under either Servicemen's Group Life Insurance (SGLI) for veterans' groups (VGLI). To find out the current status of the VA benefits available to you and your family, contact your local VA office.

Civil service

If you work for the federal government, then you and your family may be entitled to civil service benefits. Retirement and survivorship benefits are available to covered persons and their families, and if you are not familiar with the benefits to which you and your family are now entitled, you can write to the Civil Service Bureau of Retirement Insurance and Occupational Health, at 1900 E Street, N.W., Washington, DC, 20415.

Disability—the living death

What happens to all your great plans for the future if something happens to you? You have life insurance to take care of your family if you die, but what happens if some unforeseen tragedy, a serious accident or a crippling illness, knocks you out of the box, but not all the way out. Just suppose you were the victim of a permanent or long-term disability. Have you protected yourself and your family against this hazard?

Jerry and Sally Bass had it made. Jerry was a successful young lawyer, and Sally had given up her job as a teacher to stay home and raise their three lovely children, ages four, seven and ten. Jerry was a firm believer in life insurance. He had analyzed his tax situation, and felt that he had taken all the necessary steps to safeguard his family's future. When Jerry went out to interview a potential new client who was injured in an accident and couldn't leave her home, Jerry's financial house was completely in order. He had money in the bank, and plans were made to send the children to camp and take a long-awaited vacation. Jerry's business was improving, and the mortgage payments on their new home were not proving to be the burden he had anticipated.

But fate had other plans for Jerry. Coming home from the client's apartment, he became the victim of a holdup. He was struck on the head with a heavy object, his wallet was taken, and he lay on the sidewalk for some time before he was finally taken to the hospital. He was in the hospital more than two months.

If You Work for a Living

When Jerry was finally discharged from the hospital and permitted to go home, there was really nothing he could do. The blow on the head had injured his brain, and he spent much of the rest of his life at home while Sally attempted to find the highest-paying teaching job available to cover the family expenses. Jerry's social security disability payments provided for basic food and clothing, but even when added to Sally's income, they could not cover the large mortgage payments, and eventually the family had to move to a much smaller home.

Frequently, a long-term disability can be even more costly and traumatic than a death. Not only must the remaining healthy family members be able to survive financially, but there is the additional cost of taking care of the disabled breadwinner. Together with the economic hardship, the mental effect on the disabled person of being unable to contribute anything to the family is another serious result of the problems caused by prolonged disability.

Fortunately, there are plans designed to alleviate the burden caused by the type of disability that Jerry suffered. As discussed before in this chapter, if Jerry had been employed by a large corporation, chances are he might have had a disability policy that would have covered him, at least for a minimum period of time. A company might also have offered a longer-term disability policy that would have been extremely beneficial in these circumstances.

Protecting your income

What could Jerry have done to guard against long-term or permanent disability? He could have obtained his own individual disability income insurance or had a group disability plan installed in his office. Disability plans provide a specific amount of income to be payable over a set period of time (or for life). The plans often differentiate as to whether the disability was caused by accident or sickness. You should be familiar with the major provisions of disability income policies.

The company's right to cancel the policy is extremely important. The preferred type policies are those that are non-cancellable (by the insurer) *and* guaranteed renewable to age sixty-five or for life. Under the policies, the premium is guaranteed and the coverage guaranteed for the length of the renewable period. You are therefore assured that coverage will be there if you need it. Cost is a factor, and less expensive policies can be purchased that are "guaranteed renewable." Under these policies, the insurer retains the right to change the amount of the premiums on a class basis rather than an individual basis. Policies that are "renewable only at the option of the insurer" are those under which the insurance company has the right to refuse to renew the policy on its anniversary date. We recommend against this latter type of coverage.

Upon hearing of Jerry Bass's injury, his accountant, Len Moss, immediately purchased his own disability policy. The policy provided a monthly income benefit of $1,000 and had an elimination period for total disability due to sickness of ninety days and for total disability due to injury of ninety days. The maximum duration of the monthly income benefits if the disability was due to sickness was ten years, and if the disability was due to injury, the benefits could last for life. The policy was non-cancellable and guaranteed renewable to age sixty-five, and its definition of total disability was as follows:

> "Total disability" means the complete inability of the insured due to sickness or injury to perform any and every duty pertaining to his occupation until monthly income payments have been payable under the policy during any period of disability for 60 months or for a period for which monthly income benefits are payable, if less; and (b) after monthly income benefits have been payable under the policy during any period of disability due to sickness or injury for 60 months, then during the remainder, if any, of the period for which monthly income benefits are payable, "total disability" means the complete inability of the insured due to sickness or injury, as the case may be, to engage in any and every gainful occupation for which he is reasonably fitted by education, training or experience.

The choice is up to you

Let's review the different features of Len's policy to find out what options are available when purchasing an individual disability income policy.

The amount of benefits that Len will receive monthly is $1,000. This amount is arrived at by a determination of the needs of Len and his family, should he become disabled. The income needs of Len's family should then be reduced by other benefits that will be available, as well as expected income from his wife, and the return he anticipates receiving on his investments.

Insurance companies place a maximum on the amount of benefits that will be paid, based on a percentage of a person's total income. In other words, the company might be willing to give Len

75 percent of his total income if he becomes disabled, but would not agree to paying benefits that would be equal to or greater than his income had he still been working.

Len has elected an "elimination period" of ninety days both for sickness and accident. That means that during that period, no benefits accrue. In arriving at this elimination period, Len made a determination that a disability lasting three months or less would not critically affect his family's financial position. As the premium for the policy with the ninety-day elimination period was considerably cheaper than had benefits commenced after one or two weeks, Len decided to save the money and take the greater elimination period.

In selecting coverage that would last for ten years in the event of sickness and for life in the event of accident, Len based his decision mainly on the cost of the insurance. All things being equal, Len certainly would have preferred to have coverage for the longest possible time. However, after reviewing disability plans offered by several prominent companies, and considering the cost of the extended benefits for sickness, Len felt that he would rather increase the amount of his monthly benefits as opposed to having a policy that covered him up to sixty-five for sickness and lifetime for accident.

Len wanted an absolute guarantee that in the event of his disability, the coverage he was purchasing would be available, without the chance of the company either cancelling the policy or increasing the premium. Although he could have saved money by forgoing either or both of the above guarantees, he personally felt that he wanted to be certain of the coverage and the fixed premium.

It was Len's insurance agent who pointed out the differences in the definitions of disability found in this type of policy. The agent pointed out to Len that a company that defines total disability as "inability to engage in any and every gainful occupation" is providing more limited coverage than one that defines disability as "the inability to perform any and every duty pertaining to the insured's occupation." The policy that Len eventually selected contained the latter definition of disability for the first five years, and then limited it to cover any occupation thereafter.

It is impossible to predict just what type of plan you might need in the event of sickness or accident. However, it is also difficult to foresee how a plan containing any of the above variables would not be beneficial to you and your family in the event that you are prevented from working because of your physical condition. Again, the choice is up to you. Be sure to have your agent shop for you and make a comparison of cost and provisions offered by at least three companies (some insurers specialize in coverage for professionals, so demand that your agent do some extra homework if you are a doctor, lawyer, accountant or teacher).

Fill in the gaps

In this chapter, we have discussed many job-related benefits, social security benefits, and how to guard against being removed from the work force. Obviously, before doing anything, you should first take an inventory of what you already have. Many people have never taken the time to understand all of their job-related benefits. Once you know what you have, you can then fill in the gaps to reduce, to the greatest extent possible, the effect of any future event that could hamper or destroy your lifetime goals.

It should be pointed out that there are other benefits that can be available to you depending on the circumstances. If you have a job-related disability, then you could be eligible to receive workmen's compensation benefits in accordance with the laws of your state. If you are injured in an automobile accident, and your state has a no-fault insurance law, then you might automatically be entitled to wage loss benefits from your automobile insurance company. There are "accidents-only" policies that provide lump sums for losing specific parts of your body, which are extremely limited in scope, and have a relatively small premium. It should be noted that many more people are removed from the work force because of sickness than because of accident, and many more people die from illness than as a result of an accident. That's why accident-only disability policies, and accidental death insurance, are relatively inexpensive (and less likely to pay off) when compared with policies that provide protection against both sickness and accident, and with regular life insurance policies. To the best of your ability, make sure that your protection will not be limited to your becoming sick by narrowly defined diseases or being injured only in certain specified ways or times. Policies that cover you only if cancer strikes, or only if you are injured riding in a public conveyance on weekdays, and on which you suffered a loss of at least two limbs, are as out of date and old-fashioned as the five-cent ice cream cone (and can be dangerously expensive if you contract a disease or develop a sickness or are injured in a manner that is not covered). In this age of modern technology, there are excellent products that can be tailored specifically to fit your needs. Don't settle for second best. You work hard for your money, and the one asset that requires your concerted attention is yourself. Nothing else in your inventory gives you a better return than your own personal efforts, and therefore that asset (you as a working individual) must be protected to the greatest possible extent.

With today's high cost of hospitals, you are criminally underinsured if you do not have major medical coverage and grossly underinsured if your protection is less than $500,000 (most new plans are providing up to $1,000,000 of coverage or are unlimited).

18.
Minding Your Own Business

Of all the assets you may own, none will deteriorate as quickly and thoroughly, if you are taken out of the picture, as your business. Just think about it for a minute. If someone owns an automobile, or a home, or almost any kind of tangible or intangible property, the value of that property one month after that individual dies would be relatively the same as at the date of death. But suppose the deceased individual owned a restaurant that didn't open for a month, or a doctor whose office was closed for a month, or owned a small manufacturing plant for which no provision had been made following his death. In all or some of these cases, the decrease in value could be staggering.

If your spouse is in business with another person, how would you like to be associated with that individual if your spouse were to die? (Or suppose the situation were reversed?) This chapter is about what can happen to a business if something happens to the owner, or one of the owners, and what can be done to eliminate, or greatly reduce, the almost insurmountable financial and personal problems that frequently arise when there has been no advance planning.

A properly drawn and adequately funded buy-sell agreement can be worth almost as much as the business itself. A Section 303 Stock Redemption can avoid the economic hardships caused by failure to plan for the payment of federal estate taxes, state death taxes, funeral costs and administration expenses.

One way for your business to provide financial security for your family is to set up a survivor's income benefit plan. Your business can make otherwise nondeductible medical expenses completely deductible when you set up a medical expense reimbursement plan.

It sometimes takes almost a lifetime to establish a successful business or professional practice. This chapter contains the information necessary to enable you to guarantee that your family will derive the maximum value from the business in the event of your death, and also illustrates specific methods to utilize the business to obtain tax savings benefits for yourself and the members of your family. How can you stabilize and maximize the value of your business holdings? Read on.

A man alone (buy-sell agreements)

Eddie Cohen's shoe store had been a fixture in his town for twenty years. Eddie ran the business with the help of his long-time manager, Marty, and two other part-time sales people. The business provided the sole support for Eddie, his wife, Miriam, and their children, as well as for Marty and his family.

Eddie was an "old-timer" who loved his business, worked night and day, and didn't believe in planning for the future. When Eddie had a heart attack and died within three days, not only was the family hit with the emotional trauma of his death, but the problems with the store seemed insurmountable.

Miriam tried to continue to run the business, which she knew nothing about, and told Marty she would continue his salary. However, after just three months in which Miriam took most of the money out of the business to pay Eddie's bills except for Marty's salary, sales declined almost by half. Seeing the writing on the wall, Marty was only too happy to take a job with one of Eddie's chief competitors down the block. Several months later, Miriam sold the remaining inventory for approximately 50 percent of what Eddie had originally paid for it (and only a quarter of what the business was worth while Eddie was alive), and the store closed its doors for the last time.

Jerry McCormick's automobile parts shop could have suffered almost the same fate as Eddie Cohen's store, if Don Lapin, Jerry's insurance man, hadn't made his suggestions to Jerry. At Don's suggestion, Jerry and his manager, Bob, worked out a key man buy-sell agreement. Under the terms of the agreement prepared by Jerry's lawyer, in the event of Jerry's death, Bob agreed to buy the business from Jerry at a price they both felt was fair. The agreement provided that they would review the price at least once a year, to make sure that it would always reflect the fair value of the business.

In order to have the money on hand to purchase Jerry's interest, Bob bought a policy on Jerry's life in the amount of $75,000 (the value they had originally decided on), and when Jerry died, Bob collected the insurance money and paid it to Jerry's widow. Jerry's widow therefore received the full value of the business, and Bob now owned the automobile parts shop, free and clear of any obligations to Jerry's family.

Your brother's keeper

As brothers, Joe and Paul could not have been closer. They had been in business together for twenty-five years and worked very closely together. They were in a service business, and had divided their business activities right down the center. Joe was responsible for bringing in the business, as he was a super salesman, and Paul ran the day-to-day operation of the business. Joe was conservative, and lived with his wife and children in a small apartment, while Paul and his wife lived life on a higher scale.

One night, while the brothers were both in their early fifties, Joe died suddenly in his sleep. When the lawyer for Joe's estate sat down with Joe's wife, Lillian, and Paul, he heard the following story.

Lillian told the lawyer that since Joe had owned half the business, she wanted half, and wanted to continue to be able to take out of the business the money that Joe had taken, since it was in part due to his efforts that the business had reached the status that it presently enjoyed. In fact, it was absolutely necessary for her to continue to take the same amount of money out, since she had children in college.

Paul felt a very close attachment to the widow and the children of his late brother, and wanted to do everything he could for them. However, he was not a good salesman, and it was therefore necessary to hire a new salesman at a considerable salary to replace Joe, even though no new salesman would be capable of bringing in the volume of business that Joe had. However, the business could not now afford to pay three salaries where before it had only paid two. Furthermore, Paul's wife was extremely upset at having to reduce her standard of living. She cautioned the lawyer and Lillian that if the economic strain was too much for Paul and his health suffered, then nobody would realize anything from the business. Therefore, she suggested that perhaps Lillian should go out and find a good job to provide for her own needs and her children's education.

Suffice to say that, regardless of what solution was eventually worked out, whatever could be realized from the business was never enough to satisfy the needs of Lillian and her children, and was always more than Paul and his wife could afford to pay.

Could this unfortunate situation have been prevented? The answer is yes, and quite easily. If Joe and Paul, their lawyer, accountant and insurance representative had prepared and funded a buy-sell agreement, all of these problems could have been solved. A properly drawn agreement could have provided that in the event of the death of either partner, the other partner would purchase the share of the deceased partner with insurance proceeds from a policy that the surviving partner owned on the deceased partner's life. Here's what would have happened. On Joe's death, the life insurance policy that Paul owned on Joe's life would have paid Paul the amount they had agreed would represent Joe's interest in the business. Paul would have taken the money, paid it to Lillian, and would then have owned the business outright. From Lillian's standpoint, she would now have the money she needed for herself and her children, which she could invest to provide a livable income. There would be no need for her to bother Paul, because it would have been understood that this was the arrangement that Joe had made for her and the children.

On the other hand, Paul's situation would also be greatly enhanced. He would own the business free and clear, and therefore have the right to all of the income. He would then have funds available to hire a salesman to solicit new business, and should also not have to worry about being pressured by his sister-in-law and his wife. A remarkably appropriate solution to an extremely difficult situation.

Who needs it?

You probably know someone who owns a closely held corporation. You may even own stock in one yourself. If you do, and there are other shareholders, you may want to consider a buy-sell agreement. Why? The best way to answer that question is to look at the basic characteristics of a closely held business.

Gene and Gary each own 50 percent of the stock in the Marcia-D Corporation. Both Gene and Gary are active in the operation of the business. Gene handles the accounting and office work while

Gary is in charge of sales. Both Gene and Gary receive most of their income in the form of salaries or fringe benefits. The corporation has never paid dividends and probably never will. Except to the extent that Gene and Gary personally guaranteed loans that the corporation has made, they have limited their liability to corporate creditors.

What happens if either Gene or Gary dies? If either shareholder/employee dies, the legal structure of the business will probably remain intact. The Marcia-D Corporation will survive as a legal entity. But the personal structure of the corporation will change dramatically. This is because when a working shareholder dies, the surviving shareholder or shareholders have little choice. In this case, if Gary dies, the surviving shareholder can decide to stay in business with Gary's heirs, buy out Gary's heirs, sell out to Gary's heirs, or accept the individuals who purchased Gary's stock as new shareholders. What would you do if you were Gene? What would you want if you were Gary—or his heirs?

It is inevitable, if not obvious, that the interest of the surviving stockholders and the decedent/shareholder's heirs will conflict. Gene, the surviving shareholder, will seek to maintain (or increase) his salary. Why not? He's now doing the work of two men. He will want to re-invest corporate earnings and profits in the business to avoid the need to borrow at high interest rates. Gene will favor expansion, growth and other steps that build up the financial strength of the Marcia-D Corporation. Typically, dividends are the last thing that Gene will want the corporation to pay out. Paying dividends not only would put a strain on the corporation, but also would be highly taxed before Gary's heir could get to use them.

On the other hand, Robin, Gary's heir, will be very much concerned with dividends. Since she is a minor and not capable of earning a meaningful salary (or for any other reason does not go into the business), dividends will become her major source of income. This is especially true when the heir doesn't have the skill, education or temperament to carry her part in running the business. (Worse yet, the IRS would probably disallow the deduction for a high unearned salary even if the business could afford to pay it to her.)

Robin's position is not unusual. Often, heirs can't or don't want to take an active role in the business. Sometimes, a person's heirs will lack a technical understanding of the business. Quite often, they will have little training or experience or are unwilling or unable to handle the severe emotional punishment entailed in modern business management. Furthermore, surviving stockholders will seldom want to share corporate control or decision making with individuals who have not worked in the business for some time. (Would you want your coshareholder's heirs in business with you with an equal voice in major decisions? Would they be happy to accept your heirs?)

What happens if Robin remains inactive? If Robin should remain inactive, it places her fate in the hands of Gene, the surviving shareholder. This may be undesirable, because the dividends Robin would be likely to receive as an inactive heir would probably not provide adequate income. Gene, in trying to be fair to Robin, may not be fair to himself.

Could Robin sell her stock to an outsider? She could. But it is usually difficult for the heirs to sell their stock, since the price they will want (and often need) is often more than many buyers can afford or would be willing to pay. Frankly, a buyer who is aware of how much Robin needs cash to pay taxes or to provide income will use this knowledge to his advantage (and to Robin's disadvantage).

Robin, like most heirs, will probably be totally unfamiliar with the true value of the Marcia-D stock. Quite often, heirs assume (erroneously) the value of the stock should be a multiple of the deceased/shareholder/employee's salary. This is a misguided and naïve expectation. The result will probably be a forced sale of stock or other property at depressed prices to raise cash for basic living needs.

The problem is aggravated even further since Robin owns only 50 percent of the corporation's stock. Her task would be much easier if she had a controlling (51 percent or more) interest. If she owns less than 50 percent, her minority interest could make it difficult, if not impossible, to find a buyer. The reason is that the minority shareholder has little power or say over any of the major decisions to be made in a corporation. A minority shareholder can't control the hiring or firing of employees or whether the corporation will or will not pay dividends. Someone contemplating the purchase of Robin's stock will be just as powerless as she is.

A few pennies' worth of planning makes a lot of sense

Most attorneys and financial advisors will recommend a

legally binding buy-sell agreement. That document would require the surviving shareholders (or the corporation) to buy, and require the estate of a deceased shareholder to sell, the inherited stock interest. Why might Gary and Gene decide to establish a buy-sell agreement and properly "fund" it? (Funding means providing the appropriate amounts of cash to effectuate the buy-out when it occurs.)

Establishing and properly funding a buy-sell agreement makes a good deal of financial sense for all the parties for these reasons:

First, looking at the problems from the surviving shareholder's point of view, the corporation is protected against inactive, uninformed, and potentially dissident shareholders who often cause conflict over management policies such as the size of dividends, the amount of salaries, or risks the corporation should take for growth. Once a buy-sell agreement is executed and properly funded, Gene won't have to worry that Gary's heir, Robin, might try to tell him how to run his business. The buy-sell has kept the closely held corporation "close."

Second, Gene, the active shareholder, can be assured that the profits produced by his efforts will benefit him rather than someone else (such as an inactive shareholder or the person who purchases that shareholder's stock).

Third, by properly funding the agreement, Gene, the surviving shareholder, is assured of all or the bulk of the cash he'll need to purchase Robin's interest.

Fourth, Gene knows that he will not have to pay more than a fair price for the stock.

Fifth, only a buy-sell agreement can guarantee the surviving or remaining shareholders that the transition of management and control will be fluid and complete.

Sixth, the buy-sell agreement can be used by Gene as a convenient means of fulfilling the natural sense of obligation that he may have toward Gary and his family.

A legally binding and properly funded buy-sell agreement makes sense from the viewpoint of the deceased shareholder's family too. From Gary's point of view, once the agreement is in effect, he knows that Robin will receive a reasonable price for his stock. This would be especially important if Gary held less than a 50-percent interest.

Second, after Gary and Gene sign the agreement, the economic future of Gary's heirs (as well as Gene's heirs) would no longer be tied to the fate of the business. Robin will be free from worry about the financial success or failure of the business.

A third reason that a buy-sell agreement is advantageous from Gary's viewpoint is that he knows once Robin receives the cash from the buy-out, the pressure on her to liquidate other estate assets to pay estate taxes and other settlement costs would be decreased. Valuable family heirlooms would not have to be sold to pay taxes. Money from the sale of the stock at a shareholder's death is assured. Death, the event that creates the need for cash, creates the cash to satisfy the need.

Fourth, if a buy-sell agreement is arranged properly, it will practically eliminate an after-death dispute with the Internal Revenue Service as to the value of the stock. A properly drawn buy-sell helps establish the federal estate tax value.

Fifth, at Gary's death, funds paid by the corporation to Robin in payment of her stock interest can be entirely income tax free.

Just what is it we're trying to do here?

Specifically, what is it that a buy-sell agreement should do? What are the objectives that the parties want to meet in funding such an agreement?

The answer is that a corporate buy-sell agreement should be funded by a method that will facilitate a trouble free transfer of the business interest in one of four situations: (a) at some time before retirement; (b) at normal retirement age; (c) in the event of a disability of a shareholder; and (d) at the death of a shareholder. Ideally, Gene and Gary's advisors will be able to figure out a way to provide funds to meet those contingencies. Optimally, the method used to provide such funds will have a relatively low cost and be simple for Gary, Gene, Robin, and any other party to the agreement to understand. It should be easy to administer. Furthermore, the agreement and the funding mechanism that makes it work should not adversely affect the working capital or credit position of the business.

Finding funding

Steve Kandell, the insurance agent who handles all the Marcia-D Corporation's insurance, told Gene and Gary that they should consider the possibility of a buy-out at a stockholder/employee's termination, retirement, death or disability. Both Gene and Gary were shocked when Steve showed them actuarial tables illustrating the possibility of either death or disability before age sixty-five. He told them that, expressed as the number of chances out of one hundred, at least one out of two business owners in relatively good health will die before age sixty-five. The figures are:

Chances of Death before 65	Ages of Business Owners
48.5	30/30
47.4	35/35
45.8	40/40
43.5	45/45
39.8	50/50
38.0	30/35
46.6	35/40
44.7	40/45
41.7	40/45

(Source: *Funding Corporate Buy-Sell Agreements,* R & R Newkirk, Indianapolis, Indiana.)

Steve mentioned that the probability of disability would be even greater.

Both Gene and Gary immediately asked Steve how they would create the cash to effectuate the buy-sell. Steve explained that there were four alternatives available for funding the buy-sell: (1) cash; (2) borrowing; (3) installment payments; and (4) life insurance. When they asked him to compare the four methods, he explained:

Cash has the apparent advantage if no immediate outlay of cash is required. The problem is, he said, neither of you know who will be the survivor. You don't know precisely when you will need the cash or how much cash you will need. This means you will always have to keep a large amount of cash available to meet the anticipated need. Worse yet, you will have to use after-tax dollars. In other words, either you or the corporation will have to earn the money, pay taxes on it, and then use what is left to go through with the buy-out. Obviously, more than one dollar must be earned to net a dollar of purchase money. Also, Steve added, money that you or the corporation hold in reserve to meet that potential need can't possibly earn a return as high as it might earn if it were invested in the business. (But, of course, if you invest it in machinery, equipment, or other business assets, it wouldn't be available.)

Gene and Gary then asked about borrowing as a source of

funds. Why couldn't the survivor go to a bank and borrow the necessary money? Steve's answer to that was that a bank may not be willing to lend money to a corporation that has lost one of its key employees and is probably struggling to survive in the worst economic environment since the depression. But even if it did lend your corporation or the surviving shareholder money to buy out the decedent shareholder, it could be terribly expensive. Steve pointed out that the annual cash flow needed to pay off a loan of $100,000 (if you could possibly borrow money) at 15 percent would be $29,831 in the case of a five-year loan and as much as $19,925 a year in the case of a ten-year loan. The total cost of such a loan would be $149,255 in the case of a five-year loan and almost $200,000 if the loan was outstanding for ten years. Although a loan may get the deceased shareholder's family off the hook, it puts an extremely heavy weight on the back of the survivor.

Will installment payouts be the answer? Could the corporation or the surviving shareholder buy out the deceased shareholder's interest through installment payments?

Steve's answer to this was that it could be used, but the installment payout method would not provide the large sums of cash that might be needed by the deceased shareholder's family for settlement costs. The big problem, he added, is that it leaves substantial sums at the risk of the business. And from the surviving shareholder's viewpoint, the installment payout creates almost as much nuisance value as if the deceased shareholder's heirs still owned the stock. Steve then showed Gene and Gary the cost of a ten-year installment payout of $100,000 assuming 10 percent interest was paid on the balance. To repay $100,000 over ten years, $55,000 would be interest, making a total payment of $155,000. But if the surviving shareholder were in a 50-percent combined federal and state income tax bracket, to pay $155,000 would require that the stock purchaser earn as much as $282,500. it would be paying for stock with expensive dollars.

Steve explained that life insurance is the only means of guaranteeing that death, which creates the need for cash, will also create the cash to satisfy that need.

How much is enough?

Gene wanted to know how much insurance should be purchased. Steve recommended that the buy-sell agreement should, if possible, be fully funded. That means, he said, that each of you should purchase enough life insurance to allow the survivor to purchase all the stock of the other. In fact, you may even want to purchase more than that if possible. That's because the value of your business interest, and therefore the liability of the surviving shareholder, will increase—not only with the real value in the price of your stock, but also with inflationary growth. Steve explained that if the business grows at 10 percent, the price that will have to be paid will (approximately) double every 7.2 years. (He explained the rule of 72 that is used by bankers and other financial planners can be used to find out quickly how long it takes an asset to double in value, by dividing whatever growth rate you assume into the number 72.) He illustrated that a business currently worth $500,000 would be worth $1,296,871 in ten years at a compound rate of 10 percent. In twenty years, a $500,000 business would be worth over $3,300,000.

What do we do next?

Gene and Gary then asked Steve how to proceed. Steve mentioned that a joint meeting should be held as soon as possible with all the members of the estate planning "cooperative"—the insurance agent, the attorney, the CPA, and Gary and Gene.

At that meeting, their attorney explained that there are two types of buy-sell agreements, a so-called "cross purchase" agreement and a "stock redemption" agreement. A cross purchase agreement is used where the shareholders have decided to assume the obligation of purchasing a deceased coshareholder's interest personally. Another name for a cross purchase agreement, he explained, is a "criss cross" arrangement. Each stockholder owns, pays the premiums for, and is the beneficiary of, an appropriate amount of life insurance on the lives of the other shareholders. Since Gene and Gary are each 50-percent shareholders, the agreement would obligate the survivor to purchase the share of the decedent. If each has a business interest worth $100,000, Gary would purchase at least $100,000 of insurance on Gene's life and Gene would purchase at least $100,000 worth of insurance on Gary's life. If Gary dies first, Gene receives $100,000 of insurance. He then uses that insurance to buy Gary's stock from his estate or beneficiary. Gary would do the same if Gene died first.

Their attorney explained that in some cases he drafts the buy-sell agreement so that the corporation, rather than the individual shareholders, is obligated to purchase (retire or redeem) the stock of the deceased shareholder. In that case the corporation purchases, pays premiums on, and names itself the beneficiary of an appropriate amount of life insurance on each shareholder's life. When a shareholder dies, the corporation receives the insurance proceeds and then uses that money to purchase the stock from the estate or heir of the deceased shareholder.

How taxing is it?

Gene asked if the premiums were deductible. Steve's response was that no deductions were allowed where a stockholder, to fund obligations under a cross purchase agreement, purchases insurance on the life of another stockholder. Gary then asked if a stock redemption agreement made it possible for premiums to be deductible. Steve's answer was that the tax law denies deductions for premiums paid on a life insurance policy used to finance the purchaser's obligation under a buy-sell agreement, no matter who owned or was the beneficiary of the policy.

Steve also explained the taxation of premiums to stockholders. In a nutshell, he said, premiums paid by a costockholder do not constitute income to the insured under either a cross purchase or a stock redemption type of agreement.

The proceeds the policy owner receives when one of you dies will be income tax free. The proceeds are income tax free regardless of whether you use a cross purchase type of agreement or a stock redemption agreement. No matter how much money you receive, it will be entirely income tax free.

What about the estate taxation of proceeds?

The answer is that there is no double taxation. In the case of either a cross purchase or a stock redemption agreement, in a properly drawn plan, only the value of the deceased shareholder's corporate stock is includable in his estate. But since, under a cross purchase agreement, you'll each own a policy on the other's life, the value of the policy the decedent owns on the life of the surviving shareholder will be included in the decedent's estate. In the case of a stock redemption agreement, when a corporation receives the insurance proceeds, it may have the effect of increasing the value of the business interest for estate tax purposes. How much, if any, it increases the value of the stock for estate tax purposes depends on how the buy-sell agreement is drawn by your attorney.

How taxed is the seller?

Regardless of whether the buyer is the corporation (stock redemption) or the surviving shareholder (cross purchase), the estate of the deceased shareholder is selling and not giving away the stock. Unless it is arranged properly, that sale could result in a sizable tax liability. Fortunately, current tax law makes it possible for a sale to a surviving shareholder to be entirely income tax free in most cases. Extreme caution should be used in the case of a stock redemption, however, since highly complex tax law can make the entire amount received by the estate or heir subject to ordinary income tax. The problem is especially acute where the shareholders are related to each other. (We recommend that family-owned corporations use a stock redemption type buy-sell only after very careful examination by competent tax counsel.)

Is part better than whole? (Section 303 stock redemptions)

During the interview, Gary asked if it was necessary for his estate to sell his entire interest in Marcia-D Corporation. Steve's response was that favorable tax treatment in the case of a partial redemption (purchase of less than all the shares of Gary's stock) by the corporation was possible without the corporation's distribution being considered a dividend, but only if Gary's estate qualified. Steve called this partial purchase a "Section 303 redemption." Section 303 is a key section of the Internal Revenue Code. It allows a corporation to purchase enough stock so that the deceased shareholder's estate can pay federal and state death taxes, funeral costs, and allowable administrative expenses. In most cases, the estate will realize no gain on the sale of stock after the death of the shareholder; the transaction will be income tax free.

Unfortunately, not every estate qualifies for a Section 303 stock redemption. First of all, only stock includable in your estate at the time of your death will qualify. So if you give stock away more than three years before your death, since it is not includable in your estate, it does not qualify for a Section 303 redemption.

Second, the protection of Section 303 only applies if the estate tax value of that stock in your estate is more than 35 percent of your "adjusted" gross estate (gross estate less funeral, administrative expenses and debts). If your adjusted gross estate were $1,000,000 and the value of your stock were exactly $350,000 or some lesser figure, it would not qualify. What happens if the corporation buys less than all of the decedent's stock, but the tests of Section 303 are not met? The result might be that the entire payment made by the corporation to the deceased shareholder's estate would be a dividend taxable as ordinary income. But if the "more than 35 percent" test is met, the seller would realize no taxable gain and the corporation could buy enough stock so that the seller could pay off estate administrative expenses and federal and state death taxes.

As is the case with a typical buy-sell agreement, a partial buy-sell (Section 303 stock redemption) should be properly and adequately funded with life insurance. One way is for the corporation to own insurance on the life of each shareholder. At the least, the amount of insurance would be the total of the estimated combined death taxes and funeral expenses.

The alternative is to have some third party, such as an irrevocable trust or an adult child, own insurance on the life of the shareholder and then have that third party, at the shareholder's death, lend money to the corporation. The corporation could use the loan to purchase the deceased shareholder's stock. One advantage of third-party insurance ownership is that the insurance would not increase the estate tax value of the stock. Another advantage is that interest paid by the corporation to the lender would provide income that could be used for food, clothing, shelter, and other current living expenses. The corporation could deduct the interest payments it makes. Eventually, it would pay off the loan out of earnings.

The magic number

Sam Smokeville has spent his entire working lifetime building his business. He's turned years of sweat and hard work into the bricks and buildings and machinery owned by his corporation.

Starting from the day Sam dies, his executor has about nine months to turn these bricks and buildings and machinery back into cash to pay funeral costs, administrative expenses, and state and federal taxes—unless there's some alternative source to pay off these expenses. In other words, his executor may have to sell some or all of Sam's business to pay these estate settlement costs.

Sam has reason to be worried about the problem. Sam's competitor, Clarence Hambil, was in about the same position as Sam: the bulk of his assets and money were tied up in a family business. Clarence wanted to avoid a forced sale of his business when he died but never took the appropriate action. At his death, his family had no life insurance and could find no way to pay the estate's taxes or expenses. So a majority interest in the business had to be sold to someone outside the family. (No one wanted to purchase a minority interest.)

Sam wants to avoid a forced (depressed-price) sale of his business and keep at least a controlling interest in the business within his family. He'd also like to be able to use corporate funds—if possible—to pay estate taxes and other expenses.

Sam's attorney suggested that one of the best ways to handle the problem would be to use Internal Revenue Code Section 303.

One more time with no hocus-pocus

As you probably realize by now, Section 303 of the Internal Revenue Code (sure it's confusing—that's why they call it a "code") provides a safe way to use corporate dollars to pay death taxes and other expenses. Code Section 303 makes the payment of these expenses possible without fear that the estate will be treated as if it received a dividend. (The general rule of corporate taxation is that any distribution from a corporation to a party owning corporate stock is a dividend. That means money coming out of the corporation is taxed as ordinary income to the extent of earnings and profits. This is true even if the corporation calls the payment a sale or redemption of its stock. There are only a few exceptions. Section 303 is one of the safest of the exceptions.)

There are requirements your estate must meet. Knowing what they are may make it easier for your estate to qualify for this favorable treatment.

First, you must own the stock on the date of your death—or have owned it within three years of your death. (You can still qualify even if you give your stock away within three years of your death.)

Second, more than 35 percent of your "adjusted gross estate" (essentially your gross estate less funeral, administrative expenses, and debts) must be composed of the stock to be redeemed. An easy-to-use form designed by The American College, an organization that provides tax education for thousands of estate and financial planning professionals each year, can be found in the appendix. Why not check to see if your estate will qualify for a Section 303 redemption and see how much stock can be sold to your business?

Third, the redemption (corporate purchase of your stock) can be as much as (but no more than) the total of (a) the federal estate taxes, (b) state death taxes, (c) funeral costs, and (d) administrative expenses. If your corporation buys more of your stock than these limits, the difference may be taxed to the estate as ordinary income.

How to make sure the trick works

Assume your adjusted gross estate is $1,000,000. Your business interest is worth exactly $350,000 (which does *not* meet the more than 35 percent test). How do you make sure your estate will qualify?

The easiest way is to make your corporation worth more—relative to the rest of your estate. One way to do that is to have the corporation purchase and own life insurance on your life to help "swell" the value of the business relative to other estate assets. Certainly, a $100,000 policy will help put the value over the "more than 35 percent minimum."

Another way is to give away assets (other than stock) such as cash, land, or other property. But to keep it from being too easy to qualify under this favorable tax law provision, the Internal Revenue Code says property you give away within three years of your death doesn't count in meeting the more than 35 percent test. So the trick is to give it away—now. Since you can give up to $10,000 per year per donee ($20,000 if your spouse consents to "split" the gift), there are no federal gift tax costs to reduce your estate to the required level.

Remember, it's not easy for your estate to qualify; without enough money to make a Section 303 redemption work, it doesn't matter if your corporation is qualified to purchase stock. There must be cash or life insurance to enable the corporation to make a purchase of stock under Section 303 or it's worthless.

Name of the game—survivor's income benefit plan

If the name of the game is to provide for your family's security with corporate funded tax deductible dollars, here's a winner: the Survivors' Income Benefit (S.I.B.) plan. (Your attorney may call it a salary continuation plan and your insurance agent may call it a death benefit only [D.B.O.] plan.)

An S.I.B. is an agreement between your business and you as an employee. Your corporation agrees that if you die before retirement, it will pay a specified amount—or an amount determined by a specified formula—to your spouse (or other survivor). Your corporation could make that death benefit a multiple of your salary or a specified amount. It could pay your survivors a lump sum or specify that payments will be made in installments (the more typical case).

One thing that an S.I.B. does not do is provide you with retirement income.

Who would play this game?

Ed Graves is a widower. Ed is in a very high estate tax bracket. He is looking for a way to provide substantial security for his two daughters if he should die before they are financially self-sufficient.

Bob Cooper is the president of a fast-growing corporation that is looking for a special employee benefit plan to lock in three key employees and attract two new sales managers from a competitor. He's already covered most of his one hundred employees with a pension plan. Bob now wants to cover just these few special people.

Ron Dell of the RonDell Corporation recently hired Sam Bowles, a young hardworking supervisor. Ron would like a plan that would provide immediate financial security for Sam's family, but could easily be turned into a retirement plan if Sam remains with his firm.

An S.I.B. plan could meet all these objectives.

Kicking off

How do you get started with an S.I.B. plan? Simple. Let's say you are forty years old, you're an executive of a corporation that would like to provide your family with financial security (and provide you with the knowledge that you are more financially secure).

The corporation makes a legally binding promise that, in return for your agreement to continue working for the firm, if you should die while employed by the company, it will pay your surviving spouse half of your $100,000 salary, $50,000 a year, for ten years, a total of $500,000.

What does it cost the firm?

Let's say the firm insures you for $500,000. At your death, the insurer would pay that money—tax free—to your employer. The money is the corporation's and it could invest that money in any way it wants. Assume the money is put into tax free municipal bonds earning 12 percent. The income is $60,000 a year—tax free. So $60,000 a year is coming in.

Now assume that at the time the payout begins the corporation is in a combined income and estate tax bracket of 50 percent. Since payments to your widow are treated as a continuation of salary, they are deductible by the corporation. That means it costs—after taking a deduction—only $25,000 a year to pay your widow $50,000 a year. So $25,000 a year is going out.

$60,000 comes in—$25,000 goes out—so $35,000 a year more stays in than goes out. In ten years, $350,000 more comes in than goes out. And don't forget, at the end of the ten years—after your widow has received $500,000—the company's obligation is over, and it still has a $500,000 tax free municipal bond.

Are you in or out?

Before you decide whether the S.I.B. plan is right for you, consider that no deduction is allowed to your corporation for premiums it pays. On the other hand, life insurance proceeds the corporation will receive (no matter how large the amount) are income tax free. Then, when the corporation actually makes payments to your widow (or the other employer-designated beneficiary), every dime it pays is deductible, if and to the extent that (a) the payments represent reasonable compensation for services you had rendered, and (b) the plan serves a valid business (as opposed to purely stockholder) purpose. (For example, if the plan is designed to lock you into the firm with golden handcuffs, it meets a business goal.)

If the plan has been drafted carefully (don't even think about trying it without both your attorney and your accountant), none of the death benefit will be in your estate. Even if the death benefit is includable in your estate, if your spouse is your beneficiary the unlimited estate tax marital deduction shelters your estate from federal estate tax.

Second, since the insurance isn't technically tied into the plan (it's treated merely as a corporate asset that the employer may or may not use to satisfy its liability under the plan), you don't have any rights to it. That's good because it means that you're not subject to income tax each time your employer pays a premium. You pay no tax at all while you are alive and working.

How are beneficiaries taxed each time they receive a payment?

Dollars your spouse receives are treated just like salary; only it's as if the salary were paid to your spouse. It's taxed as ordinary income, at her (or his) tax bracket.

Can you think of a better way to provide estate tax free financial security for your family through your business?

Feelin' good (medical expense reimbursement plan)
You may be feeling good right now, but you know that over a long period of time sooner or later you (or someone in your family) will not. A medical expense reimbursement plan (some people call these "MERP") is an agreement provided by an employer (including a professional corporation) to reimburse one or more employees for dental expenses, cosmetic surgery, and other medical expenses which are not covered under Blue Cross/Blue Shield, or any other medical plan available to all employees.

A MERP will reimburse you for the medical expense you incur as an employee. It will also pay for medical expenses incurred by your spouse and dependents.

The nicest thing about a MERP is that it is tax free to you and tax deductible by the corporation. In other words, you pay no current income taxes regardless of how much your medical expenses are reimbursed. No matter how much the corporation pays, that amount (assuming it is reasonable) will be deductible against its ordinary income. So a MERP could be just what the doctor ordered.

Could you use a MERP? Certainly, if you own or are a shareholder in a closely held corporation and all or most of the corporation's employees are members of your family, a MERP makes sense (and dollars).

Before you install a MERP, the bulk of your family's medical expenses are paid either by insurance or out of your own pocket with expensive (after tax) dollars. After your corporation installs its MERP, those out-of-pocket expenses aren't paid out of your pocket anymore—the money comes from your corporation. And the money it uses has never been taxed to you, and never will be. Best of all, the expenses will be deductible by your corporation. So a MERP makes otherwise nondeductible medical expenses completely deductible. Let's see how it works:

Morty Berk is the president and chief executive of the Fly High Kite Manufacturing Company. Morty and his wife, Mary, are the only full-time employees of the corporation. Before establishing the MERP, expenses Morty or his wife incurred over and above their group health insurance limits had to be paid for with expensive after-tax dollars. To pay $10,000 of dental and cosmetic surgery costs, Morty (who is in a 50-percent income tax bracket) had to earn twice that amount.

Dr. Edward Nomad is an ophthalmologist who recently formed a professional corporation. He has two nurses who are receiving salaries of $15,000 each. Edward's salary is $150,000 a year. He covers both of his nurses as well as himself and his family. The MERP makes what might otherwise be nondeductible medical expenses incurred by his family deductible to Edward.

Charlie Goodwill employs sixteen people in his closely held corporation. All but three are not related to Charlie. Charlie believes that it is his responsibility to provide significant and tax-favored benefits to his employees. He also believes that providing such benefits will help attract and retain the type of employees he needs to run his highly specialized electronics corporation. He already has provided coverage for these employees under basic Blue Cross/Blue Shield and an insurance company sponsored major medical plan but would like to provide additional protection for them.

A must for your MERP

What does a MERP cost? There are requirements that must be met to qualify for the favorable tax treatment afforded to a MERP. A MERP must be insured by an insurance company, or can be "self-insured" by the employer. That means your corporation makes the promises and takes the risk, so if a covered event occurs, you pay. However, if it is self-insured, that is, if the employer is willing to pay expenses as they are incurred out of operating revenues, or from a sinking fund, the plan must be nondiscriminatory. It can't discriminate either in coverage or operation in favor of shareholders or highly compensated employees.

A MERP that discriminates will cause all or a portion of the reimbursements to be included in the income of key employees.

Gotcha covered

What types of medical expenses can you use a MERP to cover? The answer is, any medical expense that is deductible on your income tax return (including prescription eyeglasses and dental work) can be covered by a MERP plan. Why not sit down with your attorney and your accountant and see if a MERP makes sense for you?

19.
Youth, Old Age and Mental Illness

This chapter deals with two extremely important issues. The first is the proper way to safeguard your children's money, and the second, how to prepare for your old age.

There are tax advantages to having money in your children's name as opposed to your owning it, and in some cases there are important nontax considerations for placing money or property in your children's names. The "Uniform Gifts to Minors Act" illustrates how you can make gifts to a minor while avoiding many of the problems and expenses of other methods of giving property to them. The "2503(c) Trust" is an excellent vehicle in which to transfer money to children.

How you can best protect yourself against the problems associated with handling money in old age is discussed in the sections on "Protecting You Against Old Age" and "The Power of Attorney." Although you can appreciate the need for trusts or custodial accounts when children's money is involved, you often fail to provide for supervision of the funds of older people. Perhaps a "revocable living trust" is the answer, or maybe you should seriously consider a power of attorney. This relatively easy-to-prepare device is thoroughly discussed in this chapter, and is one that can prove of considerable value when an older person becomes disabled for any reason.

What do you like? (Uniform Gifts to Minors Act)
You'd like to give money or property to your children but you don't think your child is capable of managing it wisely yet. And you don't want to go to the trouble and expense of setting up a trust.

Perhaps you'd like to shift the burden of paying taxes from your tax bracket to your child's. Your accountant has told you that since you are in the 50-percent income tax bracket you'll net less than your child who isn't working—far less. In fact he/she tells you that if your child's custodian invests $10,000 at 15 percent there will be $9,414 after taxes—in only five years. But if you personally invested the same $10,000 at the same 15-percent return you'd end up with only $4,357—$5,057 less. So you are looking for a way to drop the tax on family income to your child's lower bracket.

You'd like to make irrevocable gifts to your child to move assets—and the appreciation of the assets—from your estate, but you don't want to incur any gift tax if you can help it.

If these are your goals and you don't object to your child receiving money or other property at majority (age eighteen or twenty-one in some states), the Uniform Gifts to Minors Act (UGMA) may be your solution.

What do you give and what does it take?

Most states have passed laws allowing you to put money, securities (stocks, bonds, evidences of indebtedness, certificates of interest or participation in an oil, gas mining title or lease), life insurance and annuity contracts into an account for a minor.

The UGMA provides that as an adult you can give these types of property to a minor (even if you are not related to the minor). This is accomplished by delivering it to—or having it registered in the name of—an adult or a trust company as custodian for that minor. You can even give it to yourself as custodian, but most tax authorities will recommend that you name someone else (such as a spouse, relative or friend). The reason is that if you die at a time when you are custodian and the child has not reached the age of majority, the property you have given away will be includable in your estate.

Custodial gift laws were designed to accomplish a very simple objective; to make it possible for you to make gifts to a minor but at the same time avoid many of the problems and expenses of other transfer methods, such as outright gifts, trusts, or formal guardianship arrangements.

Although (as is the case with all of these tools and techniques) you should consult your attorney and your accountant before doing anything, a UGMA gift is simple; you transfer the cash or other property to the person you have selected as custodian, or you call your stockbroker and tell him to purchase stock or mutual funds, or "money markets," and make the person you have selected the custodian for your child. That person holds the property "as custodian for (name of minor) under (your state's) Gifts to Minors Act."

If you have more than one child, and you'd like to make a gift to each, you should appoint a custodian and have that custodian keep a separate UGMA account for each child.

Keep two things in mind. First, once you make a gift it's irrevocable. You can't get it back. So don't give more than you are sure you can afford to give. And don't give property you may need personally or may regret giving (such as a controlling interest in your family corporation).

Tic tax

Mel Young transfers his hundred shares of Purple Lady, Inc., stock to his wife, Sonia, as custodian for their daughter, Melanie, age eleven. Mel does it by having the ownership of the stock registered on the company's books as follows: "Sonia Young, as custodian for Melanie Young under the Tennessee Uniform Gifts to Minors Act."

Assuming the value of the stock is $10,000 or less ($20,000 if Sonia agrees to "split" the gift and sign her consent on a gift tax return), Mel wouldn't have to pay any gift tax or use any of his gift tax credit. In fact Mel could make a gift of similar value every year—and never pay any tax.

Assuming Mel keeps each year's gifts under the $10,000 limit ($20,000 if split with Sonia), none of the gifts will be in either his or Sonia's estate even if Mel dies within three years of making the gift. In just five years, giving $20,000 a year, Mel could remove as much as $100,000 from his estate (plus the income and appreciation on the annual gifts) with absolutely no adverse gift or estate tax implication (check to see if your state has a state gift tax).

Melanie doesn't pay any income or gift tax on receiving the gift. But since the stock is hers once Sonia accepts it as custodian, if Melanie dies it will be in her estate and not in either Mel's or Sonia's estate.

Typically, whether or not she actually receives it, any income produced by the stock will be taxed at Melanie's tax bracket. There is one important exception. If income is used to discharge Mel and Sonia's support obligations (for instance to pay for Melanie's food, clothing, or shelter), it will be taxed to Mel and Sonia. That problem is solved by using such income to pay for non-necessaries such as summer camp, a trip to Europe, or toys or pleasure reading books for Melanie.

Who can play?

Most states' laws provide that you can name any adult or trust company or bank with trust powers as custodian.

If the custodian you have named wants to resign, many states allow that custodian to name a new custodian in writing (the document must be signed by the resigning custodian and should be witnessed by someone other than the new custodian).

What if the custodian dies or becomes incapacitated? In that case the successor custodian named by the original custodian takes over. If no successor custodian was ever named, typically the minor's guardian will be appointed the successor. If the child is age fourteen or over, no successor custodian has been named, and no guardian has been appointed, the child can name a successor custodian.

What does your accountant think about this device?

In tax savings we trust—the 2503(c) trust

If tax savings is the name of the game, the 2503(c) trust is its golden rule. Internal Revenue Code Section 2503(c) is a blueprint for both income and gift tax savings, if you want to accomplish those objectives by making significant gifts of income-producing property to minors.

You should look into the 2503(c) trust if your income tax bracket is high and your donee's bracket is relatively low. It's also highly useful if you own an asset that is likely to appreciate substantially over a period of time and you don't want it includable in your estate.

Why trust 2503(c)?

Why use a trust to shift cash or other property to your children? Why not give it to them outright? The answer is that there are a number of very realistic objections to outright gifts: your stockbroker wouldn't deal with securities owned directly by a minor. That's because the law allows a minor to disaffirm either a purchase of stock that subsequently falls in value or a sale of stock that later increases in value.

Another objection to putting property in your child's name

directly is that by doing so you "freeze" the title; your minor child's signature on a real estate deed doesn't give a buyer any assurance that he has acquired a permanent title.

Sure, you could petition a court to have a guardian appointed for your child. Once a legal guardian was appointed, many of the objections to an outright transfer could be overcome, but think of the cost; your child's guardian has to post bond and periodically must account for every transaction to a local court.

How's that?

Setting up a 2503(c) trust requires an attorney; the trust should be tailor-made to your situation. It should meet three requirements:

First, the trust must provide that income and principal may be expended by or on behalf of your beneficiary at any time prior to the time the beneficiary reaches age twenty-one (twenty-one is the age to be used no matter at what age a minor becomes an adult in your state).

Second, the trust must require that any income and principal will be payable to the beneficiary upon reaching twenty-one. (Actually, you can have the trust last longer than your child's twenty-first birthday. It can last as long as you want it to provided that your child is given the right, when he/she reaches age twenty-one, to take the money and other property in the trust. You could provide, for example, that your child has an absolute right to the property at that age, but if the principal is not withdrawn by a written request within three months of the child's twenty-first birthday, it remains in the trust until he/she is thirty, or whatever age you select.)

Third, if your child dies before age twenty-one, the principal must go to your child's estate or the person selected in his/her will.

Rule-of-thumb tax

If the trust pays out income to the trust beneficiary, that income will be taxed at his/her bracket.

Sometimes income is accumulated by the trust rather than paid out. In that case it's taxed to the trust. Eventually, when the accumulated income is paid out, your child is taxed on the money as if—in each of the years it was actually received by the trust—it had been received by your child. But your child, of course, receives credit for taxes paid by the trust. There's also a rule that exempts from tax all distributions of income accumulated in years he/she was under twenty-one.

Watch out for tax traps: The key one is that the income earned by the trust will be taxed back to you if trust income is—or may be—used to pay premiums on a life insurance policy on your life or your spouse's life. (It's OK to use trust principal. It's also safe to use trust income to purchase insurance on the life of your child or anyone else, including your business associates. This may make it possible to set up a buy-sell agreement and enable a child working in the business to purchase a deceased business associate's interest.)

Trust income will also be taxed to you if it is used to support your child; that is, to pay for his/her food, clothing, and shelter. (There's no prohibition against the trust's using principal for this purpose, however.)

Gifts to a 2503(c) trust qualify for the gift tax annual exclusion. As long as the three requirements described above are met, your gifts (up to $10,000 a year per donee if you are single or $20,000 if you are married) can be gift tax free.

Once a gift is made, all the future growth occurs in your child's estate—not in yours. Neither the gift nor the appreciation will be in your estate even if you die within three years of the gift.

Dr. Bruce Folbaum, a foot surgeon in the 50-percent income tax bracket, and his wife, Eileen, set up a trust for each of their three children, Rickey, Steven, and Kim. Bruce put $4,000 in cash into each of these trusts for his children (the law allows up to $20,000 gift tax free per child if Eileen signs Bruce's gift tax return and agrees to "split" the gift even if Bruce's earnings are the source of the money). This year, since the trusts meet all the requirements of Section 2503(c), Bruce's gifts are tax free; Bruce pays no federal gift tax on the transfer and the children pay no gift or income tax either.

If each $4,000 investment earns 15 percent, the trust will receive and can pay out $600 per child. No tax will be paid on any of the $1,800 total ($600 times three children), but if Bruce had not set up the trusts he would have lost $900 in taxes. Stated another way, over a ten-year period $9,000 in tax savings will help put Bruce and Eileen's children through college.

Consider the alternatives

No estate planning tools and techniques are perfect. Each

has a cost and almost all have alternatives. Many of the objectives you would accomplish through the use of a 2503(c) trust can be met through a Uniform Gifts to Minors Act account. So why use a 2503(c) trust?

If you plan to make only one property or cash transfer and you anticipate that gift will be a relatively modest one, use the UGMA account. The complexity and expense of creating a 2503(c) trust will probably outweigh its utility. But if you plan on making significant additional gifts in the future, you may want the additional flexibility of a 2503(c) trust (and the guarantee that your child can't take any principal until age twenty-one at the earliest).

Your decision may be made for you; certain property can't be held safely inside a 2503(c) trust. For instance, if a gift of stock in an S corporation (see Chapter 12) is given to a 2503(c) trust, the special treatment allowed to such corporations may be inadvertently lost. Conversely, a UGMA account can only hold certain types of property. One common type of property it can't hold is real estate. Fortunately, you can make a gift of real estate to your child through a 2503(c) trust.

Another reason you may want to use a 2503(c) trust instead of the UGMA account is custodianship. Under UGMA laws, you can only name one person as a custodian. When you establish a trust, you can name any number of trustees and have two or more of them acting together. You can even designate a line of successor trustees, but do not name yourself as either trustee or successor trustee. (If you do and you die as trustee before your child is twenty-one, the value of the assets in the trust will be in your estate and become subject to tax even if you've transferred them many years ago.)

Protecting you against old age

It is not pleasant to think of being old and alone. But aside from the social implications, what can you do about your personal security in those later years? Annie Michaels, single all of her life, was a valued employee of the Mighty Manufacturing Company. She had been retired for eight years, with an adequate pension and $45,000 in the bank. Annie had a few close friends with whom she played cards and went to the movies, but her only close relative was a brother who lived 2,000 miles away. When Annie suffered a stroke, she was found in her apartment by the building superintendent and taken to the hospital. Although Annie had a will leaving all of her assets to her brother's children, she had made no plans to take care of herself in case of her own disability.

How was Annie to receive the benefit of her pension and other assets if she was not physically capable of handling the money because of her condition? Since Annie had not designated anyone to act on her behalf, someone had to be appointed to act for her. However, there was a real problem as to who would institute the appropriate court proceedings to have someone appointed to manage Annie's property so that her assets would be used to maintain her during her disability, which might be permanent because of her advanced age. Perhaps the court having jurisdiction (which could be the Orphans' Court or other lower court in the state where Annie lived) would permit the director of the hospital where Annie was a patient to petition the court to appoint someone to care for Annie. Perhaps the court might insist that Annie's brother petition the court to name someone to take care of Annie, since he was her closest relative (even though he had no close contact with her and had not seen her for many years).

In order for the court to appoint someone to act for Annie (in most states called a "guardian" or a "committee"), Annie, in most instances, would have to be declared legally incompetent. How does a court go about deciding if someone is legally incompetent? It must have professional testimony, most likely from a psychiatrist, that Annie was incapable of handling her own money, might become the victim of designing persons, or perhaps unaware of the extent of her property, and any other standards that the court of Annie's state might use. Once appointed, Annie's "guardian" would be responsible for reporting to the court what use is made of Annie's money, a periodic accounting must be filed, fees are charged, and after all of this has taken place, Annie will, one hopes, personally benefit by the appointment.

What could Annie have done to avoid this situation? As a matter of fact, Annie had several very important options available to her.

Annie could have set up a revocable living trust, as has been discussed in Chapter 8. If Annie had sat down with a trust officer at the bank where she deposited her pension checks and had her savings, he/she might have explained the advantages to Annie of the revocable living trust. If Annie had permitted the trust department of the bank to handle her investments for her, she could have put a provision in the trust for the bank to be "Trustee" and to apply the income from her trust for her benefit if she became disabled. She also could have given her Trustee the right, in its discretion, to use as much of the principal for Annie's benefit as it felt necessary. If she had done that, then as soon as she became hospitalized, someone from the bank would have been in touch with her, would have advised the hospital that the bank was the trustee for Annie and that any bills should be forwarded to it. Annie's doctors could have been assured that there were funds available so that Annie received the best care, and arrangements could have been made for Annie to be placed in an appropriate nursing home so that her convalescence could be accelerated. Since the bank was already handling Annie's money, that Annie was disabled would have no effect whatsoever on Annie's investments, or on the bank's ability to use Annie's money for her benefit as quickly and efficiently as possible.

If Annie wanted to invest her own money while she was capable, but wanted to have someone else, either one of her girlfriends or a bank, and perhaps even her brother (although that might have been inconvenient), act for her if she became disabled and could not act for herself, Annie could have created a power of attorney. In this way, when Annie was hospitalized, someone else would have the authority to instantly receive Annie's pension and use that and any of her other assets for Annie's benefit until Annie was able to handle her own funds.

Nothing lasts forever—the power of attorney

Face it. Anyone could become disabled or have a serious accident. You probably know someone who became sick or was seriously hurt. Perhaps that person was a friend or even a close relative. It could even happen to you!

Jack Kirby is quite healthy but he's in his middle eighties. There's a good chance he could have a heart attack or a stroke, hurt himself, or become senile at any time. You are perfectly healthy and have no reason to thnk you'll be anything but healthy for years to come.

Yet Annie Michaels, Jack Kirby and you may at some time all have a common need—a need for someone to act on your behalf if you can't.

You may want to provide for the management of your legal affairs or assets in case you are physically or mentally unable. For instance, you may be out of the country and complex financial affairs may require decisions in your absence. You may wish to consider the power of attorney as a temporary and expedient substitute for a living trust. Since a trust will take much longer for an attorney to draft, a power of attorney may be an excellent stopgap measure until your trust is ready. (If you are in perfect health but worry about what would happen if you someday weren't, talk to your attorney about a standby or step up trust, one that doesn't really do anything until or unless you are disabled and give the word for the trustee to step up and take over.)

Sensible shifts

A power of attorney is a power-shifting device. Technically, it's a written document you can use to name another person (or persons) your "attorney-in-fact." That gives them the legal authority to act on your behalf.

You can make the scope of that power shift as limited (only for one purpose or for a short period of time) or as broad (any purpose and for an unlimited length of time) as you'd like.

Perhaps the best way to illustrate how broad or how many different individual powers you may want to consider using is to examine the provisions of an actual power of attorney.

POWER OF ATTORNEY

KNOW ALL MEN BY THESE PRESENTS, that I, Brett A. Rosenbloom, of Delaware County, Pennsylvania, hereby revoke any general power of attorney that I have heretofore given to any person, and by these Presents do constitute, make and appoint my brother, Eric J. Rosenbloom, of Delaware County, Pennsylvania, my true and lawful attorney.

1. To ask, demand, sue for, recover and receive all sums of money, debts, goods, merchandise, chattels, effects and things of whatsoever nature or description which are now or hereafter shall be or become owing, due, payable, or belonging to me in or by any right whatsoever, and upon receipt thereof, to make, sign, execute and deliver such receipts, releases or other discharges for the same, respectively, as he shall think fit.

2. To deposit any moneys which may come into his hands as such attorney with any bank or bankers, either in my or his own name, and any of such money or any other money to which I am entitled which now is or shall be so deposited to withdraw as he shall think fit; to sign mutual savings bank and federal savings and loan association withdrawal orders; to sign and endorse checks payable to my order and to draw, accept, make, endorse, discount, or otherwise deal with any bills of exchange, checks, promissory notes or other commercial or mercantile instruments; to borrow any sum or sums of money on such terms and with such security

as he may think fit and for that purpose to execute all notes or other instruments which may be necessary or proper; and to have access to any and all safe deposit boxes registered in my name.

3. To sell, assign, transfer, and dispose of any and all stocks, bonds (including U. S. Savings Bonds), loans, mortgages or other securities registered in my name; and to collect and receipt for all interest and dividends due and payable to me.

4. To invest in my name in any stock, shares, bonds (including U. S. Treasury Bonds referred to as "flower bonds"), securities or other property, real or personal, as to vary such investments as he, in his sole discretion, may deem best; and to vote at meetings of shareholders or other meetings of any corporation or company and to execute any proxies or other instruments in connection therewith.

5. To enter into and upon my real estate, and to let, manage, and improve the same or any part thereof, and to repair or otherwise improve or alter, and to insure any buildings thereon; to sell, either at public or private sale or exchange any part or parts of my real estate or personal property for such consideration and upon such terms as he shall think fit, and to execute and deliver good and sufficient deeds or other instruments of warranty or otherwise as he shall see fit, and to give good and effectual receipts for all or any part of the purchase price or other consideration; and to mortgage my real estate and in connection therewith to execute bonds and warrants and all other necessary instruments and documents.

6. To contract with any person for leasing for such periods, at such rents and subject to such conditions as he shall see fit, all or any of my said real estate; to give notice to quit to any tenant or occupier thereof; and to receive and recover from all tenants and occupiers thereof or of any part thereof all rents, arrears of rents, and sums of money which now are or shall hereafter become due and payable in respect thereof; and also on non-payment thereof or of any part thereof to take all necessary or proper means and proceedings for determining the tenancy or occupation of such tenants or occupiers, and for ejecting the tenants or occupiers and recovering the possession thereof.

7. To commence, prosecute, discontinue or defend all actions or other legal proceedings pertaining to me or my estate or any part thereof; to settle, compromise, or submit to arbitration any debt, demand or other right or matter due me or concerning my estate as he, in his sole discretion, shall deem best and for such purpose to execute and deliver such releases, discharges or other instruments as he may deem necessary and advisable; and to satisfy mortgages, including the execution of a good and sufficient release, or other discharge of such mortgage.

8. To execute, acknowledge and file all Federal, State and Local tax returns of every kind and nature, including without limitation, income, gift and property tax returns.

9. To engage, employ and dismiss any agents, clerks, servants or other persons as he, in his sole discretion, shall deem necessary and advisable.

10. To convey and transfer any of my property to trustees who shall hold the same for my benefit and/or the benefit of my children and other members of my immediate family upon such trust terms and conditions as to my attorney shall deem desirable.

11. To make gifts to my wife and/or issue upon such terms and conditions as he in his discretion shall determine.

12. In general, to do all other acts, deeds and matters whatsoever in or about my estate, property and affairs as fully and effectually to all intents and purposes as I could do in my own proper person if personally present, giving to my said attorney power to make and substitute under him an attorney or attorneys for all the purposes herein described, hereby ratifying and confirming all that the said attorney or substitute or substitutes shall do therein by virtue of these Presents.

13. In addition to the powers and discretion herein specifically given and conferred upon my attorney, and notwithstanding any usage or custom to the contrary, to have the full power, right and authority to do, perform and to cause to be done and performed all such acts, deeds and matters in connection with my property and estate as he, in his sole discretion, shall deem reasonable, necessary and proper, as fully, effectually and absolutely as if he were the absolute owner and possessor thereof.

14. In the event of my disability or incompetency, from whatever cause, this power of attorney shall not thereby be revoked.

IN WITNESS WHEREOF, I have hereunto set my hand and seal this   day of   , 19 .

_____ (SEAL)
BRETT A. ROSENBLOOM

STATE OF PENNSYLVANIA:
                    ss.
COUNTY OF DELAWARE

Before me, the undersigned, a Notary Public within and for the County of Delaware, Commonwealth of Pennsylvania, personally appeared Brett A. Rosenbloom, known to me to be the person whose name is subscribed to the within instrument, and acknowledged that he executed the same for the purposes therein contained.

IN WITNESS WHEREOF, I have hereunto set my hand and official seal this   day of   , 19 .

_____
NOTARY PUBLIC

(Source: *The Tools and Techniques of Estate Planning,* 4th Edition: The National Underwriter Company, Cincinnati, Ohio.)

On and on and on

To be sure a power of attorney will not be terminated by your disability or incapacity, your lawyer should insert words that convey your desire that "This power of attorney shall not be affected by the subsequent disability or incapacity of the principal" (you). That way the power you confer will be exercisable whether or not you are subsequently disabled or incapacitated. Paragraph 14 in the Power of Attorney document, providing that your designated person's power is to continue in spite of your physical or mental incapacity, makes the document a "durable" power of attorney.

When does it all end?

The power you give to someone else ends when you say it does. It could end when a particular act or transaction has been completed, upon a certain date, upon the occurrence or nonoccurrence of an event you have specified or (as all powers of attorney end) upon your death.

Your death terminates the right of a person to act under the power of attorney whether or not you have made it "durable." But in most states the "attorney-in-fact" you have named (you can name anyone who is a competent adult residing in your state—and that person does not have to be and typically is not a lawyer) can continue to act according to and under the power until that person learns of your death.

If you should become incompetent and a guardian is appointed on your behalf, that person has the same rights you would have. Therefore, the guardian could terminate the power on your behalf (just as you could if you remained competent).

Is it taxing?

Drafting of a power of attorney (which, like any other legal document, should not be attempted by anyone but a qualified lawyer) should not be expensive, since it is typically a relatively simple document. Nor will there be any adverse tax implications. The power of attorney doesn't shift any property rights; it merely authorizes someone to perform certain acts on your behalf.

But tax savings may result. Joe Mozino was extremely ill, a widower who had been hospitalized on December twentieth. Shortly before lapsing into a coma, Joe signed a power of attorney that authorized his son to make gifts up to $10,000 each to a number of related donees on Joe's behalf. These were all beneficiaries Joe had named in his will. It also authorized the son to purchase "Flower" Bonds, government bonds that could be purchased at a "discount" and used to help pay Joe's federal estate tax.

The son immediately used $100,000 of cash from Joe's checking and savings accounts to make gifts of $10,000 each to the ten children and grandchildren Joe had named in his will. Since Joe was still alive on January second of the following year, his son liquidated a number of nonappreciated assets, put the proceeds into Joe's checking account, and repeated the gift, giving $10,000 each to ten donees on Joe's behalf.

Even if Joe died within a day or two of the second round of gifts, not one penny of the $200,000 total would be in Joe's estate. Because of the $10,000 per donee annual gift tax exclusion, the entire $200,000 of gifts would be gift tax free as well. If Joe's estate were in the 40-percent federal estate tax bracket, the savings in federal estate tax would be $80,000!

The son also used his power of attorney right to buy Flower Bonds on Joe's behalf. (See Chapter 15 on Flower Bonds.) This made it possible to pay $100,000 of federal estate taxes at a cost of only $85,000 of cash.

Still further tax dollars and aggravation were saved by the power of attorney, which gave Joe's son the right to sign Joe's income and gift tax returns on his behalf.

Don't count on it

Not all states have specific laws enabling an individual to establish a durable power of attorney. Some states limit the type of property over which such powers will apply.

Naturally, as is the case with every other planning device, none should be considered a panacea or a solution to all your problems. But in many cases a power of attorney will be a powerful yet inexpensive estate planning tool.

20.
Charitable Gifts

Keeping your eye on the ball

We often don't achieve our goals because we forget what they are. If we don't remember where we are going, we'll probably wind up someplace else. The main purpose for estate planning is not to save taxes but to achieve personal objectives.

Many of us have charitable objectives. We'd like to repay society for many of its blessings and fulfill our moral obligations to give to those from whom we have taken so much.

If you have such a desire, you should know that the tax laws encourage such gifts. So why not take those favorable laws into account in your planning?

The tax laws regarding charitable contributions are highly complex and technical. Because so much is at stake, it is extremely important to "go by the book" in this area. The comments that follow are general and merely summarize the most basic and essential of the key rules and available tools.

Giving it now

One of the greatest pleasures is the joy of seeing your gift in action. To add to that enjoyment, if you make an outright gift to a qualified charity, you'll receive an income tax deduction.

The income tax law can't limit how much you can give—you can give every dollar that you have. But it does limit the size of the deduction you'll obtain for your gift—and whether or not you'll be allowed a deduction.

Here are the five requirements for an income tax deduction:

First, charitable contributions are deductible only if they are made to organizations which are "qualified." A donee will be considered qualified only if it meets three conditions: (a) it must be operated exclusively for religious, charitable, scientific, literary, or educational purposes, or to foster national or international amateur sports competition or to prevent cruelty to children or animals; (b) no part of the organization's earnings can benefit any private shareholder or similar individual, (c) the organization cannot be one disqualified for tax exemption because it attempts to influence legislation or participates in, publishes or distributes statements for, or intervenes in, any political campaign in behalf of any candidate seeking public office.

The Internal Revenue Service publishes a list of qualified charities. Examples of "qualified" organizations are nonprofit schools and hospitals, churches and synagogues, the United Fund, Community Chest, YMCA, YMHA, The American Red Cross, the Boy Scouts, Campfire Girls, the American Cancer Society, and the Heart Association.

Second, "property" must be the substance of the gift. Therefore, the value of your time or services, even if contributed to a qualified charity, is not deductible. For example, if you were a carpenter and spent ten hours building chairs for your daughter's school, you could not deduct your normal hourly wage as a charitable contribution. However, you could deduct the cost of materials you purchased and used in producing the finished product.

The donation of the use of property to a charity is not a contribution of property. This means the rent free use of an office, or even an office building, will not be considered a charitable contribution any more than a contribution of personal services.

Third, you must make a contribution in excess of the benefit you receive. For example, you donate cash to a charity. The charity in turn might pay you (and perhaps your survivors) an annuity income for life. Only the difference between the contribution you made and the value of a similar commercial annuity payable to you would be deductible.

Fourth, your gift to charity must actually be paid in cash or other property before the close of the tax year in question.

Fifth, if your lifetime transfer to charity is a gift of a "partial interest" (where your gift will be split between noncharitable and charitable beneficiaries) very strict rules apply. Generally, if a charity's interest in the transfer of property is a remainder interest (the charity receives what remains after your noncharitable income beneficiaries have received income for a specified time), a transfer in trust will qualify only if it is a so-called "annuity" or "unitrust" or a "pooled income" fund. (These terms are defined and described later in this chapter.)

If you've met these five requirements, the tax implications are:

1. A charitable contribution to a qualified charity reduces your current income taxes and therefore leaves you with more spendable income if you've donated property other than cash.

2. You pay no federal gift taxes regardless of the size of your gift.

3. The charity itself will pay no tax upon the receipt of your lifetime gift.

4. Generally, no income tax will be payable by a qualified charity on income earned by property you have donated to it.

A gift to charity can be one of the simplest estate planning techniques. While you are alive, you make a charitable gift merely by writing a check, assigning stock, transferring life insurance policies, signing a deed to real estate, or conveying property to charity in any other normal outright manner.

You can figure the cost of your gift, after your tax deduction, by this formula: Tax savings equals amount of deductible gift times effective tax bracket. For example, a $2,000 gift by a 40-percent bracket taxpayer equals $800 in tax savings. Stated another way, the out-of-pocket cost of the gift equals: Amount contributed minus tax savings. For instance, the $2,000 gift less the $800 in tax savings equals the out-of-pocket cost of the gift, $1,200.

What a charitable contribution really costs

This table shows the after-deduction cost of a $10,000 contribution to a qualified charity at various levels of taxable income. The rates used are those applicable to a married donor in 1983:

If your taxable income is	A $10,000 contribution costs about
$ 20,000	$7,500
30,000	6,700
41,000	6,100
46,000	5,600
60,000	5,100
86,000	5,000
100,000	5,000
120,000	5,000

Charitable Gifts

How high is up?

Your income tax charitable deduction is limited by the type of property you give:

(a) Rent free occupancy.
(b) Cash.
(c) Ordinary income property.
(d) Long-term capital gain property.
(e) Tangible personal property where the use of that property by the donee *is* related to the exempt functions of the donee.
(f) Tangible personal property where the use of that property is *un*related to the exempt purposes of the donee.

If the gift you make is merely to allow the charity to occupy the premises of property you own or if your gift entitles the charity to your services, you will receive no deduction no matter how valuable a right it is. To receive any deduction, you must actually donate property.

Cash gifts to so-called "public" charities generate a deduction of up to 50 percent of your adjusted gross income. So if your adjusted gross income is $100,000 this year, you would contribute and currently deduct as much as $50,000. If you give more than $50,000, you could carry over the excess deduction for up to five future years and use it to offset income in those years. Most churches and synagogues, hospitals, nonprofit schools and other charities are considered public charities and therefore qualify for this "50-percent" deduction.

"Ordinary income" type property is property that would produce ordinary income rather than capital gain if you sold it. Examples of ordinary income type property include capital assets you've held less than a year and a day, inventory or stock-in-trade, and works of art, books, letters, and musical compositions (if you are the person who created or prepared them or for whom they were prepared).

What is your deduction if you give "ordinary income" type property? Your deduction is limited to your cost (tax basis) for the property. For example, suppose you contribute real estate that you bought three months ago. You paid $15,000 for it and now it's worth

$20,000. Your deduction is limited to your cost, $15,000. The percentage limits and carry-over rules for this type of property are the same as for cash gifts. That means you can't take a current deduction for an amount in excess of one half of your adjusted gross income.

Capital gain type property is property that you would pay capital gains tax on if you sold it at a profit. The rules here are complex. The amount of your deduction depends on whether the charity is a "public" charity (as defined above) and (if your gift is tangible personal property) how the charity will use your gift.

If the charity will use your tangible personal property in a manner related to its tax-exempt functions and activities (for example, if you donate a painting to a museum that will display it to the public), the deduction is "use related." That means the full value of what you donate is deductible up to 30 percent of your adjusted gross income.

For instance, Lara Leimberg has $60,000 of adjusted gross income. She contributes stock worth $30,000 to the Girl Scouts of America. Assume the stock cost her $10,000. Her $30,000 contribution is deductible—up to 30 percent of her $60,000 adjusted gross income. In other words, she can deduct $18,000 this year. The $12,000 difference ($30,000 less $18,000) can be carried over and used as a deduction in future years. She could elect different tax treatment if it would be more advantageous. She could deduct the contribution with a limit of up to 50 percent of her adjusted gross income instead of only 30 percent. But the cost of this increased current deduction is that she must decrease her overall deduction. Why is her overall deduction reduced? Because if she makes the special election she can only deduct the sum of (a) her cost, and (b) one half the appreciation. For example, assume Lara paid $20,000 for the stock and it's now worth $50,000. This special election allows her to deduct her cost ($20,000) plus half the $30,000 appreciation ($15,000), a total of $35,000. Because of this election her deduction this year is 50 percent of $60,000—$30,000. She can carry over the other $5,000 and deduct it in future years. If she had not made the special election, she would only be able to deduct $18,000 this year (30 percent of her $60,000 adjusted gross income). But she would have the difference, $32,000 ($50,000 contribution minus $18,000 deduction), to carry over into the next five years.

Not all gifts of tangible personal property are "use related." For example, if the art museum intended to sell the painting rather than display it, or the donor donated a diamond necklace that was not a work of art the museum intended to display, the gift would not be "use related." Here the donor's deduction is limited to 50 percent of his/her adjusted gross income—but a deduction can be taken only for the donor's cost plus half the appreciation. So if Lara donated a diamond necklace worth $20,000 that cost her $12,000 and the museum sold it and used the proceeds to purchase art, since the use is "unrelated" Lara's deduction would be limited. She could only deduct her $12,000 cost plus $4,000 of her $8,000 gain, a total of $16,000. If the gift was "use related" her deduction would have been $20,000.

What's the moral of all these highly technical stories?

First, you get more tax saving mileage from giving appreciated long-term capital gain type property than from giving cash or other assets. Why? Because (with the exception of "unrelated use" tangible personal property) you can deduct the full value of the property (up to the maximum limit of your adjusted gross income) and escape the capital gain tax on the appreciation. That means the gift costs less than if you sold the same property, paid your tax, and then contributed the proceeds. For example, Mary Robinson is in a 50-percent income tax bracket. She owns capital gain stock for which she paid $2,000 and which is now worth $10,000. If she sold the stock first and then contributed what was left, she'd have an $8,000 capital gain ($10,000 less $2,000) and the capital gain tax would be $1,600. (60 percent of the $8,000 gain is deductible and the remaining 40%, $3,200, is taxable at Mary's 50-percent income tax rate). Her cost to make the contribution would be $10,000 (the value of the stock) plus $1,600 (the capital gains tax) less her $5,000 tax savings ($10,000 deduction from a 50-percent tax bracket), that is, $6,600. By giving the stock directly, Mary's cost is $5,000, that is, $10,000 (the value of the stock) less $5,000 (the tax deduction). Giving appreciated stock directly saved $1,600 ($6,600 less $5,000).

Second, it pays to hold substantially appreciated capital stock for more than twelve months before donating it. That makes it long-term capital gain property.

Third, leave ordinary income property to a charity in your will so you'll receive a full estate tax deduction. (The estate tax law doesn't treat ordinary income property any differently from long-term capital gain property.)

Fourth, leave ordinary income property—including works of art you've created—to your children, who receive a new cost basis and who could themselves receive an income tax charitable deduction for the full fair market value of their gift.

Fifth, if the property you'd like to contribute is worth less than you paid for it, sell it, take a tax deductible loss, and contribute the proceeds.

Sixth, if the property you'd like to give is tangible personal property, obtain a commitment from the donee specifying that the donated property will be used in a manner related to its (the organization's) exempt purpose.

Here's a table capsulizing these charitable deduction rules:

CHARITABLE CONTRIBUTION DEDUCTION LIMITATIONS

	Type of Property	Donee*	Adjusted Gross Income(%)	Deduction Limitation Carryover	Tax Treatment
(a)	Rent free occupancy or services	—	—	—	No deduction
(b)	Cash	Public	50%	5 yrs.	Full deduction
(c)	Ordinary income property	Public	50%	5 yrs.	Deduction limited to basis
(d)	Long-term capital gain property (except for tangible personal property)	Public	30%	5 yrs.	Full deduction for fair market value
(e)	Tangible personal property (L.T.C.G. property)		30%	5 yrs.	Full deduction for fair market value
	(1) "use related"	Public			
	(2) "non-use related"	Public	50%	5 yrs.	Deduction reduced to 40% of potential L.T.C.G.

*Regardless of the type of property given, the deduction for an individual's contributions to private charities is limited to the lesser of (a) 20 percent of the taxpayer's adjusted gross income or (b) 50 percent of adjusted gross income less any charitable contribution deduction allowed for contributions to public type charities.

What's in the future?

You can receive a current deduction even if you give the charity only a "future interest." A "future interest" is any interest or right that the charity will possess or enjoy at some time in the future. The term "future interest" includes situations where a donor purports to give tangible personal property to a charitable organization but has made a written or oral agreement with the organization reserving to a noncharitable beneficiary (himself, a member of his immediate family, or a friend) the right to use, possess, or enjoy the property. For example, suppose Dave Carnahan donates an Ansel Adams photograph to an art museum but arranges with the museum to keep the photograph in his home as long as he lives. The museum has a future interest in the photograph.

One of the basic general rules governing charitable contribution deductions is that contributions must (a) actually be paid, (b) in cash or other property, (c) before the close of the tax year. (Generally, no deductions are allowed for an outright contribution of less than the donor's entire interest in property.) Since the museum's enjoyment of the photograph was deferred, no current tax deduction would be allowed. The implication is that typically a deduction will not be allowed until the charity receives actual possession or enjoyment of the work of art. The gift of tangible personal property must be complete, in the sense that the charity must have all interests in and rights to the possession and enjoyment of the property. Generally, this means that a transfer of a future interest in property to a charity is not deductible until all intervening interests in and rights to possession held by the donor or certain related persons or organizations have expired (or unless the gift is in the form of a future interest in trust that meets the requirements discussed below).

You're probably wondering

If the general rule is that a donor receives no deduction if the charity has to wait, how can I receive a current tax deduction for such a gift? The answer is, because of certain favorable exceptions to that general rule, you can receive a current deduction even if you:

1. Make a gift of your house or farm. For example, you could give your farm to the Boy Scouts but stipulate that you had the right to live on it as long as you lived. You'd receive an income tax deduction now for the value of the farmland that would someday be received by the Scouts.

2. Make a gift that the charity will not receive until you (and/or your spouse or other designated relative) die. It is possible to put property into a trust, receive income from that property for as long as you (and/or other noncharitable beneficiaries you name) live and still obtain a deduction—today. How? By using a "charitable remainder" trust.

A charitable remainder trust is one in which the charity receives what remains after a specified number of years or after the lifetimes of specified individuals (which may include yourself).

This means there's a way to provide income for yourself and someone you love, increase your income through favored treatment, and at the same time fulfill your charitable objectives.

How? Let's say you are in a 50-percent income tax bracket. You'd like to retire next year. You know at that time your income will drop substantially. Assume also that you have securities you bought years ago that have appreciated substantially. If you sold them in order to reinvest your proceeds in some investment yielding more income, you'd have to pay an immediate capital gains tax. That would reduce the amount remaining to earn income for you.

So instead of selling the securities, you contribute them to a charitable remainder trust. That gives you an immediate tax deduction, which in turn puts money in your pocket—now. The trustee of your trust could sell the stock and reinvest the proceeds in higher-yield assets. Since you have retained the right to the income for life and since no tax is paid on the sale by the trust, the principal and therefore the income it produces for you is not reduced by any tax.

Suppose you want to provide income to your spouse after your death. You can also provide that income from the trust is to be paid to her for life if she survives you. That extra security has a cost, of course. Since the charity has to wait longer for its money, the value of its interests—and therefore the value of your current deduction—is reduced.

You could also reverse the process. You could set up a trust, put income-producing assets in it and give the charity the right to the income for a specified period of time. At the end of that time, your beneficiary would receive the property. This is called a charitable "income or lead" trust and has a number of tax advantages especially useful for individuals who have particularly high-income years followed by low-income years (as is common at retirement).

One popular type of remainder trust is the so-called Charitable

Charitable Gifts

Remainder "Unitrust." You create a "unitrust" by transferring money or securities to a trustee. The gift is irrevocable. The trustee in turn pays you (and perhaps your spouse) an income each year you live. At your death(s), the assets in the trust become the sole property of the charitable donee. You receive payments based on a fixed percentage of the fair market value of the trust assets. The percentage stays the same, but the assets are revalued each year. For instance, if you decide on a 10-percent return, each year you'll be paid an amount equal to 10 percent of the value of the trust (in that year), so if the trust has increased in value your income increases. If the trust has decreased in value, you'll receive less.

You receive an immediate income tax charitable deduction in the year you create the trust and transfer the assets to it. The deduction is measured by the value of the charitable organization's right to eventually receive the assets of the trust; that is, the deduction is affected by your age at the time of the gift, the amount involved, and what percentage of the trust's assets you choose to receive each year.

You pay no capital gains tax when you contribute property to the trust, even if the stocks you transfer to the trust have appreciated substantially. If the trust should sell assets at a gain, those gains are taxed neither to you nor to the trust.

When you receive your income payments from the trust, some of the payment may be tax free, a portion taxable as capital gains, and the balance as ordinary income. The exact percentages depend on how the assets of the trust are invested.

Another popular type of remainder trust is the Charitable Remainder "Annuity" Trust. Here's how the annuity trust works: you transfer money or securities to a trust. The trustee, in turn, pays you a fixed dollar amount for the rest of your life, regardless of whether the assets in the trust increase or decrease in value. At your death, the remaining principal of the trust goes to the charitable beneficiary.

Your deduction is based on the present worth of the right to receive the trust assets upon your death (determined by reference to IRS tables).

The table on page 256 shows the charitable deduction you'd be allowed for a $100,000 gift if you requested annual payments of $5,000.

Income Beneficiary's Age	Male	Female
50	$ 43,335	$ 37,103
55	48,520	41,784
60	54,123	47,312
65	59,823	53,497
70	65,588	60,383

Take stock in this gift

Giving a charity shares of stock in your closely held business may yield substantial dividends. Here's how.

First, you donate some of your stock to the charitable organization you have selected. You receive a charitable contribution deduction measured by the value of the stock you contributed. Then your corporation buys the stock back from the charity. (Had the corporation redeemed the stock directly from you, dividend treatment would probably have resulted.)

One person who used this device was a controlling shareholder who gave a school about 200 shares of his corporation's stock each year. He took an annual deduction for the present value of the gifts, about $25,000. The terms of the gift provided that the university could not dispose of the shares without first offering them to the corporation at their book value. The corporation was not required to purchase the stock but did have a 60-day option in which to purchase any stock offered to it. Within a year or two after the shares were received by the school, they were offered to the corporation, which purchased them. The proceeds of these redemptions were then invested by the school.

If you do it properly, you can siphon funds from your business free of income tax by making a charitable contribution of your personally owned stock followed by an unrelated redemption of that stock by your corporation. This technique may eliminate or reduce the threat of a corporate accumulated earnings tax problem, generate a current income tax deduction for you, and provide cash for your favorite charity with no out-of-pocket outlay on your part.

The keys for success are (1) make your gifts of stock complete and irrevocable; (2) don't insist upon any formal or informal agreement that your charitable donee will sell the stock back to your corporation; and, (3) don't promise the charity either directly or indirectly that your business will buy the stock you've given to it.

Where there's life there's hope—and charity

Many successful and charitably minded people use life insurance on their lives as a way to make their charitable contributions. Why? For a number of reasons.

First, the death benefit going to the charity is guaranteed as long as premiums are paid. This means that the charity will receive an amount that is fixed in value and not subject to the potential downside risks of securities.

Second, life insurance provides an "amplified" gift that can be purchased on the installment plan. Through a relatively small annual cost (premium) on your part you can provide a large future benefit for the charity. A significant gift can be made without impairing or diluting the control of your family business interest or other investments. Assets earmarked for your family can be kept intact.

Third, life insurance is a self-completing gift. If you live, guaranteed cash values, which can be used by the charity currently, grow constantly from year to year. If you become disabled, the policy will remain in full force through the waiver-of-premium feature. This guarantees both the ultimate death benefit to the charity and the same cash values and dividend build-up that would have been earned had you not become disabled. Even if your death occurs after only one premium payment, the charity is assured of your full gift.

Fourth, the death proceeds can be received by your designated charity free of federal income and estate taxes, probate and administrative costs and delays, brokerage fees, or other transfer costs. This means the charity receives "one hundred percent" dollars. Compare this prompt cash payment with the payment of a gift to the selected charity under the terms of your will. In that case, probate delays of up to several years are not uncommon.

Fifth, because of the contractual nature of the life insurance contract, large gifts to charity are not subject to attack by disgruntled heirs. Life insurance proceeds also do not run afoul of the so-called state "mortmain statutes," which prohibit or limit gifts made to charities within a short time before death.

Finally, a substantial gift may be made with no publicity. Since the life insurance proceeds on your life that are paid to charity can be arranged so they will not be part of your probate estate, the proceeds can be paid confidentially. Of course, if you want publicity you can have it.

Here's how to obtain a current income tax deduction. Have the charity own the policy on your life and name itself the beneficiary. The premiums you pay can then be fully and currently deductible as charitable contributions.

Make your check out to the charity. Have it pay the premiums to the life insurance company. That will insure the most favorable tax results. Your cancelled check will serve as proof of (1) the fact that your gift was made to the charity; (2) the date the gift was made; and (3) the amount of the gift. It will also assure you of a full deduction up to 50 percent of your adjusted gross income. (When an "indirect" gift is made to a charity, the annual deduction limit is lowered to 20 percent of the taxpayer's income. A gift in trust is one such example. Another example of an indirect gift is where premiums on a policy owned by a charity are remitted directly to the life insurance company instead of to the charity itself.)

Records, records, records

When you make a gift to charity, be sure to keep records of your gift. Keep all receipts, cancelled checks, or other evidence of the date of the actual payment, the name of the charity, the amount, and the type of gift you've made. Your receipts should be held at least three years from the date your tax return is due or filed, or two years from the time you paid your tax if that date was later. Keep your tax returns and tax payment checks permanently.

Giving it later

Not everyone can or wants to give up either income or principal while they are alive—even if the recipient will be a charity that is near and dear. Many, however, would like to make a meaningful and significant gift upon death.

The estate tax law (and most states' death tax laws) favor charitable gifts by providing an unlimited charitable deduction. In other words, you could leave your entire estate—no matter how large—to charity and not have to pay one nickle in estate taxes.

If there is a charity you love—or feel you "owe," why not contact the charity directly? It probably has a person or department in charge of fund-raising who can assist you in deciding what to give and how to give it.

Many colleges and universities can provide your attorney with helpful—and cost saving—specimen documents or will provisions.

21.
Dying and Death: What Can Be Done—Before and After

Death is inevitable—taxes are not

We hope this book has already helped you avoid taxes. Although we think it's a very good book, it's not good enough to help you avoid the other inevitable—death. But we can outline some of the preparations you should make for it and explain to survivors what to do next.

The single most important thing you can do for your family is to plan and execute a "Financial Firedrill." It may seem grim, but you can save your family more money and grief by sitting down and sharing your thoughts about what should be done and who should do it than anything else you could do.

What to do when your time is limited

The truth is—we are all dying. The death trajectory of a patient with inoperable cancer differs from that of a healthy athlete only in terms of time. Some of us will die "before our time"—others after a long and happy life. Many of us will know that we have a limited time. Those of us who do know that we have less than a normal life expectancy have an opportunity to attach a value, a meaningfulness to our remaining days to make them fulfilling in terms of significant accomplishments.

What can you do if you are aware that the death of a family member—or your own—is imminent? A great deal. An incredible amount of tax and administration expense dollars can be saved if you are willing to act decisively.

Easing administration

Sign a durable power of attorney. This will give the person of your choice the power to act as your agent if you can't. (See Chapter 19 for more details.)

Consider a revocable trust. This device can provide for the management of property both before and after your death. Assets inside the revocable trust will avoid probate. This should result in administration expense savings. You can name yourself both primary trustee and beneficiary. This gives you full control and enjoyment over your property, for as long as you want, but enables the successor(s) you have chosen to take over should you become incapacitated (physically or mentally) or upon your death. A revocable trust could be especially useful to keep your family business operating.

A "living will"

Consider a "living will." In this era of modern technology, we all have thought about the "right to die." Many people have expressed a desire that extraordinary means should not be employed to prolong their lives. Some states (these include Arkansas, California, Idaho, New Mexico, North Carolina, Oregon and Texas) have already enacted laws making it easier for doctors or family members to honor your wishes. In other states, a specimen document will have no legal effect. But certainly, the declaration of desires (see opposite page), if properly executed while you are competent, will help a physician follow your wishes more readily than if you had signed no such document, even in states that have not passed "right to die" laws. Give a copy of the signed living will (designed in a project of the Yale Law School) to your personal physician and to appropriate family members and discuss your thoughts and desires with them (and with your attorney).

How to increase the overall size of your estate

Certain bank loans for car loans, home mortgages, home improvements and other business and personal loans permit or may even require the purchase of group (no exam required) creditor life insurance. Spread out the repayment of the loan over as long a period as possible.

If you own permanent life insurance and you are disabled, call your agent to see if you have "disability waiver of premium." If you do, and you've met the requirements, the insurer will repay every

Proposed Living Will

DECLARATION MADE THIS _____ DAY OF _____

I, _____ being of sound mind, willfully and voluntarily make known my desire that my dying shall not be artificially prolonged under the circumstances set forth below, do hereby declare:

If at any time I should have an incurable injury, disease or illness certified to be a terminal condition by two physicians who have personally examined me, one of whom shall be my attending physician, and the physicians have determined that my death will occur whether or not life-sustaining procedures are utilized and where application of life-sustaining procedures would serve only to artificially prolong the dying process, I direct that such procedures be withheld or withdrawn and that I be permitted to die naturally with only the administration of medication or the performance of any medical procedures deemed necessary to provide me with comfort care.

In the absence of my ability to give directions regarding the use of such life-sustaining procedures, it is my intention that this declaration shall be honored by my family and physicians as the final expression of my legal right to refuse medical or surgical treatment and accept the consequences from such refusal.

I understand the full import of this declaration and I am emotionally and mentally competent to make this decision.

Signed _____

City, County, State of Residence _____

_____

The declarant has been personally known to me and I believe him or her to be of sound mind.

Witness _____

Witness _____

dollar of premium you've paid after you became totally disabled and take over the premium payments for you, and your policy will stay in full force.

If you don't have waiver of premium or it doesn't apply, talk to your insurance agent and other counsellors about "extended term." You can stop paying premiums and still be covered for the full death benefit under the policy.

Buy "Flower Bonds" if your advisors have guesstimated there will be significant federal estate taxes to be paid. Flower Bonds (see Chapter 15) are special U.S. government bonds you can buy even on your death bed (or have the person with your power of attorney purchase for you). These bonds can be bought at a discount and are redeemable at their face value in payment of the federal estate tax. Keep in mind that these bonds must be purchased while you are alive—your executor can't do it for you.

Increasing your salary may enlarge death benefits under certain fringe benefit plans. If you control your business and your pension, group insurance or other benefits are based on a multiple of salary, an increase in salary could have a multiplier effect. In other words, if your group insurance, for example, is two times your salary, every dollar of increased salary increases your group coverage by two dollars.

How to reduce transfer taxes

If you haven't changed your will since September 13, 1981, your estate may not be eligible for the unlimited federal estate marital deduction. Roughly half of your estate may be subjected to federal estate tax—needlessly! Call your attorney to review your will and/or trust.

Repay life insurance policy loans. Why? Because in most states a dollar of life insurance is worth more to your beneficiaries than a dollar of cash in the bank (or anyplace else). The reason is that most states treat life insurance more favorably than other assets. Some states exclude life insurance totally from state death taxes. Many other states exempt a large part of insurance proceeds.

Repaying policy loans will also reduce the size of your probate estate and help save on administrative expenses.

If you've named your estate as beneficiary of your life insurance, change it—NOW! You may have needlessly subjected the insurance to state inheritance taxes. For instance, in Pennsylvania, $100,000 of life insurance payable to your estate will be diminished by a 6 percent state inheritance tax, even if your child or spouse were your sole beneficiary. If you had named that same person directly, there would be no tax and he/she would receive $6,000 more. Since the state tax on property left to brothers, sisters, aunts, uncles, cousins, or friends is 15 percent in Pennsylvania, the savings would be a whopping $15,000—plus the savings realized by avoiding administrative costs.

Use the $10,000 per donee annual federal gift tax exclusion. You can give—gift tax free—$10,000 to anyone you want and as many people as you want year after year. None of that money will be in your estate even if you die within a day of making the gift. Furthermore, all the income and the appreciation is removed from your estate—starting the day of the gift. You can double the $10,000 to $20,000 per donee to an unlimited number of donees if you are married. (See Chapter 9.) All these gifts also avoid probate, and you can be sure they've gone to the persons you've wanted to have them.

Many states have a "gifts in contemplation of death" rule which brings back gifts into your estate for state death tax purposes if you die within a specified period of time. But many states have surprisingly liberal laws with many escape holes if you act quickly enough. For instance, Pennsylvania law doesn't bring a gift back if you've made it more than two years prior to your death. Even if you have, it still isn't subjected to Pennsylvania inheritance tax unless it comprised a significant portion of your estate, and even then it wouldn't be brought back if your executor can prove the gift was made primarily to achieve "living" objectives.

How to decrease income taxes

If you plan to make gifts to a charity in your will, don't wait—do it NOW! A lifetime gift results in an income tax deduction that you wouldn't have had otherwise.

Personal touches

There are a number of things you can do to make it easier for your executor and other family members. These include:

Tell the appropriate people where your safe deposit box is and the location of your keys.

Arrange for successor management—or sale—of your business. (It's far easier for you to do these things than your uninformed and emotionally distraught successors.)

Prepare a list of advisors (names, addresses, phone numbers) and discuss with your family which ones can be relied upon for various advice and assistance.

Prepare a letter to various family members (some people call these "letters of instructions"). This is a personal nonlegal document explaining your wishes with respect to how family heirlooms are to be distributed, your thoughts about the remarriage of your spouse, and other highly personal matters that you don't want disclosed in your will or other public documents.

Make an up-to-date list of all your investments and be sure all important documents (wills, trusts, deeds, birth certificates, and so forth) are in your safe deposit box. Be sure the right person has the key and knows where the box is.

After death

Immediately following death, there are decisions to be made that require prompt action. In certain instances, anatomical gifts have been anticipated by the deceased and must be implemented by the survivors. (See the Uniform Donor Card on page 332.)

Funeral arrangements must be made, either in accordance with the prior wishes of the decedent, if known, or at the discretion of the surviving family members.

The personal representative of the decedent must be formally appointed. If there was a will, then the deceased's choice of executor or executrix will be formally approved. Otherwise, the law of the state where the decedent was domiciled will determine who is eligible to represent the decedent's interests. In Chapter 7, you will find a check list of the executor's primary duties, which outlines the formal obligations of the personal representative. In order to have all of the essential information available to perform his or her duties properly, expeditiously and completely, the personal representative must have a clear picture of what's in the estate. Included in the Appendix is a comprehensive inventory of information needed by executors or administrators, together with the most commonly used forms. These were prepared by Edward F. Graves, Assistant Professor of Insurance at The American College in Bryn Mawr, Pennsylvania, for his excellent article "Procedural Aspects Following Death," and are reprinted in the Appendix with the permission of Mr. Graves and The American College.

22.
Wrapping It Up

Taking stock of yourself

If you have understood the ideas presented in this book, something you've read must have hit home.

One of the stories used to illustrate an estate planning idea or one of the tax savings special situations could have been applicable to your specific needs. In fact, it is almost impossible for you not to have increased your knowledge of where you stand in regard to planning for the future, regardless of your previous technical background. You have probably learned a lot about yourself, your property and your family that were not evident before. What's more important, you have some definite goals that you now feel are attainable. What happens next?

Getting it together and going for help

If you have not already done so, then it is certainly time to turn to the Appendix and fill in your Personal Fact-Finder and accumulate as much information as you can about yourself. There is a great deal of helpful information and advice you can obtain at no cost. Your local IRS office can provide you with booklets on estate and gift tax laws; your bank's trust department is an important source of information on wills, trusts and state property laws; many insurance agents are highly trained in computing the probable costs of dying and the income and capital needs of your survivors.

You should not need help in accumulating all of the pertinent papers that are necessary to any well thought out plan. Obtain your deed and make sure it is set up with you and your spouse as the owners and that the survivor will own the entire property at the death of the first spouse, if that's your understanding. Make sure that the stock that was supposed to be set up in a custodian's name for your son has been set up that way and was not put in your name by mistake. Make absolutely certain that you have named contingent beneficiaries in your life insurance policy, and if the policy does not indicate it, write to the insurance company to be sure. All of these steps may seem basic, but they are three of the most frequently occurring "oversights" that only become apparent following death.

Once you've done all you can for yourself, then it is time to find professionals with whom you want to work.

Get a lawyer you like

The keystone of the estate planning team is the lawyer. If you do not think you will have any of the serious death tax problems discussed and perhaps only need a will and to rearrange your life insurance, then your only expense might be your legal fees. A will that spells out your wishes for your family and at the same time distributes your assets as efficiently as possible, while being completely coordinated with your insurance and other benefits, need not be an expensive undertaking.

In most cases, it is to your advantage to utilize the services of an experienced lawyer who specializes in estate planning. Most lawyers are competent and have experience in preparing wills, but in the age of specialization, all lawyers cannot be experts in all areas of the law. Ask the attorney about his or her tax background or what special estate planning courses he/she has taken. Look on the office walls to see if he/she belongs to an estate planning council—or ask.

How do you know you have the right lawyer? Make certain that at the initial interview the lawyer understands what you have and what you want to do with it. Has he explained the law to you as it applies to your situation, what the tax consequences will be, and how best to achieve your goals in the most efficient manner possible? Demand a written statement of what the charges will be and how they are calculated. (But give the attorney a chance to understand your situation and what type of work will have to be done for you before quoting a fee. In all fairness, you wouldn't call a clothing store and ask how much a suit of clothes would cost. You would first have to stop in, look over the merchandise, make your selection, and then find out the price. By the same token, a lawyer cannot quote a price for services when he does not know what type of services he or she will be called on to perform.)

Lastly, as with all professionals whom you ask to work for you, make sure that you have confidence that they are working in your best interest. Lawyers, like doctors, teachers and businessmen, are only people. Some people are great to do business with, and there are some people, who because of their attitude toward you or their outlook on life, make them the type of person whom you would rather not patronize. Most people have excellent relationships with their professional advisors, and there is no reason whatsoever for not being able to find a qualified attorney to assist you with your planning.

The addition of an accountant

Do you require the services of an accountant? If you own your own business, or don't take standard deductions on your income tax return, you probably have—or should have—your own accountant. Most people with moderate to high incomes find that the expense of having a qualified accountant review their tax returns is more than made up by the ideas and tax savings they realize from this association. The same holds true with estate planning.

In many cases, your lawyer is competent to review the tax implications of your situation and make recommendations and draw the appropriate instruments. It is often a good idea to insist that the attorney contact and discuss your situation with your accountant before drafting any instruments. In estimating the value of a business, the input of an accountant is often essential. What you can or can't afford to save, whether you are or are not utilizing the most efficient retirement savings plans available to you, and how best to provide funds for the death or disability of a business partner or associate are some of the kinds of information that are particularly within the knowledge of your accountant. Even if you think your income is too modest to have an accountant review or prepare your returns, it is often a good idea, at least every few years, to secure some professional advice in this area. There might be one or two easily available tax savings plans that you are not utilizing solely because no one has ever told you about them. The accountant therefore is often a valued member of the estate planning team.

How do you choose the services of an accountant if you do not already have one? If your purpose is to assist in your estate plans, then it is obviously best to have an accountant who specializes in estate planning situations and death taxes. There is a national organization, the National Association of Estate Planning Councils, which is comprised of local estate planning councils throughout the country. They include accountants, attorneys, banking officers from the estate planning and trust departments, and representatives of the life insurance industry. Accountants belonging to this organization have indicated by their membership that they specialize in estate planning and would be prime candidates to assist in your estate plan. Membership lists can be obtained from the trust officer or estate planning officer of your commercial bank or by looking in your phone book under Estate Planning Councils. Your attorney and insurance representative, as well as your banker, might also be in the position to recommend a qualified accountant.

The agent who works for you

Quite often, the professional who first gets you thinking about estate planning is your insurance agent. Quite often, the insurance agent is more responsible for initiating estate planning than the other members of the estate planning team. Life insurance, as has been indicated, is a key and integral part of most estate plans and one of the cheapest and simplest ways to leave property to your heirs. Choosing whom you buy your insurance from is an important decision. While accountants and attorneys have to have certain formal qualifications to act as such, this is not always the case with insurance people. Therefore, you are perfectly within your rights to question the qualifications of the insurance representative with whom you come in contact. A person holding the degree of Chartered Life Underwriter (CLU) has been exposed to many courses in income and estate and gift tax law as well as in all facets of estate planning. Certainly, a CLU can be of considerable help to you.

Formal qualifications alone do not guarantee satisfactory results, and you should therefore apply some of the other criteria indicated above, as well as your own intuition, in determining whether the individual with whom you are doing business has considered your overall situation and your best interest in making recommendations to you. Ask your agent how recently he took a course in estate planning. Ask if he/she belongs to an estate planning council.

Bank on the right man—or woman

Most commercial banks have estate planning and trust departments, with qualified people ready and anxious to give both advice and assistance with your personal estate plans. Quite often, if you are a customer of the bank, there will be no charge for conferring with the bank representative. This is sometimes a desirable starting point for you in attaining some initial advice or in following through with some of the ideas presented in this book. Obviously, the bank involved would be more than pleased if you decided to include it in your estate plan—as executor of your will, or as a trustee under one or more trusts that might be indicated. No charge is imposed by the bank for being named executor or trustee of a trust that will not begin until your death, when you initially appoint it to act as such. In other words, until the bank actually begins its work, there are no charges for merely appointing it now to act after your death. (As in the case of the purchase of any other service, banks charge fees. Ask what these fees are and request your banker to explain the pros—and cons—of using the bank as your executor or trustee.)

One more point, shop around for a bank the same way you'd shop for any other service. All trust departments are not equally equipped to help your estate plan.

Your executor—an appointment to be carefully considered

Being an executor involves a tremendous amount of responsibility. Before naming someone to be your executor in your will, or volunteering to act as an executor for someone, you should be aware of the nature of the job.

What does the executor do?

When a person dies, the law requires that his property must be collected. After debts, taxes and expenses are paid, the remaining assets are distributed to whoever is entitled to that property. That distribution is determined by the person's will if he has one or the intestate laws of the state in which he dies, if he does not have a will. It is the executor's responsibility to collect and distribute the assets and to pay the death taxes and expenses of the deceased.

In trying to accomplish all this, the executor can run into a number of problems. For example, if there was a business in the estate, and the executor handles it improperly, he/she can be sued by the beneficiaries of the estate for certain mistakes. In many cases, businesses are continued following a person's death by the executor, without authority in the will to continue the business and without court authorization. The executor can be held personally liable for any loss to the estate suffered by continuation of the business in those cases. Executors have also been held responsible for not investing the proceeds properly, for filing tax returns late, and for failing to exercise options that were available to them for the benefit of the estate. Because of changes in the Economic Recovery Tax Act of 1981, the executor may have to make decisions that can have serious death tax consequences.

The bottom line, therefore, is that in choosing your executor be sure you select someone who is aware of the size and value of your estate, the persons who will share in your estate, and who is knowledgeable about the proper way to handle your property. He/she must act with your wishes for the welfare of your beneficiaries, and also must be familiar with the various tax ramifications involved in properly closing out your estate. Be sure to consider a bank if your estate is large or consists of many assets.

Trustees

Where you have thought it best to have property held in trust for a beneficiary, you have decided that a person or institution should have the responsibility for holding and investing the property that you are leaving in trust, and making payments of income and/or principal to the beneficiary or to the recipient. Your best bet would probably be to use a professional (typically a bank) trustee, unless: (a) there is a small amount involved; or (b) where there is a close family situation where the trustee undoubtedly will have the interest of the beneficiary at heart, the time and skill to properly invest the funds, and be in a position to systematically pay the proceeds to the beneficiaries or else apply it for them, by payment either directly to a college, hospital or for rent, or for other purposes. Trust companies, usually commercial banks with a trust department, are best situated to act in these cases, unless the amount involved is so small as to not warrant your paying the bank its minimum fees. Sometimes there is an individual who will fit these requirements, such as a brother who has had experience as a stockbroker or accountant, but more often than not, the best interest of the estate, yourself and your beneficiaries will be served by using the services of someone who does this on a regular basis and has the time, skill and patience to act accordingly. You can, of course, appoint an individual or several individuals to work as co-trustees with the bank.

Guardians

Where you are appointing someone to act as "guardian of the property" of a child or an incompetent, basically the same rules will apply as indicated for trustees. However, where you want someone to act as "guardian of the person" of your minor children and to more or less stand in the position to your children that you were at the time of your death and actually take care of them personally, as opposed to merely handling money for them, an individual would be the proper choice.

Relatives usually come to mind first, but remember that your parents are much older than your children. Their personal health might not warrant them acting as guardians and caring for your children until your children attain their majority. If, in fact, your parents are the logical or only natural choice available at the time, then consider naming alternate guardians in your will in the event that they, for any reason, become incapable of assuming the responsibility of caring for your minor children. Brothers and sisters are sometimes logical choices, and quite often, close friends with whom your children have warm personal relationships could be considered. Be certain that you discuss your selection with the proposed persons or institutions beforehand so you will be sure that they will accept this serious responsibility and what, in fact, can be a prolonged imposition on their family life. Many friends and relatives, aware of the serious implications that the death of both parents can cause, have reciprocal arrangements. Neil and JoAnne Harmon and Steve and Sue Parker each have two children and have been friends and neighbors for ten years. The Harmons have named the Parkers as guardians for their children in their wills, and the Parkers have named the Harmons. The Harmons left their property and insurance to a trust with the Great Valley Bank. If Mr. and Mrs. Harmon are killed in an automobile accident, the Parkers will raise the Harmons' children, with the bank giving to the Parkers the necessary money to care for the children and to facilitate their moving in with the Parker family. In that way, the children can be assured of a home in which they can be well cared for, in circumstances that are not much different than their former home. In such cases, your will or trust should specifically provide for money to be available to these guardians, in the event that any additions are necessary to their home, to accommodate your children. Sometimes it is mutually agreed that in fact the other family can move into your home to live with your children, in the event that you and your spouse die. Remember also that only the surviving spouse can name the guardian for your children. As long as one parent is alive, then of course he/she is the natural parent and guardian of any minor children.

Educate your survivors—before they are

Not only is it necessary to select your professional advisors and those persons or institutions who will take an active part in handling your affairs after your death, but you should also let everyone know what plans have been made.

Years ago, when husbands worked and wives stayed home, serious problems occurred when the husband died and the wife was forced to come to grips for the first time with the world of business and economics. Today, this is hardly the normal case, but there can be unfortunate results if your beneficiaries are not aware of the plans you have made or don't have the training or experience to execute those plans. Certainly, the amount, extent and location of your assets should be made available to your executor, so that time will not be lost or assets not uncovered because no one knew where they were. Why have a conflict caused by having an executor or trustee who is not familiar to your beneficiaries start with a lack of communication? Why not tell your beneficiaries—and certainly discuss with your spouse—your plans and desires, so that any accommodation can be made at this time, rather than at a time of emotional stress?

Die rich

Even though it is often a sacrifice, there is a good feeling in knowing you have money in the bank, insurance protection for your family and peace of mind caused by the security of proper planning. Do yourself a favor. Don't make a lot of mental notes that this and that must be done and then conveniently put this book away for that sometime in the future when you know you must get to it. Put yourself on your own payroll and on your own time schedule. Put some time away now or in the immediate future, take care of those things that must be done, and then relax without the pressure of what an unsecured future can mean.

Let's be serious—no one wants to think of dying—even dying rich. However, most of us like the additional bonus we get every time we can remove a little more pressure from our daily lives. With the information in this book, you can institute a plan that definitely can remove some of the problems and unknowns that create insecurity. By planning in advance, you can have a more secure future for yourself and your family plus the pleasure of knowing you have lived a full and happy life and can die rich.

Appendixes

[NOTE: This section contains many documents and forms for use as worksheets by the reader. It is suggested that duplicates be made on readily available copying machines wherever needed. When all the information is complete, it can be transferred to the book for a permanent record.]

Appendix A. Your Personal Fact-Finder

PERSONAL DATA

Name			
Spouse's Name			
Address (Home)		Phone	
Address (Business)		Phone	

Consultants for Financial and Business Planning	Name	Address	Phone
Attorney			
Accountant			
Trust Officer			
Other Bank Officer			
Life Underwriter			
Insurance Agent			
Stock Broker			
Other			

Name	Date of Birth	Age	Occupation	Health Problems or Special Needs	No. and Age of Grandchildren	Amount of Support by Self/Spouse
Self						
Spouse						
Children and Grandchildren						
Your Family						
Spouse's Family						

Notes:

Citizenship	Husband	United States ☐	Other (Specify) ☐
	Wife	☐	☐
Marital Status	Single ☐ Married ☐ Divorced ☐ Widowed ☐		
	Date married, divorced, widowed:		
	Any former marriages? ☐ Yes ☐ No		
	Are you paying alimony? ☐ Yes ☐ No Child support? ☐ Yes ☐ No		
Wills & Marital Agreements	Do you have a will? ☐ Yes ☐ No Date of will:		
	Does your spouse have a will? ☐ Yes ☐ No Date of will:		
	Have you named guardians for children? ☐ Yes ☐ No Whom?		
	Do you have a pre- or post-nuptial agreement? ☐ Yes ☐ No		
Trusts	Have you created a living trust? ☐ Yes ☐ No Who is the trustee?		
	Who are the beneficiaries?		
	Has your spouse created a living trust? ☐ Yes ☐ No Who is the trustee?		
	Who are the beneficiaries?		

Custodianships	Have you or your spouse ever made a gift under the Uniform Gift to Minors Act? ☐ Yes ☐ No	
	Who is the custodian? Who are the donees?	
Trust Beneficiary	Are you or any members of your immediate family beneficiaries of a trust? ☐ Yes ☐ No	
	If so, who?	
Gifts or Inheritances	Do you or your spouse expect to receive gifts or inheritances? ☐ Yes ☐ No	
	If so, who? How much? From whom?	
Social Security Numbers	Your social security number:	
	Your spouse's social security number:	
	Have social security benefits been reviewed lately? ☐ Yes ☐ No	
Military Service	Did you serve in the military? ☐ Yes ☐ No If so, from to	
	Any service-connected benefits? ☐ Yes ☐ No	
	Did your spouse serve in the military? ☐ Yes ☐ No If so, from to	
	Any service-connected benefits? ☐ Yes ☐ No	

PROPERTY (EXCEPT FOR LIFE INSURANCE OR BUSINESS)

Item No.	Family Property	Fair Market Value and Titled Owner(s)						Present Indebtedness	Cost	When and How Acquired
		Husband	Wife	Children	Joint (survivor-ship rights)	Joint (no survivor-ship rights)	Community Property			
	REAL ESTATE									
( )	Residence									
( )	Seasonal Residence									
( )	Other Real Property									
( )										
( )										
	SECURITIES (Marketable)									
( )	Corporate Bonds									
( )	Municipal Bonds									
( )	U.S. Govt. Bonds									
( )	Listed Stocks									
( )	Money Market Funds									
( )	Mutual Funds									
	MISCELLANEOUS									
( )	Survivor Annuities									
( )										
( )										
( )										
	MORTGAGES, ACCOUNTS RECEIVABLE, NOTES (Unpaid Balance Due You)									
( )	Mortgages Owned									
( )	Accounts Receivable									
( )	Notes Receivable									
	Notes:									

PROPERTY (Continued)

Item No.	Family Property	Fair Market Value and Titled Owner(s)						Present Indebtedness	Cost	When and How Acquired
		Husband	Wife	Children	Joint (survivorship rights)	Joint (no survivorship rights)	Community Property			
	PERSONAL PROPERTY									
( )	Household									
( )	Auto(s)									
( )	Boat(s)									
( )	Jewelry-Furs									
( )	Collection-Hobby Equip.									
( )	Interests in Trusts									
( )	Royalties, Patents, Copyrights									
( )	Other									
( )										
	CASH OR EQUIVALENT									
( )	Savings Accounts, Average Balance (Include certificate of deposit and life insurance dividend accumulations)									
( )	Checking Accounts, Average Balance									
( )	Ready Cash									
	MISCELLANEOUS PROPERTY									
( )										
( )										
( )										

LIFE INSURANCE

Item #	( )	( )	( )	( )	( )
Policy Numbers					
Name of Insurance Company					
Issue Age					
Insured					
Owner of Policy					
Type of Policy					
Premium Cost and Mode					
Cash Value					
Extra Benefits (e.g., waiver of premium, accidental death, etc.)					
Amount of Base Policy					
Dividends (Value & Option)					
Term Rider(s)					
Loan Outstanding					
Net Amount Payable at Death					
Beneficiaries and Settlement Option Elected					
1st to					
2nd to					

Item #	( )	( )	( )	( )	( )	( )
Policy Numbers						
Name of Insurance Company						
Issue Age						
Insured						
Owner of Policy						
Type of Policy						
Premium Cost and Mode						
Cash Value						
Extra Benefits (e.g., waiver of premium, accidental death, etc.)						
Amount of Base Policy						
Dividends (Value & Option)						
Term Rider(s)						
Loan Outstanding						
Net Amount Payable at Death						
Beneficiaries and Settlement Option Elected						
1st to						
2nd to						

HEALTH INSURANCE

Disability Income	Policy #1	Policy #2	Policy #3	Policy #4
Disability Income Policy Numbers				
Name of Insurance Company				
Insured				
Owner of Policy Premium Payer				
Premium Cost and Mode				
Type of Continuance or Renewal Provision				
Definition of Disability				
MONTHLY DISABILITY INCOME				
Accident				
Sickness				
PARTIAL DISABILITY				
Accident				
Sickness				
WAITING PERIOD				
Accident				
Sickness				
BENEFIT PERIOD				
Accident				
Sickness				
Supplementary Benefits				

HEALTH INSURANCE (Continued)

Medical Expense	Policy #1	Policy #2	Policy #3	Policy #4
Medical Expense Policy Numbers				
Name of Insurance Company or Service Type Plan				
Insured				
Owner of Policy				
Premium Cost and Mode				
Type of Continuance or Renewal Provision				
Termination Date for Child Coverage				
BASIC HOSPITAL				
Room Rate				
No. of Days				
Hospital Extras				
Other Benefits				
SURGICAL				
Maximum				
Type of Schedule				
MAJOR MEDICAL				
Deductible				
Percentage Participation (Coinsurance)				
Inside Limits				
Overall Maximum				

BUSINESS INTEREST

Full Legal Name _____ Phone No. _____

Address _____

Business now operates as

☐ Proprietorship ☐ Corporation, Fiscal Year Ending _____

☐ Partnership ☐ Subchapter S Corporation

Principal business activity is: _____

In what year did this business begin operation? _____

Date of incorporation, if it began other than as a corporation? _____

What is your function in the business? _____

Do you have an employment contract? _____

PRESENT OWNERS

		Corporation		Other
(A) You _____	Owns ____ % common	____ % preferred	____ %
(B) _____	Owns ____ % common	____ % preferred	____ %
(C) _____	Owns ____ % common	____ % preferred	____ %
(D) _____	Owns ____ % common	____ % preferred	____ %
(E) _____	Owns ____ % common	____ % preferred	____ %

Do you want your business interest retained or sold if you

Retire?   Become Disabled?   Die?

IF RETAINED   **IF SOLD**

Who will own your interest and how will he (she, or they) acquire it?   Who will buy your interest?

_____   How is purchase price to be determined?

_____   _____

Who will replace you in your job?   How will the buyer(s) pay for it?

_____   _____

_____   Is this already arranged by legal agreement?

_____   _____

What is your estimate of the lowest price for which the entire business might be sold as a going concern today?

What is the lowest price you would accept for your interest today?

BUSINESS INTEREST (Continued)

If you were not an owner, what is your estimate of the highest price you would pay today for the entire business as a going concern?	What is the highest price you would pay to buy the interest of your co-owners today?	What is the average business indebtedness? _____ Estimate of highest it has ever been? _____ Estimate of lowest it has ever been? _____	Are there any patents or special processes used by but not owned by the business? If yes, who owns what, and under what terms is each used or leased? What are the prospects for growth, sale, merger, or going public?

SURVIVOR CONTROL (letters in parentheses refer to owners named above):

IF (A) DIES	IF (B) DIES	IF (C) DIES	IF (D) DIES	IF (E) DIES
B wants ____ % control	A wants ____ % control	A wants ____ % control	A wants ____ % control	A wants ____ % control
C wants ____ % control	C wants ____ % control	B wants ____ % control	B wants ____ % control	B wants ____ % control
D wants ____ % control	D wants ____ % control	D wants ____ % control	C wants ____ % control	C wants ____ % control
E wants ____ % control	E wants ____ % control	E wants ____ % control	E wants ____ % control	D wants ____ % control
* wants ____ % control	* wants ____ % control	* wants ____ % control	* wants ____ % control	* wants ____ % control

*New owner to acquire control is: _____

BUSINESS ATTORNEY

Name _____

Address _____

Phone _____

BUSINESS ACCOUNTANT

Name _____

Address _____

Phone _____

EMPLOYEE CENSUS DATA

Listing below includes: ☐ Key Employees Only   ☐ All Employees

	Name				Date of Birth			Date Employed			Earnings		Occupation		Marital Status
Sex	First	Middle	Last		Mo.	Day	Year	Mo.	Day	Year	Amount	Payable	Title	Key Person	
1															
2															
3															
4															
5															
6															
7															
8															
9															
10															
11															
12															
13															
14															

Sex	Name			Date of Birth			Date Employed			Earnings		Occupation		Marital Status
	First	Middle	Last	Mo.	Day	Year	Mo.	Day	Year	Amount	Payable	Title	Key Person	
15														
16														
17														
18														
19														
20														
21														
22														
23														
24														
25														
26														
27														
28														
29														

BENEFITS ARISING FROM CONTINUED EMPLOYMENT

PART I

You _____

Employer _____

Who could provide specific information that you do not have?

Department: _____ Title: _____ Phone: _____

	Benefit Is Currently Provided	Complete Description or Contract Is in Possession of Whom?
EMPLOYEE GROUP INSURANCE		
Life	_____	_____
Survivorship Annuity	_____	_____
Dependent Life	_____	_____
Accidental Death	_____	_____
Travel Accident	_____	_____
Dismemberment	_____	_____
Hospitalization	_____	_____
Surgical Expense Benefits	_____	_____

	Benefit Is Currently Provided	Complete Description or Contract Is in Possession of Whom?
EMPLOYEE GROUP INSURANCE (Continued)		
Major Medical	_____	_____
Dental Care	_____	_____
Disability Income	_____	_____
Legal Services — Prepaid by Employer	_____	_____
CONTINGENT FUTURE TAX EXCLUDABLE BENEFITS		
Sick Pay	_____	_____
Employer-paid Health Care	_____	_____
BARGAIN PURCHASE, USE AND ENJOYMENT		
Split-Dollar Life Insurance	_____	_____
Company Car Provided	_____	_____
Club Memberships	_____	_____
OTHER (specify)		
_____		_____
_____		_____

BENEFITS ARISING FROM CONTINUED EMPLOYMENT
PART II

QUALIFIED PLAN ☐ PENSION ☐ PROFIT SHARING ☐ NONE

Amount of Current Death Benefit $ _____ Estimated Pension at Age 65 $ _____

Beneficiary: Primary _____ Contingent _____

Percent Contributed by Employer _____ % by Employee _____ %

Death Benefit Funded by Life Insurance $ _____ Other $ _____

Mode of Settlement _____

HR-10 PLAN ☐ YES ☐ NO

Type of Funding _____

Annual Contribution _____ Total Contributions _____ Date Started _____ No. of Employees Covered _____

(Self) $ _____ (Self) $ _____

Primary _____ Primary _____ Contingent _____

Beneficiary _____ Beneficiary _____ Beneficiary _____

Death Benefit $ _____

Mode of Settlement _____

IRA PLAN YOU ☐ YES ☐ NO SPOUSE ☐ YES ☐ NO

Primary _____ Contingent _____

Beneficiary _____ Beneficiary _____

Death Benefit $ _____

Mode of Settlement _____

SPLIT-DOLLAR PLAN ☐ YES ☐ NO

Describe Plan of Insurance, Death Benefit, Ownership, and Beneficiary _____

_____

| **TAX-DEFERRED ANNUITY PLAN** | ☐ YES | ☐ NO |

Employer: ☐ Public School ☐ Other

Primary   Contingent
Death Benefit $ _____ Beneficiary _____ Beneficiary _____

DEFERRED COMPENSATION AGREEMENT   ☐ YES   ☐ NO

Describe Provisions and Funding _____
_____
_____

STOCK BONUS, STOCK OPTION, STOCK PURCHASE, THRIFT PLANS, SHADOW STOCK   ☐ YES   ☐ NO

Describe Provisions _____
_____
_____

DEATH BENEFIT ONLY (salary continuation) PLAN   ☐ YES   ☐ NO

Describe Provisions _____
_____
_____

FAMILY INCOME

	You	Spouse	Dependent Children
ANNUAL INCOME			
(1) Salary, Bonus, etc.	$	$	$
(2) Income as Business Owner (self-employment)			
(3) Real Estate (net after taxes, etc.)			
(4) Dividends:			
(a) Closed Corporation Stock			
(b) Investments			
(5) Interest			
(a) Bonds			
(b) Savings Accounts			
(c) Money Market Funds			
(6) Trust Income			
(7) Other Sources			
TOTAL ANNUAL INCOME	$	$	$
INCOME TAX (Federal and State)			
Last Year	$	$	$
Quarterly Estimated Tax This Year	$	$	$
FUTURE INCOME			
Estimated Annual Income Next Year	$	$	$
Five Years	$	$	$

FAMILY FINANCES

Do you live on a monthly budget? ☐ YES ☐ NO How much?	
How much do you save annually? In what form? Why?	
How much do you invest annually? In what form? Why?	
How much do you think you should be able to save and invest annually?	
For what?	

In order to assist you to accumulate funds would you enter into any of the following plans:

	YES	NO	Check if Now Using
Allotment from salary	☐	☐	☐
Contractual mutual fund plan	☐	☐	☐
Cash value life insurance plan	☐	☐	☐
Money market fund or certificates	☐	☐	☐

On a scale of from one to five, with one being slight preference and five being substantial preference, rate, in the order of YOUR preference, the following methods of saving or investing:

	1	2	3	4	5	Check if Now Using
Savings Account	☐	☐	☐	☐	☐	☐
Cash Value Life Insurance	☐	☐	☐	☐	☐	☐
Government Bonds	☐	☐	☐	☐	☐	☐
Corporate Bonds	☐	☐	☐	☐	☐	☐
Tax-exempt Bonds	☐	☐	☐	☐	☐	☐
Mutual Funds	☐	☐	☐	☐	☐	☐
Money Market Funds	☐	☐	☐	☐	☐	☐
Variable Annuities	☐	☐	☐	☐	☐	☐
Common Stocks	☐	☐	☐	☐	☐	☐
Real Estate	☐	☐	☐	☐	☐	☐
Tax Shelters (oil, cattle, etc.)	☐	☐	☐	☐	☐	☐
Other (specify)	☐	☐	☐	☐	☐	☐

(Continued)

FAMILY FINANCES (Continued)

Compare, in terms of your own priorities, the importance of adequate funds in order to do the following (indicate ranking by first, second, etc.):

Enjoy a comfortable retirement. _____

Take care of yourself and family during a period of long-term disability. _____

Provide college educations for all children. _____

Take care of your family in the event of your death. _____

Any others that are important to you. _____

_____

_____

OBJECTIVES REQUIRING ADDITIONAL INCOME OR CAPITAL

Education Fund

Name of Child	Age	Number of Years Required	Estimate of Fund Required
			$
			$
			$
			$
Other (specify)			$
			$

INCOME AND CAPITAL NEEDS FOR
FINANCIAL INDEPENDENCE WITHOUT WORKING

At what age would you like to retire? _____

Estimated Required Monthly Income .... $ _____

Expected Sources of Funds (check those now expected) ☐

    Social Security Benefits .... ☐

    Other Government Pension .... ☐

    Self-Employed Retirement Plan (Keogh) .... ☐

    Pension Plan .... ☐

    Profit-Sharing Plan .... ☐

    Tax-Deferred Annuity .... ☐

    Nonqualified Deferred Compensation .... ☐

    Nonqualified Annuity .... ☐

    Life Insurance Cash Values .... ☐

    Independent Income (from p. 296) .... ☐

    Other (specify) _____ ☐

Check sources of independent income (see p. 296)

(1) _____, (2) _____, (3) _____, (4) (a) _____,

(4) (b) _____, (5) (a) _____, (5) (b) _____,

(5) (c) _____, (6) _____, (7) _____.

Will income from any of the sources above decrease or terminate in the event that either you or your spouse dies after it begins? _____

Will basic health care and major medical coverage be continued after retirement?   ☐ Yes   ☐ No

INCOME AND CAPITAL NEEDS DURING DISABILITY

Estimated Required Monthly Income .... $ _____

Expected Sources of Funds (check those now expected)

Social Security Benefits	☐
Other Government Pension	☐
Self-Employed Retirement Plan (Keogh)	☐
Pension Plan	☐
Profit-Sharing Plan	☐
Tax-Deferred Annuity	☐
Nonqualified Deferred Compensation	☐
Salary Continuation Plan	☐
Disability Insurance	☐
Independent Income (from p. 296)	☐
Other (specify) _____	☐

Check sources of independent income (see p. 296)

(1) _____, (2) _____, (3) _____, (4) (a) _____,

(4) (b) _____, (5) (a) _____, (5) (b) _____,

(5) (c) _____, (6) _____, (7) _____.

Estimated Required Monthly Income if Spouse
Were Disabled .... $ _____

Expected Sources of Funds (check those now expected)

Disability Insurance	☐
Other (specify) _____	☐

Will basic health care and major medical benefits be continued after disability?   ☐ Yes   ☐ No

INCOME AND CAPITAL NEEDS FOLLOWING DEATH

For surviving spouse and dependent children following your death—

INCOME NEEDS

What is your estimate of the monthly income which will be needed during the following periods:

(1) Adjustment period (adjustment of standards of living without you—the breadwinner—in the transitional period following your death)   (_____) years . . . . $ _____

(2) Until your youngest child is self-supporting . . $ _____

(3) To provide life income for surviving spouse after your youngest child is self-supporting . . $ _____

CAPITAL NEEDS

Emergency Fund . . . . $ _____

Mortgage Cancellation Fund (if surviving spouse will continue to live in family house) . . . . $ _____

Notes and Loans Payable . . . . $ _____

Accrued Taxes (income, real estate, etc.) . . . . $ _____

Educated Expense . . . . $ _____

　　　　　　　　　　　　TOTAL . . . . $ ══════

Will Basic Health Care and Major Medical Coverge be continued?   ☐ Yes   ☐ No

INCOME AND CAPITAL NEEDS FOLLOWING DEATH (Continued)

Expected Sources of INCOME (check those now expected)

- ☐ Social Security Benefits
- ☐ Other Government Benefits
- ☐ Self-Employed Retirement Plan (Keogh)
- ☐ Pension Plan
- ☐ Profit-Sharing Plan
- ☐ Nonqualified Deferred Compensation Plan
- ☐ Salary Continuation Plan
- ☐ Independent Income (from p. 296)
- ☐ Other (specify) _____

Check sources of independent income (see p. 296)

(1) _____, (2) _____, (3) _____, (4) (a) _____, (4) (b) _____, (5) (a) _____,
(5) (b) _____, (5) (c) _____, (6) _____, (7) _____.

Expected Sources of CAPITAL (check those now expected)

Group Life Insurance .... ☐
Personal Life Insurance .... ☐
Real Estate .... ☐
Proceeds of Sale of Business Interests by Agreement ..... ☐
Other (specify) _____ ☐

For You and Children Following Spouse's Death

Additional Income Needs .... $ _____
Source (specify) _____
Capital Needs .... $ _____
Source (specify) _____

LIABILITIES

Loans or Other Obligations Outstanding	Creditor	Amount	Insured	Secured

Any other liabilities your estate may be called upon to pay?

Do you foresee any future liabilities (business expansion, new home, etc.)?

ADDITIONAL FACTORS AFFECTING YOUR PLAN

Have you or your spouse ever made substantial gifts to family members, to educational institutions, to tax-exempt beneficiaries? (give details) _____

Special bequests intended, including charity _____

Is your spouse good at handling money? _____

If left on his or her own, would spouse's judgment and emotional stability serve the best interests of the family? _____

What is your estimate of the emotional maturity of your children? _____

What are your feelings about the possible remarriage of your spouse? _____

Tax consideration aside, in what manner would you want your estate to be distributed? _____

Appendix B. Income Tax Tables

Rates for Tax Years Beginning in 1982
(Income tax rates for individuals, estates and trusts)

1. Married Individuals Filing Joint Returns and Surviving Spouses

Taxable income:	Amount of tax:
Not over $3,400	No tax
Over $3,400 but not over $5,500	12% of the excess over $3,400
Over $5,500 but not over $7,600	$252 plus 14% of the excess over $5,500
Over $7,600 but not over $11,900	$546 plus 16% of the excess over $7,600
Over $11,900 but not over $16,000	$1,234 plus 19% of the excess over $11,900
Over $16,000 but not over $20,200	$2,013 plus 22% of the excess over $16,000
Over $20,200 but not over $24,600	$2,937 plus 25% of the excess over $20,200
Over $24,600 but not over $29,900	$4,037 plus 29% of the excess over $24,600
Over $29,900 but not over $35,200	$5,574 plus 33% of the excess over $29,900
Over $35,200 but not over $45,800	$7,323 plus 39% of the excess over $35,200
Over $45,800 but not over $60,000	$11,457 plus 44% of the excess over $45,800
Over $60,000 but not over $85,600	$17,705 plus 49% of the excess over $60,000
Over $85,600	$30,249 plus 50% of the excess over $85,600

2. Heads of Households

Taxable income:	Amount of tax:
Not over $2,300	No tax
Over $2,300 but not over $4,400	12% of the excess over $2,300
Over $4,400 but not over $6,500	$252 plus 14% of the excess over $4,400
Over $6,500 but not over $8,700	$546 plus 16% of the excess over $6,500
Over $8,700 but not over $11,800	$898 plus 20% of the excess over $8,700
Over $11,800 but not over $15,000	$1,518 plus 22% of the excess over $11,800
Over $15,000 but not over $18,200	$2,222 plus 23% of the excess over $15,000
Over $18,200 but not over $23,500	$2,958 plus 28% of the excess over $18,200
Over $23,500 but not over $28,800	$4,442 plus 32% of the excess over $23,500
Over $28,800 but not over $34,100	$6,138 plus 38% of the excess over $28,800
Over $34,100 but not over $44,700	$8,152 plus 41% of the excess over $34,100
Over $44,700 but not over $60,600	$12,498 plus 49% of the excess over $44,700
Over $60,600	$20,289 plus 50% of the excess over $60,600

3. Unmarried Individuals (Other Than Surviving Spouses and Heads of Households)

Taxable income: — *Amount of tax:*

Taxable income	Amount of tax
Not over $2,300	No tax
Over $2,300 but not over $3,400	12% of the excess over $2,300
Over $3,400 but not over $4,400	$132 plus 14% of the excess over $3,400
Over $4,400 but not over $6,500	$272 plus 16% of the excess over $4,400
Over $6,500 but not over $8,500	$608 plus 17% of the excess over $6,500
Over $8,500 but not over $10,800	$948 plus 19% of the excess over $8,500
Over $10,800 but not over $12,900	$1,385 plus 22% of the excess over $10,800
Over $12,900 but not over $15,000	$1,847 plus 23% of the excess over $12,900
Over $15,000 but not over $18,200	$2,330 plus 27% of the excess over $15,000
Over $18,200 but not over $23,500	$3,194 plus 31% of the excess over $18,200
Over $23,500 but not over $28,800	$4,837 plus 35% of the excess over $23,500
Over $28,800 but not over $34,100	$6,692 plus 40% of the excess over $28,800
Over $34,100 but not over $41,500	$8,812 plus 44% of the excess over $34,100
Over $41,500	$12,068 plus 50% of the excess over $41,500

4. Married Individuals Filing Separate Returns

Taxable income: — *Amount of tax:*

Taxable income	Amount of tax
Not over $1,700	No tax
Over $1,700 but not over $2,750	12% of the excess over $1,700
Over $2,750 but not over $3,800	$126 plus 14% of the excess over $2,750
Over $3,800 but not over $5,950	$273 plus 16% of the excess over $3,800
Over $5,950 but not over $8,000	$617 plus 19% of the excess over $5,950
Over $8,000 but not over $10,100	$1,006 plus 22% of the excess over $8,000
Over $10,100 but not over $12,300	$1,468 plus 25% of the excess over $10,100
Over $12,300 but not over $14,950	$2,018 plus 29% of the excess over $12,300
Over $14,950 but not over $17,600	$2,787 plus 33% of the excess over $14,950
Over $17,600 but not over $22,900	$3,661 plus 39% of the excess over $17,600
Over $22,900 but not over $30,000	$5,728 plus 44% of the excess over $22,900
Over $30,000 but not over $42,800	$8,852 plus 49% of the excess over $30,000
Over $42,800	$15,124 plus 50% of the excess over $42,800

5. Estates and Trusts

Taxable income: — *Amount of tax:*

Taxable income	Amount of tax
Not over $1,050	12% of taxable income
Over $1,050 but not over $2,100	$126 plus 14% of the excess over $1,050
Over $2,100 but not over $4,250	$273 plus 16% of the excess over $2,100
Over $4,250 but not over $6,300	$617 plus 19% of the excess over $4,250
Over $6,300 but not over $8,400	$1,006 plus 22% of the excess over $6,300
Over $8,400 but not over $10,600	$1,468 plus 25% of the excess over $8,400
Over $10,600 but not over $13,250	$2,018 plus 29% of the excess over $10,600
Over $13,250 but not over $15,900	$2,787 plus 33% of the excess over $13,250
Over $15,900 but not over $21,200	$3,661 plus 39% of the excess over $15,900
Over $21,200 but not over $28,300	$5,728 plus 44% of the excess over $21,200
Over $28,300 but not over $41,100	$8,852 plus 49% of the excess over $28,300
Over $41,100	$15,124 plus 50% of the excess over $41,100

© 1981 by The American College as part of **Advanced Estate Planning Casebook.**

Rates for Tax Years Beginning in 1983
(Income tax rates for individuals, estates and trusts)

1. Married Individuals Filing Joint Returns and Surviving Spouses

Taxable income:	Amount of tax:
Not over $3,400	No tax
Over $3,400 but not over $5,500	11% of the excess over $3,400
Over $5,500 but not over $7,600	$231 plus 13% of the excess over $5,500
Over $7,600 but not over $11,900	$504 plus 15% of the excess over $7,600
Over $11,900 but not over $16,000	$1,149 plus 17% of the excess over $11,900
Over $16,000 but not over $20,200	$1,846 plus 19% of the excess over $16,000
Over $20,200 but not over $24,600	$2,644 plus 23% of the excess over $20,200
Over $24,600 but not over $29,900	$3,656 plus 26% of the excess over $24,600
Over $29,900 but not over $35,200	$5,034 plus 30% of the excess over $29,900
Over $35,200 but not over $45,800	$6,624 plus 35% of the excess over $35,200
Over $45,800 but not over $60,000	$10,334 plus 40% of the excess over $45,800
Over $60,000 but not over $85,600	$16,014 plus 44% of the excess over $60,000
Over $85,600 but not over $109,400	$27,278 plus 48% of the excess over $85,600
Over $109,400	$38,702 plus 50% of the excess over $109,400

2. Heads of Households

Taxable income:	Amount of tax:
Not over $2,300	No tax
Over $2,300 but not over $4,400	11% of the excess over $2,300
Over $4,400 but not over $6,500	$231 plus 13% of the excess over $4,400
Over $6,500 but not over $8,700	$504 plus 15% of the excess over $6,500
Over $8,700 but not over $11,800	$834 plus 18% of the excess over $8,700
Over $11,800 but not over $15,000	$1,392 plus 19% of the excess over $11,800
Over $15,000 but not over $18,200	$2,000 plus 21% of the excess over $15,000
Over $18,200 but not over $23,500	$2,672 plus 25% of the excess over $18,200
Over $23,500 but not over $28,800	$3,997 plus 29% of the excess over $23,500
Over $28,800 but not over $34,100	$5,534 plus 34% of the excess over $28,800
Over $34,100 but not over $44,700	$7,336 plus 37% of the excess over $34,100
Over $44,700 but not over $60,600	$11,258 plus 44% of the excess over $44,700
Over $60,600 but not over $81,600	$18,254 plus 48% of the excess over $60,600
Over $81,800	$28,430 plus 50% of the excess over $81,800

3. Unmarried Individuals (Other Than Surviving Spouses and Heads of Households)

Taxable income: *Amount of tax:*

Not over $2,300 .... No tax
Over $2,300 but not over $3,400 ..... 11% of the excess over $2,300
Over $3,400 but not over $4,400 ..... $121 plus 13% of the excess over $3,400
Over $4,400 but not over $8,500 ..... $251 plus 15% of the excess over $4,400
Over $8,500 but not over $10,800 ..... $866 plus 17% of the excess over $8,500
Over $10,800 but not over $12,900 .... $1,257 plus 19% of the excess over $10,800
Over $12,900 but not over $15,000 .... $1,656 plus 21% of the excess over $12,900
Over $15,000 but not over $18,200 .... $2,097 plus 24% of the excess over $15,000
Over $18,200 but not over $23,500 .... $2,865 plus 28% of the excess over $18,200
Over $23,500 but not over $28,800 .... $4,349 plus 32% of the excess over $23,500
Over $28,800 but not over $34,100 .... $6,045 plus 36% of the excess over $28,800
Over $34,100 but not over $41,500 .... $7,953 plus 40% of the excess over $34,100
Over $41,500 but not over $55,300 .... $10,913 plus 45% of the excess over $41,500
Over $55,300 .... $17,123 plus 50% of the excess over $55,300

4. Married Individuals Filing Separate Returns

Taxable income: *Amount of tax:*

Not over $1,700 .... No tax
Over $1,700 but not over $2,750 ..... 11% of the excess over $1,700
Over $2,750 but not over $3,800 ..... $115 plus 13% of the excess over $2,750
Over $3,800 but not over $5,950 ..... $252 plus 15% of the excess over $3,800
Over $5,950 but not over $8,000 ..... $574 plus 17% of the excess over $5,950
Over $8,000 but not over $10,100 ..... $923 plus 19% of the excess over $8,000
Over $10,100 but not over $12,300 .... $1,322 plus 23% of the excess over $10,100
Over $12,300 but not over $14,950 .... $1,828 plus 26% of the excess over $12,300
Over $14,950 but not over $17,600 .... $2,517 plus 30% of the excess over $14,950
Over $17,600 but not over $22,900 .....$3,312 plus 35% of the excess over $17,600
Over $22,900 but not over $30,000 .... $5,167 plus 40% of the excess over $22,900
Over $30,000 but not over $42,800 .... $8,007 plus 44% of the excess over $30,000
Over $42,800 but not over $54,700 .... $13,639 plus 48% of the excess over $42,800
Over $54,700 .... $19,351 plus 50% of the excess over $54,700

5. Estates and Trusts

Taxable income: *Amount of tax:*

Not over $1,050 .... 11% of taxable income
Over $1,050 but not over $2,100 ..... $115 plus 13% of the excess over $1,050
Over $2,100 but not over $4,250 ..... $252 plus 15% of the excess over $2,100
Over $4,250 but not over $6,300 ..... $574 plus 17% of the excess over $4,250
Over $6,300 but not over $8,400 ..... $923 plus 19% of the excess over $6,300
Over $8,400 but not over $10,600 ..... $1,322 plus 23% of the excess over $8,400
Over $10,600 but not over $13,250 .... $1,828 plus 26% of the excess over $10,600
Over $13,250 but not over $15,900 .... $2,517 plus 30% of the excess over $13,250
Over $15,900 but not over $21,200 .... $3,312 plus 35% of the excess over $15,900
Over $21,200 but not over $28,300 .... $5,167 plus 40% of the excess over $21,200
Over $28,300 but not over $41,100 .... $8,007 plus 44% of the excess over $28,300
Over $41,100 but not over $53,000 .... $13,639 plus 48% of the excess over $41,100
Over $53,000 .... $19,351 plus 50% of the excess over $53,000

Rates for Tax Years Beginning after 1983
(Income tax rates for individuals, estates and trusts)

1. Married Individuals Filing Joint Returns and Surviving Spouses

Taxable income:	Amount of tax:
Not over $3,400	No tax
Over $3,400 but not over $5,500	11% of the excess over $3,400
Over $5,500 but not over $7,600	$231 plus 12% of the excess over $5,500
Over $7,600 but not over $11,900	$483 plus 14% of the excess over $7,600
Over $11,900 but not over $16,000	$1,085 plus 16% of the excess over $11,900
Over $16,000 but not over $20,200	$1,741 plus 18% of the excess over $16,000
Over $20,200 but not over $24,600	$2,497 plus 22% of the excess over $20,200
Over $24,600 but not over $29,900	$3,465 plus 25% of the excess over $24,600
Over $29,900 but not over $35,200	$4,790 plus 28% of the excess over $29,900
Over $35,200 but not over $45,800	$6,274 plus 33% of the excess over $35,200
Over $45,800 but not over $60,000	$9,772 plus 38% of the excess over $45,800
Over $60,000 but not over $85,600	$15,168 plus 42% of the excess over $60,000
Over $85,600 but not over $109,400	$25,920 plus 45% of the excess over $85,600
Over $109,400 but not over $162,400	$36,630 plus 49% of the excess over $109,400
Over $162,400	$62,600 plus 50% of the excess over $162,400

2. Heads of Households

Taxable income:	Amount of tax:
Not over $2,300	No tax
Over $2,300 but not over $4,400	11% of the excess over $2,300
Over $4,400 but not over $6,500	$231 plus 12% of the excess over $4,400
Over $6,500 but not over $8,700	$483 plus 14% of the excess over $6,500
Over $8,700 but not over $11,800	$791 plus 17% of the excess over $8,700
Over $11,800 but not over $15,000	$1,318 plus 18% of the excess over $11,800
Over $15,000 but not over $18,200	$1,894 plus 20% of the excess over $15,000
Over $18,200 but not over $23,500	$2,534 plus 24% of the excess over $18,200
Over $23,500 but not over $28,800	$3,806 plus 28% of the excess over $23,500
Over $28,800 but not over $34,100	$5,290 plus 32% of the excess over $28,800
Over $34,100 but not over $44,700	$6,986 plus 35% of the excess over $34,100
Over $44,700 but not over $60,600	$10,696 plus 42% of the excess over $44,700
Over $60,600 but not over $81,800	$17,374 plus 45% of the excess over $60,600
Over $81,800 but not over $108,300	$26,914 plus 48% of the excess over $81,800
Over $108,300	$39,634 plus 50% of the excess over $108,300

3. Unmarried Individuals (Other Than Surviving Spouses and Heads of Households)

Taxable income: *Amount of tax:*

Taxable income:	Amount of tax:
Not over $2,300	No tax
Over $2,300 but not over $3,400	11% of the excess over $2,300
Over $3,400 but not over $4,400	$121 plus 12% of the excess over $3,400
Over $4,400 but not over $6,500	$241 plus 14% of the excess over $4,400
Over $6,500 but not over $8,500	$535 plus 15% of the excess over $6,500
Over $8,500 but not over $10,800	$835 plus 16% of the excess over $8,500
Over $10,800 but not over $12,900	$1,203 plus 18% of the excess over $10,800
Over $12,900 but not over $15,000	$1,581 plus 20% of the excess over $12,900
Over $15,000 but not over $18,200	$2,001 plus 23% of the excess over $15,000
Over $18,200 but not over $23,500	$2,737 plus 26% of the excess over $18,200
Over $23,500 but not over $28,800	$4,115 plus 30% of the excess over $23,500
Over $28,800 but not over $34,100	$5,705 plus 34% of the excess over $28,800
Over $34,100 but not over $41,500	$7,507 plus 38% of the excess over $34,100
Over $41,500 but not over $55,300	$10,319 plus 42% of the excess over $41,500
Over $55,300 but not over $81,800	$16,115 plus 48% of the excess over $55,300
Over $81,800	$28,835 plus 50% of the excess over $81,800

4. Married Individuals Filing Separate Returns

Taxable income:	Amount of tax:
Not over $1,700	No tax
Over $1,700 but not over $2,750	11% of the excess over $1,700
Over $2,750 but not over $3,800	$115 plus 12% of the excess over $2,750
Over $3,800 but not over $5,950	$241 plus 14% of the excess over $3,800
Over $5,950 but not over $8,000	$542 plus 16% of the excess over $5,950
Over $8,000 but not over $10,100	$870 plus 18% of the excess over $8,000
Over $10,100 but not over $12,300	$1,248 plus 22% of the excess over $10,100
Over $12,300 but not over $14,950	$1,732 plus 25% of the excess over $12,300
Over $14,950 but not over $17,600	$2,395 plus 28% of the excess over $14,950
Over $17,600 but not over $22,900	$3,137 plus 33% of the excess over $17,600
Over $22,900 but not over $30,000	$4,886 plus 38% of the excess over $22,900
Over $30,000 but not over $42,800	$7,584 plus 42% of the excess over $30,000
Over $42,800 but not over $54,700	$12,960 plus 45% of the excess over $42,800

5. Estates and Trusts

Taxable income:	Amount of tax:
Not over $1,050	11% of taxable income
Over $1,050 but not over $2,100	$115 plus 12% of the excess over $1,050
Over $2,100 but not over $4,250	$241 plus 14% of the excess over $2,100
Over $4,250 but not over $6,300	$542 plus 16% of the excess over $4,250
Over $6,300 but not over $8,400	$870 plus 18% of the excess over $6,300
Over $8,400 but not over $10,600	$1,248 plus 22% of the excess over $8,400
Over $10,600 but not over $13,250	$1,732 plus 25% of the excess over $10,600
Over $13,250 but not over $15,900	$2,395 plus 28% of the excess over $13,250
Over $15,900 but not over $21,200	$3,137 plus 33% of the excess over $15,900
Over $21,200 but not over $28,300	$4,886 plus 38% of the excess over $21,200
Over $28,300 but not over $41,100	$7,584 plus 42% of the excess over $28,300
Over $41,100 but not over $53,000	$12,960 plus 45% of the excess over $41,100
Over $53,000 but not over $79,500	$18,315 plus 49% of the excess over $53,000
Over $79,500	$31,300 plus 50% of the excess over $79,500

Appendix C. Unified Rate Schedule for Estate and Gift Taxes

If the amount with which the tentative tax to be computed is:	The tentative tax is:
Not over $10,000	18% of such amount
Over $10,000 but not over $20,000	$1,800 plus 20% of the excess over $10,000
Over $20,000 but not over $40,000	$3,800 plus 22% of the excess over $20,000
Over $40,000 but not over $60,000	$8,200 plus 24% of the excess over $40,000
Over $60,000 but not over $80,000	$13,000 plus 26% of the excess over $60,000
Over $80,000 but not over $100,000	$18,200 plus 28% of the excess over $80,000
Over $100,000 but not over $150,000	$23,800 plus 30% of the excess over $100,000
Over $150,000 but not over $250,000	$38,800 plus 32% of the excess over $150,000
Over $250,000 but not over $500,000	$70,800 plus 34% of the excess over $250,000
Over $500,000 but not over $750,000	$155,800 plus 37% of the excess over $500,000
Over $750,000 but not over $1,000,000	$248,300 plus 39% of the excess over $750,000
Over $1,000,000 but not over $1,250,000	$345,800 plus 41% of the excess over $1,000,000
Over $1,250,000 but not over $1,500,000	$448,300 plus 43% of the excess over $1,250,000
Over $1,500,000 but not over $2,000,000	$555,800 plus 45% of the excess over $1,500,000
Over $2,000,000 but not over $2,500,000	$780,800 plus 49% of the excess over $2,000,000

For 1982 — *In the case of decedents dying and gifts made in 1982:*

Over $2,500,000 but not over $3,000,000	$1,025,800 plus 53% of the excess over $2,500,000
Over $3,000,000 but not over $3,500,000	$1,290,800 plus 57% of the excess over $3,000,000
Over $3,500,000 but not over $4,000,000	$1,575,800 plus 61% of the excess over $3,500,000
Over $4,000,000	$1,880,800 plus 65% of the excess over $4,000,000

For 1983 — *In the case of decedents dying and gifts made in 1983:*

Over $2,500,000 but not over $3,000,000	$1,025,800 plus 53% of the excess over $2,500,000
Over $3,000,000 but not over $3,500,000	$1,290,800 plus 57% of the excess over $3,000,000
Over $3,500,000	$1,575,800 plus 60% of the excess over $3,500,000

For 1984 — *In the case of decedents dying and gifts made in 1984:*

Over $2,500,000 but not over $3,000,000	$1,025,800 plus 53% of the excess over $2,500,000
Over $3,000,000	$1,290,800 plus 55% of the excess over $3,000,000

For 1985

Over $2,500,000	50%

Appendix D. Determination of Whether Estate Qualifies for Section 303 Stock Redemption

(Husband's) (Wife's) Estate When (He) (She) Dies (First) (Second)

(1) FEDERAL ESTATE TAX VALUE CORPORATE STOCK
 INCLUDED IN GROSS ESTATE .... $ _____
 (The value of stock of two or more corporations can be
 aggregated if 20% or more of the value of the outstanding
 stock of **each** such corporation is included in the decedent's
 gross estate.)

(2) 35% of ADJUSTED GROSS ESTATE .... $ _____

☐ Does Qualify   Does **Not** Qualify

If line 1 **exceeds** line 2, a redemption under Section 303 is
considered a sale or exchange rather than a dividend **to the
extent** the selling stockholder's interest is reduced directly
or the stockholder is bound to contribute to the payment of

    (a) Deductible funeral and administration expenses ...... $ _____

    (b) Federal estate taxes .... $ _____

    (c) State death taxes .... $ _____

    (d) Interest collected as part of above taxes .... $ _____

Maximum Allowable Section 303 Redemption .... $ ══════════

Appendix E. Inventory of Important Information Needed by Executors or Administrators

This Inventory and the following forms were prepared by Edward E. Graves, Assistant Professor of Insurance at The American College in Bryn Mawr, Pennsylvania, for his excellent article on Procedural Aspects Following Death, and are reprinted with the permission of Mr. Graves and The American College.

PERSONAL INFORMATION

Name _____

Address _____

Date of Birth _____ Location of Birth _____

Date of Death _____ Location of Death _____

Death Certificate # _____ Social Security # _____

Military Service # _____ Veterans Administration Claim # _____

DEPENDENTS

Name	Address	Date of Birth	Social Security #	Relationship
_____	_____	_____	_____	_____
_____	_____	_____	_____	_____
_____	_____	_____	_____	_____
_____	_____	_____	_____	_____
_____	_____	_____	_____	_____

Employer _____ Address _____ Phone # _____

ADVISERS

	Name	Address	Phone #
Accountant			
Lawyer			
Investment Broker			
Insurance Agent			
Trust Officer			
Clergy			
Funeral Director			
Executor or Administrator			

CERTIFICATES

Where Located:

- [ ] Birth Certificate(s) (every family member)

- [ ] Marriage Certificate

- [ ] Divorce Papers

- [ ] Military Records (especially discharge papers certificate)

- [ ] Passport(s) (every family member)

- [ ] Citizenship Papers

- [ ] Death Certificate (any deceased family member)

- [ ] Adoption Papers

WILL

I have made a will (yes) _____ (no) _____

The original copy is located at _____ dated _____

Name of attorney who drafted the will _____

Attorney's address _____ Phone # _____

TRUST AGREEMENT

Location of trust agreement _____

Name of Trustee _____

Trustee's address _____ Phone # _____

FINAL ARRANGEMENTS

- [ ] Burial Location of cemetery plot _____
             Location of deed _____
- [ ] Cremation   [ ] Funeral
- [ ] Donation of organs and/or body to medical science
- [ ] Prepaid arrangements Location of agreement _____
                            Name of organization _____
                            Address _____ Phone # _____

INSURANCE

LIFE

Policy # _____ Company _____ Policy Location _____
Agent Address _____ Phone # _____

* * *

Policy # _____ Company _____ Policy Location _____
Agent Address _____ Phone # _____

* * *

Policy # _____ Company _____ Policy Location _____
Agent Address _____ Phone # _____

* * *

Policy # _____ Company _____ Policy Location _____
Agent Address _____ Phone # _____

* * *

Policy # _____ Company _____ Policy Location _____
Agent Address _____ Phone # _____

* * *

Policy # _____ Company _____ Policy Location _____
Agent Address _____ Phone # _____

* * *

Policy # _____ Company _____ Policy Location _____
Agent Address _____ Phone # _____

* * *

Policy # _____ Company _____ Policy Location _____
Agent Address _____ Phone # _____

* * *

Policy # _____ Company _____ Policy Location _____
Agent Address _____ Phone # _____

INSURANCE

LIFE

Policy # _____ Company _____ Agent _____ Phone # _____

_____ _____ Address _____ _____

Location of Policy(ies) _____

HEALTH

Policy # _____ Company _____ Agent _____ Phone # _____

_____ _____ Address _____ _____

Location of Policy(ies) _____

DISABILITY

Policy # _____ Company _____ Agent _____ Phone # _____

_____ _____ Address _____ _____

Location of Policy(ies) _____

Disability benefits are included in my life insurance policies with:

Company _____ Policy # _____

_____ _____

INSURANCE (continued)

AUTO

Policy # _____ Company _____ Agent _____ Phone # _____
_____ Address _____

Location of Policy(ies) _____

HOME

Policy # _____ Company _____ Agent _____ Phone # _____
_____ Address _____

Location of Policy(ies) _____

BOAT

Policy # _____ Company _____ Agent _____ Phone # _____
_____ Address _____

PLANE

Policy # _____ Company _____ Agent _____ Phone # _____
_____ Address _____

TRAILER

Policy # _____ Company _____ Agent _____ Phone # _____
_____ Address _____

OTHER

Policy # _____ Company _____ Agent _____ Phone # _____
_____ Address _____

Location of Policy(ies) _____

BANK ACCOUNTS

CHECKING

Account # _____ Bank _____ Location _____ Phone # _____

SAVINGS

Account # _____ Bank _____ Location _____ Phone # _____

CERTIFICATE OF DEPOSIT

Certificate # _____ Bank _____ Location _____ Phone # _____

CREDIT UNION

Account # _____ Address _____ Phone # _____ Records located _____

INCOME TAX

Location of tax returns _____

Location of receipts _____

SECURITIES

STOCK

Company	# of Shares	Location of Shares	Location of Purchase Records
1.			
2.			
3.			
4.			
5.			

Note any stocks that are held in street name by the broker

BONDS

Issuer	Serial #	Maturity Date	Location
1.			
2.			
3.			
4.			
5.			

BROKER

Name _____ Address _____ Phone # _____

LOANS TO OTHERS (Notes Receivable)

Debtors Name	Address	Phone #	Location of Record Payment
_____	_____	_____	_____
_____	_____	_____	_____

Location of Loan Agreement _____

Business Agreements	Subject	Location
_____	_____	_____
_____	_____	_____

CREDIT CARDS*

Company	Account #	# of Cards	Company Address	Phone #
1.				
2.				
3.				
4.				
5.				
6.				
7.				
8.				
9.				
10.				

*Check for existence of credit life insurance that will pay the debt upon proof of death.

UNPAID DEBTS*

Owed to	Address	Phone #
1.		
2.		
3.		
4.		

Purpose of Debt	Agreement Location	Payment Record Location
1.		
2.		
3.		
4.		

*Check for existence of credit life insurance that will pay the debt upon proof of death.

PERSONAL PROPERTY

☐ **SAFE-DEPOSIT BOX** # _____ Location _____

☐ **HOUSEHOLD FURNITURE** (List most valuable items)

Description	Location
_____	_____
_____	_____
_____	_____
_____	_____
_____	_____
_____	_____
_____	_____
_____	_____
_____	_____
_____	_____
_____	_____

☐ **JEWELRY**
Description — *Location*

☐ **FURS**
Description — *Location*

☐ **CAMERAS**
Make — *Location* — *Serial #*

☐ **COLLECTION (Stamps/Coins/Books/Paintings)**
Item — *Location* — *Value*

PERSONAL PROPERTY (continued)

☐ **TOOLS & SHOP EQUIPMENT**

Item	Serial #	Location
_____	_____	_____
_____	_____	_____
_____	_____	_____
_____	_____	_____

☐ **AUTOMOBILE(S)**

	(1)	(2)	(3)
Make	_____	_____	_____
Year	_____	_____	_____
Model	_____	_____	_____
Serial #	_____	_____	_____
Location of title	_____	_____	_____
Location of registration	_____	_____	_____

☐ **TRAILER(S)**

           (1)   (2)

Type _____ _____

Manufacturer _____ _____

Serial # _____ _____

Location _____ _____

☐ **BOAT(S)**

           (1)   (2)

Type _____ _____

Manufacturer _____ _____

Serial # _____ _____

Location _____ _____

☐ **PLANE(S)**

Manufacturer _____ Model _____ Serial # _____

Location _____

REAL ESTATE

PROPERTY(IES)   *Location*

1. _____   _____
2. _____   _____
3. _____   _____
4. _____   _____

TYPE OF OWNERSHIP OF PROPERTIES ABOVE

     Sole Owner   *Held Jointly With*

1.   ☐   _____
2.   ☐   _____
3.   ☐   _____
4.   ☐   _____

MORTGAGES ON PROPERTIES ABOVE

    Mortgagee

1. Mortgage held by _____   Mortgage # _____
   Address _____   Phone # _____

2. Mortgage held by _____   Mortgage # _____
   Address _____   Phone # _____

3. Mortgage held by _____   Mortgage # _____
   Address _____   Phone # _____

4. Mortgage held by _____   Mortgage # _____
   Address _____   Phone # _____

DEED LOCATION FOR ABOVE PROPERTIES

1. _____
2. _____
3. _____
4. _____

RETIREMENT PLANS

Identify each plan administrator and indicate how to contact.
(Give telephone number and address)

☐ Pension _____
_____
_____

☐ Annuity Contracts _____
_____
_____

☐ Associations or Fraternal Organizations _____
_____
_____

☐ Union _____
_____
_____

☐ Keogh Plan (HR 10) _____
_____
_____

☐ Individual Retirement Account_____
_____
_____

FORMS COMMONLY INVOLVED IN THE SETTLEMENT OF DEATH

UNIFORM DONOR CARD

OF _____
Print or Type name of donor

In the hope that I may help others, I hereby make this anatomical gift, if medically acceptable, to take effect upon my death. The words and marks below indicate my desires.

I give: (a) ____ any needed organs or parts

(b) ____ only the following organs or parts

_____
Specify the organ(s) or part(s)

for the purposes of transplantation, therapy, medical research or education,

(c) ____ my body for anatomical study if needed.

Limitations or special wishes, if any: _____

Signed by the donor and the following two witnesses in the presence of each other:

_____ _____
Signature of Donor   Date of Birth of Donor

_____ _____
Date Signed   City & State

_____ _____
Witness   Witness

This is a legal document under the Uniform Anatomical Gift Act or similar laws.

Instructions for the Forms Shown on Pages 334, 335 and 336

HOW TO PREPARE FORM

It is not necessary to employ the services of anyone to present this statement to XYZ Co. Please send this completed form, and the policy, to a duly authorized representative of XYZ Co. or to the Office from which this form was received.

1. **Statement of Person Requesting Payment**

   a. The Statement is to be signed by the person legally entitled to receive the proceeds of the policy.

   b. If such person is an Executor, Administrator, Guardian or other legal representative, please furnish a certificate of appointment. A Trustee not named in the policy should submit evidence of authority.

   c. If there has been any change in the name of the person requesting payment from that stated in the policy, and XYZ was not previously notified of the change, please furnish a statement explaining the difference.

   d. If the person requesting payment is a secondary beneficiary, please furnish a statement giving details and date of death of primary beneficiary. If a co-beneficiary has died, please furnish a similar statement as to death.

   e. If the policy is payable in one sum and it is desired to have the proceeds paid as income, the necessary forms to be completed will be furnished upon request. Generally income settlements are available only if the policy is payable to a natural person in his or her own right. Ask your XYZ representative about this.

2. **Proof to be Furnished**

   a. The Completed "Statement of Person Requesting Payment" on reverse side of this form is required, and

   b. An Official Certificate of Death OR the "Attending Physician's Statement" below. HOWEVER, if a policy was issued or reinstated within two years prior to death or death was by Suicide, Homicide or Accident, the "Attending Physician's Statement" must be completed (if there was an attending physician.)

   c. If newspaper clippings concerning the death are available, please send them with the request for payment.

334   **Proof of Death—Claimant Statement**

DATE RECEIVED IN AGENCY

REQUEST FOR PAYMENT OF DEATH BENEFIT   PLEASE READ INSTRUCTIONS ON REVERSE SIDE

This form is supplied by XYZ upon request without verification of the status of the insurance. Verification will be made upon receipt of the completed form at the Home Office.

Policies under which payment is requested:

Number _____ Number _____

STATEMENT OF PERSON REQUESTING PAYMENT

1. Name of Insured Person in full (Please Print) _____

2. Date of birth of Insured Person _____ Place of birth _____

3. Date of death of insured Person _____ Place of death _____

4. Last residence of Insured Person
   Street or R.F.D. No. ____ City ____ County ____ State or Province ____ Zip Code ____

5. Occupation of Insured Person at Death—date last worked _____

6. Principal cause of death _____

7. When did health of Insured Person first begin to be affected. _____

8. Are you the beneficiary named in the policy?   Yes ☐   No ☐
   (If not, state in what capacity you request payment.)

9. Are you entitled to receive the entire amount payable on the policy?   Yes ☐   No ☐
   If not, how much of the amount?

10. If an income settlement has not previously been elected, check one of the following:
    ☐ Settle proceeds as directed on attached form.
    ☐ Withhold proceeds pending my election of payment in cash or of type of income settlement. (Unless election is made within one month, payment will be made in one cash sum.)
    ☐ Pay proceeds in cash.

11. Information on all Beneficiaries and Payees.

Name (Last, First, Mid. Init.)	Address Street or R.F.D., City, State, Zip Code	Date of Birth Mo. Da. Yr.	Taxpayer I.D. or Social Security Number
(1)			
(2)			
(3)			
(4)			

12. Please list all other insurance on the life of the Insured Person.

COMPANY	AMOUNT	COMPANY	AMOUNT

I have read any attending physician's statement furnished by me herewith and ask that it be made a part of this request.

AUTHORIZATION

In connection with the case of _____

I hereby authorize any physician, practitioner, hospital, clinic, institution, insurance company, Medical Information Bureau, or other organization or person that has records or knowledge of the above named person or of such person's health to give any such information to an authorized representative of XYZ Life Insurance Company.

A photostatic copy of this authorization shall be as valid as the original

Date _____ **SIGNATURE IN FULL OF PERSON REQUESTING PAYMENT** _____

_____ _____
Residence   Street and Number

_____ _____ _____
City or Town   County   State or Province   Zip Code

(The authorization above will be used only if a policy was issued or reinstated within
two years prior to the date of death or if death was by suicide, homicide or accident.)

POLICY RECEIPT

Received from _____ Policy No. _____ 19___ issued by _____ to be sent to the Home Office in connection with Request for Payment of Death Benefit.

(over)

335

Proof of Death—Physician's Statement

ATTENDING PHYSICIAN'S STATEMENT

(This is the Uniform Statement recommended by The International Claim Association)

Full Name of Deceased _____   Date of Death _____

Residence at Death _____   Place of Death _____ (if hospital or institution, give name)

Age at Death—or Date of Birth _____

Cause of Death (enter only one cause for each of A, B, and C)
Disease or Condition Directly Leading to Death: (this does not mean the mode of dying, such as heart failure, asthenia, etc. It means the disease, injury or complications which caused death.)

	Interval between onset and death
A) _____	A) _____

Antecedent Causes. (Morbid conditions, if any, giving rise to the above cause (A) stating the underlying cause last)

Due to B) _____	B) _____
Due to C) _____	C) _____

NOTE: ANSWER FOLLOWING QUESTIONS ONLY IF DEATH WAS BY SUICIDE, HOMICIDE OR ACCIDENT, OR IF XYZ REQUESTS THEY BE COMPLETED.

Date of First Attendance in Last Illness _____   Date of Last Attendance in Last Illness _____

If Death was due to Accident, Suicide or Homicide,
Specify Which: ☐ Suicide ☐ Homicide ☐ Accident
Describe Briefly:

Was an Inquest Held? Yes ☐ No ☐
Was an Autopsy Performed Yes ☐ No ☐
If so, by whom and with what conclusion?

Have you treated or advised the deceased during the last 2 years, prior to illness? Yes ☐ No ☐
Did the deceased to your knowledge, receive treatment during the last 2 years from any other physician, or in any hospital or institution? Yes ☐ No ☐
If "Yes" to either question, please furnish the following:

Name	Address	Nature of Illness or Injury	Dates

Date _____   Signed by _____ M.D

Residence _____

Portion of a Typical Certificate of Death

Social Security Administration Claim Form
(Page 1 of a 5-Page Form Required)

DEPARTMENT OF HEALTH AND HUMAN SERVICES
Social Security Administration

APPLICATION FOR LUMP-SUM DEATH PAYMENT*

I apply for all insurance benefits for which I am eligible under Title II (Federal Old-Age, Survivors, and Disability Insurance) of the Social Security Act, as presently amended, on the named deceased's Social Security record. (This application must be filed within 2 years after the date of death of the wage earner or self-employed person.)

*This may also be considered an application for insurance benefits payable under the Railroad Retirement Act.

1.	(a) PRINT name of Deceased Wage Earner or Self-Employed Person (herein referred to as the "deceased")	*(First name, middle initial, last name)*
	(b) Check (✓) one for the deceased	☐ Male ☐ Female
	(c) Enter deceased's Social Security Number	___ ___ ___ / ___ ___ / ___ ___ ___ ___
2.	PRINT your name	*(First name, middle initial, last name)*
3.	Enter date of birth of deceased *(Month, day, year)*	
4.	(a) Enter date of death *(Month, day, year)*	
	(b) Enter place of death *(City and State)*	
5.	(a) Did the deceased ever file an application for Social Security benefits, a period of disability under Social Security, supplemental security income, or hospital or medical insurance under Medicare?	☐ Yes ☐ No ☐ Unknown *(If "Yes," answer (b) and (c).)* *(If "No" or "Unknown," go on to item 6.)*

(b) Enter name(s) of person(s) on whose Social Security record(s) other application was filed. _____

(c) Enter Social Security Number(s) of person(s) named in (b). ___ ___ ___ / ___ ___ / ___ ___ ___ ___
(If unknown, so indicate)

6. ANSWER ITEM 6 **ONLY** IF THE DECEASED WORKED WITHIN THE PAST 2 YEARS.

(a) About how much did the deceased earn from employment and self-employment during the year of death? → Amount $ _____

(b) About how much did the deceased earn the year before death? → Amount $ _____

7. ANSWER ITEM 7 **ONLY** IF THE DECEASED DIED PRIOR TO AGE 66 AND WITHIN THE PAST 4 MONTHS.

(a) Was the deceased unable to work because of a disabling condition at the time of death?
☐ Yes *(If "Yes," answer (b).)* ☐ No *(If "No," go on to item 8.)*

(b) Enter date disability began *(Month, day, year)* _____

8.

(a) Was the deceased in the active military or naval service (including Reserve or National Guard active duty or active duty for training) after September 7, 1939?
☐ Yes *(If "Yes," answer (b) and (c).)* ☐ No *(If "No," go on to item 9.)*

(b) Enter dates of service. _____

From: *(Month, Year)* | To: *(Month, Year)*

(c) Has anyone (including the deceased) received, or does anyone expect to receive, a benefit from any other Federal agency?
☐ Yes ☐ No

9. Did the deceased work in the railroad industry at any time on or after January 1, 1937?
☐ Yes ☐ No

Form **SSA-8-F5** (1-82) Page 1
DESTROY PRIOR EDITIONS

Glossary

Accidental death benefits The accidental death, or "double indemnity," feature of a life insurance policy will provide a larger additional benefit, often twice the face amount of the policy, if death arises from accidental means.

Adjustable life An adjustable life insurance policy permits the insured to change from term to permanent, apportion premium dollars and change the type of coverage without cancelling the policy. This flexibility is subject to the limitations of the specific policy in question.

Administration The management of the estate of a deceased person. It includes collecting the assets, paying the debts and taxes and making distribution to the persons entitled to the decedent's property.

Administrator (m) administratrix (f) The person appointed to manage the estate of a deceased person in the case that the decedent had no valid will, or when the will did not provide for an executor (m) executrix (f) to settle the decedent's estate.

Alternate value date For federal estate tax purposes, the value of the gross estate six (6) months after the date of death, unless property is distributed, sold, exchanged or otherwise disposed of within six (6) months. In that case the value of such property is determined as of the date of disposition.

Annual exclusion For federal gift tax purposes, an exclusion of $10,000 is allowed the donor each year provided the gift is one of a present interest in property (the donee must be given an immediate right to use, possession or enjoyment of the property interest).

Attestation clause The paragraph at the end of a will indicating that certain persons by their signatures have heard the testator (testatrix) declare the instrument to be his (her) will and have witnessed the signing of the will.

Automatic premium loan A provision in permanent life insurance policies which permits the company to borrow from the cash value of the policy to pay the premium, if the insured has elected this provision.

Beneficiary The person who inherits a share or part of the decedent's estate. One who receives a beneficial interest under a trust or insurance policy is also called a beneficiary.

Bequest A gift of property by will. A specific bequest is a gift of specified property (my watch or automobile). A general bequest is one that may be satisfied from the general assets of the estate (I give $100 to my brother, Sam). If the specific bequest (watch) was sold before the decedent died, the gift will fail.

Buy-sell agreements A buy-sell agreement, or business purchase agreement, is an arrangement for the disposition of a business interest in the event of the owner's death, disability, retirement or upon withdrawal from the business at some earlier time. Business purchase agreements can take a number of forms: (1) an agreement between the business itself and the individual owners (a stock redemption agreement); (2) an agreement between the individual owners (a cross-purchase agreement); and (3) an agreement between the individual owners and key person, family member or outside individual (a third party) business buy-out agreement.

Charitable contributions A charitable contribution is a gratuitous transfer of property to charitable, religious, scientific, educational and other specified organizations. If the donee of the gift falls within a category designated by the law, a charitable deduction may be taken for income, gift or estate tax purposes. Charitable contributions have tax value, therefore, because they result in a current income tax reduction, may reduce federal estate taxes and can be made gift tax free.

Charitable deductions A deduction allowed against a reportable gift to a charitable organization (equal to the value of the gift). For estate tax purposes there is no limit on the amount of the deduction.

Charitable remainder annuity trust A charitable remainder annuity trust is a trust that permits payment of a fixed amount annually to a non-charitable beneficiary, with the remainder going to charity.

Charitable remainder unitrust A charitable remainder unitrust is a trust that is designed to permit payment of a periodic sum to a noncharitable beneficiary, with the remainder going to charity.

Codicil A supplement or addition to an existing will to effect some revision, change or modification of that will. A codicil must meet the same requirements regarding execution and validity as a will.

Community property Property acquired during marriage in which both husband and wife have an undivided one-half interest. Not more than half can be disposed of by the will. In some Community Property States, the husband can control and dispose of community property during marriage. There are currently eight (8) Community Property States: Arizona, California, Idaho, Louisiana, New Mexico, Nevada, Texas and Washington.

Contingent interest A future interest in real or personal property that is dependent upon the fulfillment of a stated condition that may never come into existence.

Contingent remainder A future interest in property dependent upon the fulfillment of a stated condition before the termination of a prior estate. For example, husband leaves property to bank in trust to pay the income to his wife during her lifetime. After his wife's death the trustee is to transfer the property to his son if the son is then living. Otherwise, to his daughter. The son has a contingent remainder interest which is contingent upon his outliving his mother. The daughter has a contingent remainder interest which she will only receive if the son does not outlive their mother.

Convertible term A right to exchange your term policy for a "whole life" or "endowment" type of policy without evidence of insurabilty.

Corporation A separate and distinct legal entity whose exact nature and status are determined by the State of incorporation. For federal tax purposes, a corporation is an organization that has a preponderance of the following elements: (1) associates; (2) limited liability; (3) free transferability of interests; (4) centralized management; (5) continuity of life; and (6) an objective to carry on business and divide the gains therefrom.

Corpus A term used to describe the principal or trust estate as distinguished from the income. When we speak of the corpus of a trust we are talking about the assets in the trust.

Credit estate tax A tax imposed by a State to take full advantage of the amount allowed as a credit against the Federal Estate Tax.

Decedent The person who died. It refers to both men and women.

Decreasing term Similar to mortgage insurance in that the death benefit decreases over the specific period of time in which the insurance is in effect.

Defined benefit pension plan A type of pension plan under which definitely determinable retirement benefits are computed using a predetermined benefit formula established when the plan is created. Each employee is promised a specific amount of retirement benefits. The employer's contribution to provide that benefit is based on an actuarial determination of the cost of benefits promised.

Disclaimer The refusal to accept property that has been devised or bequeathed. It's a renunciation by the beneficiary of his or her right to receive the property in question.

Dividend options Options available to owners of "participating" insurance policies in which the insured can elect to take dividends in any of the following ways: (1) in the form of cash; (2) to reduce the premiums; (3) to buy "paid up" additional insurance; (4) to leave the dividends with the company to earn interest; (5) to purchase one-year term insurance; (6) to pay off the policy at an earlier date; and (7) to use a combination of the above.

Domicile An individual's permanent home. The place to which, regardless of where he or she is then living, an individual has the intention of returning.

Donee The person who received a gift. The term also refers to the person who is the recipient of the power of appointment from another person.

Donor The person who makes a gift. The term also refers to the person who grants a power of appointment to another person.

Durable power of attorney A "durable" power of attorney is a power of attorney which is not terminated by subsequent disability or incapacity of the principal.

Endowment insurance Endowment insurance pays the face amount at the sooner of the time of "endowment"—the maturity of the contract, or at the death of the insured prior to the endowment date.

Estate tax A tax imposed upon the right of a person to transfer property at death. This type of tax is imposed not only by the federal government but also by a number of States.

Executor (m) executrix (f) The person named by the deceased in his or her will to manage the decedent's affairs. This personal representative of the decedent stands in the shoes of the decedent, and collects the assets of the estate, pays the debts and taxes, and makes distribution of the remaining property to the beneficiaries or heirs.

Fair market value The value at which estate property is included in the gross estate for federal estate tax purposes. The price at which property would change hands between a willing buyer and a willing seller, neither being under a compulsion to buy or sell and both having knowledge of the relevant facts.

Federal estate tax An excise tax levied on the right to transfer property at death, imposed upon and measured by the value of the estate left by the deceased.

Fiduciary One occupying a position of trust. An executor, administrator, trustee and guardian all stand in a fiduciary relationship to those persons whose affairs they are handling.

Flower Bonds Flower Bonds are certain U.S. Treasury obligations (which are traditionally traded at a discount) owned by a decedent at death that can be redeemed at par value (plus accrued interest) in payment of federal estate taxes. They are called Flower Bonds because they "blossom" at death, and while purchased at a discount, can be redeemed at their full par value in payment of federal estate taxes.

Gift For gift tax purposes, property rights or interests voluntarily and gratuitously passed on or transferred during lifetime for less than an adequate and full consideration in money or money's worth to another, whether the transfer is in trust or otherwise, direct or indirect.

Gift splitting (For federal gift tax purposes) A provision allowing a married couple to treat a gift made by one of them to a third person as having been made one-half by each, provided it is consented to by the other.

Gift tax A tax imposed on the lifetime voluntary gratuitous transfer of property. There is a federal gift tax, and some states also impose a tax on transfers during lifetime.

Gift tax exclusion (For federal gift tax purposes) Anyone, married or single, can give up to $10,000 in cash or other property each year to any number of persons (whether or not they are related to the donor) with no gift tax liability.

Grace period A safety device provision included in life insurance policies which permits the insured to have an extra period of time (usually thirty days) in which to pay the premium without losing the benefits of the policy.

Grantor A person who creates a trust; also called a settlor, creator, donor, or trustor.

Gross estate An amount determined by totaling the value of all property in which the decedent had an interest and which is required to be included in the estate by the Internal Revenue Code for federal estate tax purposes.

Guaranteed insurability rider An additional benefit that can be added to a life insurance policy guaranteeing the insured the right to purchase additional life insurance without evidence of insurability on certain option dates—usually available only up to certain ages.

Guardian There are two classes of guardians. A guardian of the person is appointed by the surviving spouse in his or her will to take care of the personal affairs of their minor children. Since each parent is the natural guardian of the minor children, only the surviving parent can name the guardian of the person. A guardian of the property of a minor or incompetent is a person or institution appointed or named to represent the interests of a minor child or incompetent

Glossary

adult. A guardian of property can be named in a will, or will be appointed by a court.

Heir A person designated by law to succeed to the estate of the person who dies intestate (without a will). Sometimes an heir is designated as next of kin.

HR-10 (Keogh retirement plan) Under an HR-10 (Keogh Plan) a self-employed individual is allowed to take a tax deduction for money he or she sets aside to provide for retirement. The HR-10 plan is also a means of providing retirement security for employees working for the self-employed individual.

Incontestable clause A provision contained in life insurance policies which prevents the insurance company from denying a claim because of any error, concealment or misstatement after the contestable period has expired (usually two years).

Individual retirement account (IRA) A provision in the tax laws which permits individuals to set aside the lesser of $2,000 a year or 100% of compensation, in the form of an individual retirement account. Money set aside in an IRA is deductible from gross income, and the earnings of the IRA account, between the time they are deposited and the time they are received, accumulate tax free. Under current law an individual must be at least 59½ years old (unless disabled) to receive an IRA payment without tax penalty.

Inheritance tax A tax levied on the rights of the heirs to receive property from a deceased person, measured by the share passing to each beneficiary, sometimes called a succession tax. The federal death tax is an estate tax, and while some states have estate taxes, most have inheritance taxes.

Installment payments of estate tax under Section 6166 Section 6166 of the Internal Revenue Code provides for the payment of federal estate tax in installments in certain cases in which the deceased had an interest in a closely held business that represented a considerable part of his estate. Under present law, to receive special tax treatment under 6166, the value of the business interest must comprise more than 35% of the adjusted gross estate.

Installment sale The installment sale is an elective device for spreading out the taxable gain and thereby deferring income tax from the sale of property. Essentially, the major ingredient is that the seller agrees to accept the purchase price in installments over a period of years (or agrees to accept no payment in the year of the sale and one or more payments in later years).

Insurance trust A trust composed partly or wholly of life insurance policy contracts.

Intangible property Property that does not have physical substance. The item itself is only the evidence of value. Examples are a certificate of stock or bond, and goodwill or an oral contract.

Interest free loans A loan of money to a party who will be charged no interest, or in some cases interest which will be much less than the going rate for similar loans from commercial institutions. Interest free and low interest loans are commonly made by a corporation to an employee or from a parent to a child, or between other family members, with a primary intent of shifting income, and the taxation, to the taxpayer with the lower tax bracket.

Interpolated terminal reserve The reserve on any life insurance policy between anniversary dates, regardless of whether further premium payments are due. It is determined by a pro rata adjustment upward (or downward in the case of certain long duration term policies) between the previous terminal reserve and the next terminal reserve.

Inter vivos trust A trust created during the grantor's lifetime. It becomes operative during lifetime as opposed to a trust under a will, called a testamentary trust, which does not go into effect until after the grantor dies.

Intestacy laws Individual state laws that provide for distribution of property of a person who has died without leaving a valid will.

Intestate Without a will—a person who dies without a valid will dies intestate.

Irrevocable trust A trust that cannot be revoked or terminated by the grantor. To qualify as irrevocable for tax purposes, the grantor cannot retain any right to alter, amend, revoke or terminate. The trust can be revoked or terminated by the grantor only with the consent of someone who has an adverse interest in the trust.

Joint tenancy The holding of property by two persons in such a way that on the death of either, the property would go to the survivor. If the persons are husband and wife, then the property is said to be held "by the entireties." This is contrasted to tenancy in common in which each of the owners has an undivided interest, which upon the death of one is passed by probate.

Lapse The failure of a testamentary gift due to the death of the recipient during the life of the testator (the person who made the will).

Legacy Technically a gift of personal property by will, but in practice it includes any disposition by will.

Legatee A person to whom a legacy is given.

Letters of administration A written document issued to the administrator, administratrix (if no will) or to the executor named in a will authorizing him to act as such. After the will is probated or is taken to the appropriate office for formal approval (Register of Wills, Probate, Orphans' or Surrogate Court) the letters of administration (no will) or letters testamentary (will) are granted. They serve as official recognition of the fact that the administrator or administratrix or the executor or executrix has the right to take any action that the deceased would have taken in regard to handling and disposing of the decedent's property.

Life estate The title of the interest owned by a life tenant. A person whose interest in property terminates at his or her death.

Life tenant The person who receives the income from a legal life estate or from a trust fund during his or her own life. This right terminates at death.

Liquid assets Cash, or assets which can be readily converted into cash without any serious loss (bank accounts, life insurance proceeds, government bonds).

Living will A living will is a written expression of an individual's desire that extraordinary means should not be employed to prolong his or her life. Living wills are legal in some states. In other states, where the living will itself has no legal effect, it can be of help to physicians by enabling them to know of a patient's wishes.

Marital deduction For federal estate tax purposes, the portion of a decedent spouse's estate that may be passed to the surviving spouse without its becoming subject to the federal estate tax levied against the decedent spouse's estate. Under present federal estate tax law the marital deduction is unlimited, provided that the property passes to the surviving spouse in a qualified manner.

Marital trust A trust set up to take advantage of the marital deduction provisions of the federal estate tax. It can take the form of a Q.T.I.P. trust or a general power of appointment trust, defined elsewhere in this glossary. The trust property that will pass outside the marital trust will be in a "non-marital" or residual trust. Typically, the beneficiaries of the non-marital trust will be the children of the spouse setting up the trust. Assets in the marital trust are taxed when the surviving spouse dies, while assets in the non-marital trust are not in the surviving spouse's estate and therefore not taxed when the spouse dies.

Medical expense reimbursement plan A medical expense reimbursement plan (MERP) is an agreement provided by an employer to reimburse one or more employees for dental expenses, cosmetic surgery and other medical expenses which are not covered under a medical plan available to all employees. Typically, a medical expense reimbursement plan reimburses employees for medical expenses incurred by the employee, his or her spouse and dependents.

Money purchase pension plan A type of pension plan which bases the retirement benefit upon an employer's commitment to make an annual contribution. Benefits are directly dependent upon the length of time an employee participates in the plan and the amount of money contributed on his or her behalf each year, plus interest and appreciation on such funds.

Non-cancellable and guaranteed renewable A provision in a disability policy under which the premium is guaranteed and the coverage guaranteed for the length of the renewable period. The company has no right to cancel the policy or change the amount of the premium. This is contrasted with policies that are only "guaranteed renewable" under which the insurance company retains the right to change the amount of the premiums on a class basis, and policies that are "renewable only at the option of the insurance company." Under these latter policies, the company has the right to refuse to renew the policy on its anniversary date.

Non-forfeiture values Options in an insurance policy which give the insured the right to elect either "reduced paid-up" life insurance, or "extended term" life insurance, as well as receiving the cash value of the policy, at any time that the insured no longer wishes to continue paying premiums.

Non-liquid assets Assets that are not readily convertible into cash for at least nine (9) months without a serious loss. (Real estate and business interests.)

Non-probate property Property that passes outside the administration of the estate. It passes other than by will or the intestacy laws (jointly held property, pension proceeds and life insurance proceeds paid to a named beneficiary are examples of non-probate property, as is property in an inter vivos trust).

Pension plan A pension plan is a retirement plan established and maintained by an employer for the benefit of the employees and their beneficiaries. The primary purpose of a pension plan must be to provide benefits for the employees upon their retirement because of age or disability.

Personal holding company A personal holding company is a corporation which meets two particular tests (and is not specifically excluded from such status). These two tests are: (1) a stock ownership test; and (2) an income test. Such tests must be met in the same taxable year so that it is possible for a corporation to attain personal holding company status in one year and not in the next.

Pour over A term referring to the transfer of property from an estate or trust to another estate or trust upon the happening of an event that is provided in the instrument. For example, a provision in a will can provide that certain property be paid to an existing trust.

Power of appointment A property right given to a person to dispose of property that he or she does not fully own. There are two types of powers of appointment. A general power of appointment is a power over the distribution of property exercisable in favor of any person the donee of the power may select, including himself, his estate, his creditors or the creditors of his estate. A limited power of appointment is the power granted to a donee that is limited in scope. This is sometimes called a special power. An example of a limited power would be giving the donee of the power the right to distribute the property at his death to any of his sister's children that he designates.

Power of attorney A power of attorney is a written document which enables an individual, or "principal," to designate another person or persons as his or her "attorney in fact," that is, to act on the principal's behalf. The scope of the power can be severely limited or quite broad.

Present interest A present right to use or enjoy property.

Principal The property comprising the estate or fund that has been set aside in trust, or from which income has been expected to accrue. The trust principal is also known as the trust corpus or res.

Private annuity A private annuity is an arrangement between two parties, neither of whom is an insurance company. One party, the transferor, conveys complete ownership of property to the other, the transferee. In return, the transferee promises to make periodic payments to the transferor for some period of time—usually for the transferor's life or for the life of the transferor and his or her spouse.

Probate The process of proving the validity of the will and executing its provisions under the guidance of the appropriate public official. The title of the official varies from state to state. Wills are probated in the Register of Wills office, and in the Probate or Surrogate Court. When a person dies the will must be filed before the proper officer and this is called filing the will for probate. When it has been filed and accepted, it is said to be "admitted to probate." The process of probating the will involves recognition by the court of the executor named in the will (or appointment of an administrator if none has been named).

Probate property Property that can be passed under the terms of the will, and if no will under the intestacy laws of the state, is probate property. Property held

Glossary

in the individual name of the decedent, or in which the decedent had a divisible interest, is probate property.

Profit sharing plan A profit sharing plan is a plan for sharing employer profits with employees. A profit sharing plan must not provide a definite, predetermined formula for determining the amount of profits to be shared. However, there must be a definite formula for allocating these profits to each participant. But without a definite contribution formula, an employer must make recurring and substantial contributions to a profit sharing plan.

Q.T.I.P. trust The Q.T.I.P. trust (qualified terminal interest property trust) is a trust that can qualify for the marital deduction under current tax laws, even though under the trust a spouse is given the income of the trust for life. Assets at death pass to the beneficiaries named by the spouse who set up the trust. Under prior law, only a trust in which the spouse had a general power of appointment over the trust property would have qualified for the marital deduction. This type of trust is called a general power of appointment trust.

Reinstatement A privilege contained in life insurance policies which enables the insured to reinstate the policy when it has lapsed for nonpayment.

Residuary estate The remaining part of the decedent's estate, after payment of debts and bequests. Wills usually contain a clause disposing of the residue of the estate that the decedent has not otherwise bequeathed or devised.

Reversionary interest A right to future enjoyment by the transferor of property that is now in the possession or enjoyment of another party. For example, a son creates a trust under which his father is going to enjoy the income for life with the principal of the trust to be paid over to the son at his father's death. The son's interest is the reversionary interest.

Revocable trust A trust that can be changed or terminated during the grantor's lifetime and the property in the trust recovered by him.

Sale/gift-leaseback A sale-leaseback involves one party selling property (or in the case of a gift-leaseback, giving property) to another party and then leasing back the same property. This type of transaction is usually intended to secure a number of income and/or estate tax advantages.

Section 303 stock redemption Section 303 of the Internal Revenue Code establishes a way for a corporation to make a distribution in redemption of a portion of the stock of a decedent that will not be taxed as a dividend. A Section 303 partial redemption can provide cash and/or other property from the corporation without resulting in dividend treatment and provides cash for the decedent, shareholders or executor to use to pay death taxes and other expenses.

Short term trust (also known as a Clifford trust) An irrevocable trust running for a period of at least ten years or the life of the beneficiary, whichever is shorter, in which the income is payable to a person other than the grantor and established under the provisions of the Internal Revenue Code. The income is taxable to the income beneficiary and not to the grantor. The agreement may provide that on the date fixed for termination of the trust, or on the prior death of the beneficiary, the assets of the trust shall be returned to the grantor.

Shrinkage The reduction in the amount of property that passes at death caused by loss of capital and income resulting from the sale of assets to pay death costs.

Simplified employee pension plan (S.E.P.P.) A simplified employee pension plan is a retirement savings program with most of the same rules, but higher limits than a regular IRA. Unlike the IRA, the S.E.P.P. is available only to employees. As in the case of an IRA, contributions to an S.E.P.P. are currently deductible, earnings grow income tax free and you pay no tax until you begin to receive benefits.

Sole ownership Holding a property by one person in such a manner that upon death it passes either by the terms of the will or if no will then according to the intestacy law.

Sprinkling or spray trust A trust under which the trustee is given discretionary powers to distribute any part or all of the income among beneficiaries in equal or unequal shares, and direction to accumulate any income not distributed.

Stock option A stock option is a right to buy stock in the company you work for within a certain period of time and at a fixed price regardless of what the stock is selling for at the time the option can be exercised.

S corporation An S corporation (previously called a subchapter S corporation) is a corporation that elects not to be taxed as a corporation for federal income tax purposes. In all non-tax respects it is a typical corporation.

Survivors' income benefit plan A survivors' income benefit plan (S.I.B.P.) often called a death benefit only plan, or "D.B.O.," is an agreement between a corporation and an employee. The corporation agrees that if the employee dies before retirement, it will pay a specified amount, or an amount determinable by a specified formula, to the spouse of the employee or another employer-designated class of beneficiary such as employee's "children." Typically, the amount may be a multiple of salary such as two or three times the average base pay in the three years preceding death.

Tangible property Property that has physical substance—may be touched, seen or felt. The thing itself has value (a house, car or furniture).

Taxable estate An amount determined by subtracting the allowable deductions from the gross estate.

Tenancy by the entireties The holding of property by husband and wife in such a manner that, except with the consent of each other, neither husband nor wife has a disposable interest in the property during the lifetime of the other. Upon the death of either, the property goes to the survivor.

Tenancy in common The holding of property by two or more persons in such a manner that each has an undivided interest which, upon the death of one, is passed by probate. It does not pass to the surviving tenant in common.

Terminal reserve The reserve on a life insurance policy at the end of any contract year and, for policies on which premiums are still due, the amount of the reserve prior to the payment of the next premium.

Term insurance Under this type of coverage you must die before the term expires in order to collect the insurance. Several forms of term insurance include annual renewable term or yearly renewable or "YRT" term. This type of policy is renewable each year while at the same time the premiums also increase.

Testamentary The disposition of property by will. A testamentary document is an instrument disposing of property at death, either a will in fact or in the nature of a will.

Testamentary trust A trust of certain property passing under a will and created by the terms of the will.

Testate A term used when a person dies having left a will.

Testator A person who leaves a will in force at death.

Transfer for value rule The income tax rule that taxes otherwise exempt life insurance proceeds when a life insurance policy (or any interest in a policy) has been transferred for any kind of valuable consideration. There are specific exceptions to this rule, but a transfer of a policy for value should never be made to anyone without consulting an attorney or accountant.

Trust A fiduciary arrangement whereby the legal title of the property is held, and the property managed, by a person or institution for the benefit of another.

Trustee The holder of legal title to property for the use or benefit of another.

2503(c) trust A 2503(c) trust is a gift tax tool that enables someone to make a gift to a minor in trust and still obtain the $10,000 annual exclusion. The use of this irrevocable funded trust for gifts to minors eliminates many of the practical objections to giving young children outright gifts.

Unfunded insurance trust An insurance trust that is not provided with cash or securities to pay the life insurance premiums. Such premiums are paid by someone other than the trustee.

Unified credit (for federal gift and estate tax purposes) The unified credit is a dollar-for-dollar reduction against the federal estate and gift tax. In 1983 the credit is $79,300 and protects an estate of $275,000. In 1984 the credit is $96,300 and protects an estate of $325,000. In 1985 the credit is $121,800 and protects an estate of $400,000. In 1986 the credit is $155,000 and protects an estate of $500,000. In 1987 and thereafter, the unified credit is $192,800 and protects an estate of $600,000.

Uniform gifts to minors' act The Uniform Gifts to Minors' Act (U.G.M.A.) provides that an adult, while he or she is alive, may make a gift of certain types of property, such as securities, money or a life insurance contract to a minor, by having it registered in the name of and/or delivering it to the donor or another adult person or trust company as custodian for the minor. The minor acquires equitable title to the subject matter of the gift. This method avoids many of the problems and expenses of other methods of transferring property to a minor such as outright gifts, trusts or guardianship arrangements.

Universal life A form of life insurance under which the cash values are generally invested in equities and other securities to provide a better rate of return than a typical cash value life insurance policy. Features include flexibility in the amount of premium payments, and adjustments in the amount of death protection without the necessity of taking out a new contract.

Vested interest An immediate fixed interest in real or personal property, although the right to possession and enjoyment may be postponed until some future date or until the happening of some event. For example, if a husband leaves real property and securities to a trustee in trust to pay the income to his wife during her lifetime and at her death to transfer the property to his son and his heirs, the wife has a present vested life interest in the right to the income, and the son has a future vested interest in the right to property. If contributions are made to a pension or profit sharing plan, and the property regardless of any other event is going to the employee, then the employee has a vested interest in that property.

Whole life insurance Permanent insurance in which the face amount of the insurance and the premium remain level throughout the life of the contract. A reserve is built into the policy that can be borrowed from, or received in cash or in the form of other non-forfeiture values at the option of the insured.

Will Technically, a legal expression of what you want to happen to your property when you die. Formal requirements vary by states, but usually at a minimum a will must be in writing and signed at the end. Requirements for witnesses vary according to states.